PROLEGOMENA TO RELIGIOUS PLURALISM

Also by Peter Byrne

A COMPANION ENCYCLOPEDIA OF THEOLOGY
(*editor, with Leslie Houlden*)
ETHICS AND LAW IN HEALTH CARE AND RESEARCH (*editor*)
HEALTH RIGHTS AND RESOURCES (*editor*)
MEDICINE IN CONTEMPORARY SOCIETY (*editor*)
MEDICINE, MEDICAL ETHICS AND THE VALUE OF LIFE (*editor*)
NATURAL RELIGION AND THE NATURE OF RELIGION
RELIGION DEFINED AND EXPLAINED (*with Peter B. Clarke*)
RIGHTS AND WRONGS IN MEDICINE (*editor*)
THE PHILOSOPHICAL AND THEOLOGICAL
FOUNDATIONS OF ETHICS

Prolegomena to Religious Pluralism

Reference and Realism in Religion

Peter Byrne
Senior Lecturer in the Philosophy of Religion
King's College, London

First published in Great Britain 1995 by
MACMILLAN PRESS LTD
Houndmills, Basingstoke, Hampshire RG21 6XS
and London
Companies and representatives
throughout the world

A catalogue record for this book is available
from the British Library.

ISBN 0–333–60108–4

First published in the United States of America 1995 by
ST. MARTIN'S PRESS, INC.,
Scholarly and Reference Division,
175 Fifth Avenue,
New York, N.Y. 10010

ISBN 0–312–12843–6

Library of Congress Cataloging-in-Publication Data
Byrne, Peter, 1950–
Prolegomena to religious pluralism : reference and realism in religion / Peter Byrne.
p.   cm.
Includes bibliographical references and index.
ISBN 0–312–12843–6
1. Religious pluralism.   2. Religion—Philosophy.   I. Title.
BL85.B97   1995
291.1'7—dc20

95–10839
CIP

10   9   8   7   6   5   4   3   2   1
04   03   02   01   00   99   98   97   96   95

Printed and bound in Great Britain by
Antony Rowe Ltd, Chippenham, Wiltshire

Contents

Preface

This work is a study of religious pluralism. By 'pluralism' I refer not to the fact that there is a plurality of religions in the world, but to one intellectual response to that fact. It is a response asserting some measure of equal standing between the major religious traditions. Correspondingly, it denies types of uniqueness and absoluteness claimed for one tradition or another. The precise measure of equality it asserts between the faiths varies from one version of pluralism to another. Some versions of the pluralist response focus on truth, affirming that all religions are equally true. Other versions focus on salvation, affirming that all religions are equally valid paths to salvation. Yet others focus on the notions of religious experience and encounter, affirming all religions to be equally good means of encountering a divine or transcendent reality. It is of course possible to find pluralist theories which contain elements of all these ways of asserting equality between the major religious traditions.

Pluralism is one important intellectual response to the fact of religious diversity. It is well known in contemporary Western theology and philosophy of religion through the writings of, amongst others, Paul F. Knitter, Wilfred Cantwell Smith and John Hick. Hick has been particularly important in making the pluralist response to religious diversity known and a vast literature has grown up around his writings. Much of this literature is highly critical of Hick and the pluralist project. It is my belief that the debate sparked off by Hick has become thoroughly confused, hence the need for this book. It aims to unscramble it.

The debate needs unscrambling for a number of reasons. One is that the merits or otherwise of pluralism as a thesis about religion and the relations between religions have become entangled with much that is in my view irrelevant, such as the rights and wrongs of methods of inter-religious dialogue. Why entanglement with the project of dialogue is mistaken is explained in Chapter 1. Another reason for making the effort of sorting out the pros and cons of pluralism is found in the extent to which many recent writers on the subject think that pluralism in general,

and John Hick's version of it in particular, is refutable by pointing to simple errors and confusions. Pluralism is too frequently
sneered at. I aim to show that this approach to pluralism's claims
is mistaken. There is a good deal to be said for pluralism as a
thesis in the philosophy of religion. Once it is properly stated, it
does not fall because it commits ground-floor errors. It is a thesis
worth giving some time and attention to.

The sneering response to pluralism and to Hick in particular
is a regrettable feature of contemporary debate. The animus
against pluralism and Hick which comes from some quarters is
partly explained through the perceived links between pluralism
and Christian theology. Writers such as Hick are as much theologians as philosophers and his pluralism has a theological as
well as a philosophical message. Pluralism is seen by many as a
betrayal of key Christian commitments. Hence it and its proponents are felt to deserve hostility and ridicule. Since the pluralism defended here separates itself at the outset from the merits
and demerits of revisionary programmes in Christian dogmatics,
it can initially leave these kinds of concerns behind.

A particularly clear example of a critique which holds pluralism and Hick to be refutable by reference to simple and quick
arguments is to be found in Byrne 1982. I now repent of such
naiveté. In the present work I do conduct an argument with
Hick, for I contend throughout (and *ad nauseam*) that the theory
of knowledge Hick employs to make his version of pluralism
work creates more problems than it solves. I try to show that at
the heart of pluralism lies a realist perspective on religion. Indeed, such realism is one of the features which makes pluralism
interesting. I argue that a realist perspective on human religious
thought is best represented by a pluralist view of the religions.
Hick's Kantian epistemology, I allege, threatens the realist perspective on religious discourse. In contrast to my earlier, feeble
foray into this field, the argument with Hick in this book is meant
to be constructive. It builds upon and tries to take further Hick's
own thoughts, while criticising them. Its response to Hick is not
a stark 'No!' but a qualified 'Yes, but'. In this respect, like all
recent work on the topic, it is indebted to Hick's writings, and
particularly to *An Interpretation of Religion*.

The subtitle of this book is 'Reference and Realism in Religion'.
As already noted, pluralism implies realism and defending

pluralism can be viewed as one way of defending realism with regard to religion. The argument of this book is that the key to making pluralism plausible as a philosophical theory about the religions is through exploration and application of a particular brand of realism: referential realism. Hence pluralism, realism and reference are linked throughout this study.

Referential realism is an outlook on the connection between language and the world drawn from writers in the philosophy of science such as Rom Harré, and from semantic theorists such as Michael Devitt. A good deal of this book is about 'the literature'. In particular, it explores issues in religious pluralism by comparing them with issues about reference and realism raised in the philosophy of science and the philosophy of language. The need for a programmatic discussion of this kind has already been indicated. As befits a prolegomenon this work bids those interested in the relations between religions as cognitive endeavours to call a halt and re-think how an ordered, philosophical discussion of the issues should proceed. Like all great books it is also a seamless web, with the result that a stock of themes and allusions keeps reappearing in chapter after chapter. In particular the character and importance of referential realism for thinking about pluralism is continually harped upon.

A central concern of pluralism is the postulation of a common object of reference for at least many of the world's great religions. In this book I avoid using the word 'God' to indicate this alleged common referent, for the obvious reason that 'God' is too closely associated with personalist conceptions of the focus of religious life. Instead, I write of the 'sacred' and the 'transcendent'. As I use these terms, 'sacred' invokes an evaluative category and 'transcendent' an ontological one. The sacred is that which is conceived as being of the highest possible value and, on some conceptions, as the source of all value in the world. The transcendent is an object of reference whose reality is not exhaustively contained within the spatio-temporal and which, in consequence, is crucially unlike in certain respects ordinary objects of reference. As discussion proceeds, I associate the notion of the sacred, transcendent reality with the further ideas of that which is the seat of final, complete, liberating human good and that which is the ground of all reality. This richer notion of the sacred and transcendent is then linked to the search in Western and Eastern philosophy for a ground of being, be it personal or impersonal. As the richer notion emerges in my discussion, I take it to be an open question whether all religious traditions have such a conception and I debate how its putative absence in forms of Buddhism affects a pluralist outlook.

Throughout this work I write of 'the religions' and refer to these entities by the familiar names of 'Christianity', 'Islam', 'Hinduism', and so on. There are strong arguments for concluding that such usage hides the fact that the religions are semi-fictional entities. The case for saying this is pressed throughout Cantwell Smith's *The Meaning and End of Religion* and has been supported by a number of recent writers. Smith contends that we (Westerners) falsely reify fluid, multi-form traditions of thought and experience by means of such labels as 'Hinduism' and that our practice in so doing is a legacy of concerns in early modern Europe over the identity of different forms of the Christian creed. So we have looked for, and found through our own projections, a misleading credal unity and definiteness in Oriental traditions. I must acknowledge the force of this point, but regard it as no more than showing that talk of the religions is over-simple rather than being an outrageous distortion. That is to say, we must understand by 'the religions' a series of fluid traditions, and families of traditions, of thought, experience, action and institution. These traditions and families are labelled as distinct religions for convenience sake only. Cantwell Smith thinks that his arguments prove much more, that indeed the very notions of 'religion' and 'religions' should be abandoned. Elsewhere, I have summarised the case for saying that this is too drastic a response to the admitted simplification involved in the customary vocabulary (Byrne 1989, 222–6). At one point (in Chapter 3), the fuzziness of religions becomes relevant to my argument and is explicitly addressed.

Yet another point arising out of our talk of 'religions' is glossed over in what follows. I ignore throughout the Barthian distinction between religions and a Gospel, enshrined in the view that Christianity *as a religion* is to be treated like any other humanly-produced tradition, but *as a Gospel* stands in judgement of *all* those traditions. This distinction is ignored because I think it ultimately rests on an incoherence, shown when we reflect that the only way in which the Gospel is publicly identifiable is via human writings and traditions. Therefore the Barthian view of the faiths has, like any confessional view, to elevate one tradition, or 'religion', above others. Naturally, this last charge would need to be developed to provide a full reason for side-stepping a Barthian approach to religious diversity.

This Preface has already acknowledged a debt to the writings of John Hick for stimulating my interest in the topic. In addition I should like to thank colleagues and students in the University of London who offered comments on parts of the text read to various seminars over the last few years. My colleague Friedhelm Hardy provided advice on those parts of the book which mention Buddhist material in a vain attempt to rid me of my limited, Occidental perceptions of religion. Dr Mark Wynn, once of King's College and now of the Australian Catholic University, has given generously of his time in providing written comments on all the chapters. I am sure, however, that he would not wish to be associated with anything which can be found in the following pages.

PETER BYRNE

1
Definition

This book is an examination of the philosophical merits of religious pluralism. Pluralism is one intellectual response to that fact of religious diversity. The starting point in discussion of pluralism is then the fact that there are many religious traditions in human history and they exhibit diversity. Many facets of this diversity are not of primary interest to pluralism. As a thesis in the philosophy of religion, pluralism's first focus is on the fact that religions implicitly or explicitly claim cognitive successes and achievements of various kinds. Thus they claim to have a true account of the nature of transcendent, sacred reality, or of the way human beings must act toward that reality, or of human nature, or of how human salvation or liberation from evil is to be achieved. They hold that their spiritualities capture genuine encounters with and experience of the transcendent and/or that they have genuine revelation.

Diversity in claimed cognitive achievements creates cognitive conflict between the faiths. Prima facie if the cognitive successes of one religion in all these areas are genuine, then at least some, perhaps many, of the alleged achievements of other faiths are illusory. In ways which vary from case to case, depending on the closeness or otherwise of relations between traditions, explicit and implicit claims to cognitive success across the array of human religions appear to conflict. Such apparent conflict raises philosophical issues. In part this is because philosophy likes to get involved in cognitive disputes that throw up interesting puzzles and arguments. More importantly, judgement as to the character and meaning of these alleged conflicts has very important bearings on what interpretation and explanation we give to religion as a whole. Now, for good or ill, one of the most important tasks taken up by the philosophical study of religion since its emergence as a separate branch of reflection in the eighteenth and nineteenth centuries has been to provide an interpretation of religion. The character of such an interpretation will be crucially affected by a verdict on the cognitive achievements of the religions. Conflict in claims for cognitive success can suggest a number of possibilities whose truth would be vitally important for the interpretation of religion: perhaps it shows that the cognitive pretensions of all the religions are phoney, or that one tradition possesses success and the others are failures, or that these conflicting claims to success can all be reconciled, or that we must remain agnostic about these cognitive pretensions. These and other answers will evidently affect how we answer the question 'What is religion?'

Pluralism's response to the problem of diversity entailing cognitive conflict needs to be expounded by reference to a range of other responses to the same problem. We may list the following as worth setting out (the list is not meant to be exhaustive): naturalism, confessionalism (divided into exclusivist and inclusivist variants), pluralism, relativism and varieties of neutralism in the interpretation of religion.

Naturalism is dismissive of the possibility of finding any genuine cognitive achievement in religion. Where we have cognitive conflict between the religions it is easy to say that this indicates that the entire way of thinking, acting and experiencing that is human religion is unreliable. Diversity discredits the entire enterprise because there are no agreed methods of adjudicating the resulting conflicts and because it shows that there is no accumulation of reliable belief in this area of life. Religion is not an area of human discovery. Indeed the character of its diversity shows that alleged cognitive achievements are in fact explicable by rational- and truth-blind causes, such as social power, custom and personal need. Naturalism is displayed in a variety of radical theories of religion which endeavour to show how religion arises out of a mixture of the kind of causes mentioned. It is displayed in the writings on religion of the likes of Feuerbach, Freud and Marx. Naturalism need not in fact deny all cognitive achievement to religion. Feuerbach, for example, allows religion to contain genuine awareness of facets of human nature and human aspiration. Cognitive failure is alleged in the crucial area of religion's pretension to achieve successful cognitive relations with a level of reality that transcends the human and the mundane. So far as contact with or orientation toward transcendent, sacred reality is concerned, diversity between faiths is one important indication that they are systems of illusion, with a corresponding explanation.

The naturalist might contend that the fact that the religions are seen to be in conflict when interpreted as making cognitive claims should incline us not to take these claims at face value. The character of religion might be seen more clearly if we discount religion's alleged cognitive character and reinterpret religious language accordingly. Perhaps religious discourse is more properly a vehicle for the expression of emotion rather than of belief and thus it has no referential function.

In contrast, confessionalism, pluralism and relativism are all agreed on the point that religion succeeds in relating human beings to religious reality in some mode or other (be it through salvific success, doctrinal truth, genuine religious experience or whatever). So in this respect they can be said, in contrast to forms of naturalism, to be all realist interpretations of religion (though doubts about relativism in this respect will be entered below).

Confessionalism finds cognitive success in religion but locates it solely or primarily in one confession. In exclusivist confessionalism the ethics or salvific scheme or revelation or doctrines of one religion have cognitive merit to the exclusion of merit in all others. So it holds a deeply divisive view of the human religious scene. Confessional inclusivism modifies this divisive picture while accepting that the prime measure of cognitive achievement is provided by the elements of one faith. Other faiths (or at least a considerable number of other faiths) achieve cognitive success because they at some level approach the success of the favoured faith. Both forms of confessionalism then maintain that one religion is sufficiently certain in its dogmatic formulations to be the means of interpreting the whole that is human religion. The exclusivist interpretation holds that the other religions are cognitive failures in the light of the dogmatic structures of the favoured religion, the inclusivist that the other religions are cognitive successes when they are interpreted in the light of the favoured religion. The crux here is the belief that one confession has the correct account in some detail of what right relation to transcendent, sacred reality consists in (say, that it is defined through the belief that Jesus is *the* Son of God and *the* redemption for human sin). Confessionalism then seeks either to exclude other religions from that right relation or to include them.

I have defined inclusivism so far very crudely. Christian versions of it are summarised fully and clearly in D'Costa 1986, while DiNoia 1990a (119–21) contains an interesting account of Buddhist versions of inclusivism. Thinkers from many different traditions offer versions of it. What has to be narrowed down is the nature of the claim that an inclusivist position makes in favour of the selected tradition that is somehow to be the seal of all the others. Recent defenders of Christian inclusivism admit that, if 'other religions' contain an implicit awareness of the triune God of Christianity and are in part shaped by the operations of the Holy Spirit (as Christians define it), then avowed and explicit Christianity will have much to learn from non-Christian faiths (see D'Costa 1990, 23; and Schwöbel 1990, 42). The premise behind this admission is that God is revealed in the 'other religions'. Yet the definitive character of one faith's account of the transcendent remains unaltered at root, for the God that is generally revealed is '. . . the God disclosed in Christ' (D'Costa 1990, 19). Hence, inclusivism adheres to the belief that the favoured religion has the norm for understanding the others. Christ, for D'Costa, is the norm for understanding God – albeit a flexible norm; our understanding of it grows and develops as we apply it to non-Christian religions (1990, 23). For inclusivism to retain its character it must maintain that modifications, in the light of other religions, to the confessional norm on which it takes its stand can never go so far as to imply that some other religion has as full a grasp (or a better grasp) of sacred reality.

In a recent work, J.A. DiNoia has argued that there is a further confessional interpretation of religion that is beyond exclusivism and inclusivism (DiNoia 1992). He is impressed by the tendency for confessionalists (particularly Christian ones) to think of 'other religions' in terms of a stark 'either or': either they do not offer their adherents salvation in the terms defined by the favoured faith, or they do offer implicit salvation in these terms despite their other cognitive failings. For reasons which will become clear in Chapter 4, he thinks that religions are so utterly and irreducibly different that the beliefs and practices of one cannot be said to lead to the goal defined by another. So far exclusivism is on the right lines. But this is not to say that relation to the sacred is excluded for the non-favoured faiths, for genuine salvation is prospective. It is attained in a future state. The non-favoured faiths are not surreptitious ways of preaching the mode of salvific life now offered by the favoured faith. That denies their uniqueness. But we can be confident that they will lead their adherents to the prospective salvation that lies ahead for all who live well. The Christian can be confident of this, says DiNoia, while also being confident that whatever prospective salvation consists in it will turn around Jesus as the unique and unsurpassable source of divine aid (1992, 78). This might give us a third form of confessionalism: prospective confessionalism. But for the purposes of simplicity I shall treat it as a variant of inclusivism. It defines cognitive success in religion by primary reference to one faith but yet does not exclude other faiths from enjoying the fruits of that success, at least prospectively.

Pluralism can take many forms. Common to them all must be ascription of cognitive success to a great many of the world's religious traditions. (Neither inclusivism nor pluralism need attribute such success to everything that has counted as a religious tradition in history.) The essential minimum to pluralism must be the assertion of *one* kind of equality among religious traditions, namely that of each providing folk with real contact with a single transcendent focus. How versions of pluralism define relation with the transcendent will differ. It must at least include a mode of cognitive contact which enables all faiths covered by the pluralist thesis to be vehicles for salvation or liberation: the journey to the ultimate human good. Without this basic equality and achievement, others pertaining to religion are worthless. Pluralists will also differ on what further equalities follow from this one.

We should be clear from the outset that pluralism is not as such committed to saying that all major religions are equal in every aspect of cognitive endeavour or that no judgements of superiority of any kind between religions or their component elements are possible. If a writer claims a thoroughgoing equality of this sort, that appears to reflect his or her own concerns and arguments rather than the essence of pluralism itself (compare Hick 1981 and 1983). All that is required as a matter of definition is equality in some effective cognitive contact with the transcendent capable of supporting a thesis about religions as vehicles of salvation or liberation.

This way of putting the matter does not as yet secure a distinction between pluralism and confessional inclusivism, for the latter maintains this basic equality while of course making a decisive judgement of cognitive superiority in favour of one confession. To a minimal definition of pluralism we must add the element of scepticism or agnosticism with regard to the detailed dogmatic or mythical structure of any specific form of faith. The pluralist must be someone who, on reasoned grounds, doubts whether the detailed dogmatics of any particular religion can be known with sufficient certainty to enable such a faith to be the means of interpreting human religion. That is to say, pluralism must take its stand on a grand negative: there is not the certainty in any particular religion to enable its world-view to be the basis of a viable interpretation of religion. This draws a boundary between pluralism and confessional inclusivism, but given that, as noted above, some inclusivists take it that their favoured confession can borrow insights from other faiths, it is not a hard and fast one. Some writers do indeed hover between the camps of inclusivism and pluralism (see Gilkey 1988 and Pannikar 1988). Throughout this study it will be the epistemological stance outlined above, and particularly a kind of religious scepticism, that will be used to keep pluralism and inclusivism from eliding into one another.

So far then we have in pluralism three minimal elements: a fundamental realist commitment arising out of the faiths to the existence of a transcendent, sacred reality; a basic cognitive equality between faiths in putting human beings in contact with this reality and enabling them to be vehicles of salvation; and finally agnosticism toward, and therefore disengagement from, the specifics of any confessional interpretation of religion. With some later refinements, I shall stick with this definition of pluralism and thus distance myself from the richer versions of pluralism in the writings of the likes of Knitter, Cantwell Smith and Hick. Why? Well, the aim of this study is to show how pluralism might be plausible as a philosophical interpretation of religion (note: it is not to *prove* pluralism) and the less intellectual baggage that comes with pluralism the easier will be that task. Moreover, I have specific reasons for objecting to facets of the versions of pluralism in such authors. For example, it will be a constant complaint that Hick brings to his account of pluralism an epistemology that calls into question the first and second elements in its minimal definition, those that define its realist thrust.

Pluralism can be further placed by comparing it with the relativistic response to the fact of religious diversity. This has been developed in the recent writings of Joseph Runzo (1986 and particularly 1993, Chapter 9). The key feature of relativism is the granting of cognitive success to all religions by dint of making them conceptual schemas (or facets of such schemas) which each create or constitute their own worlds. The relativist says that truth and reality are relative to the manifold conceptual schemas into which human cognition divides. Relativism thereby has a pluriform account of the nature of reality. It rejects the idea that there is a single, mind-independent reality which is the terminus of our cognitive endeavours. So the religious relativist can award cognitive success to many religions despite their apparent conflicts by allowing that religious reality is pluriform, because constituted in different ways by the conceptual structures in or behind the religions. This license is only possible given that, in turn, relativism depends on a form of idealism. There is no one true account of the object of cognition because that object is not independent of us as knowing subjects. The mind must make, in some substantial way, the reality it knows. Relativism in this way compromises the basic realist thrust that is characteristic of pluralism.

Despite the superficial similarities that may exist between pluralism and relativism they are, in this respect, to be sharply opposed. For example, pluralism is bound (for reasons which will be reiterated over and over again in this study) to preach an agnosticism about many cognitive claims in the religions. Its message is that religions have massive cognitive limitations, yet despite this provide cognitive contact with the real. Relativists can be agnostic about some things but the tendency of relativism is to eschew such sweeping agnosticism, because relativism closes the gap between the object and subject of cognition, thus making this kind of agnosticism inappropriate. We shall see that pluralism's characteristic agnosticism toward much in religion trades on some of the points that fuel a full-blooded relativism, in particular on the fact that many facets of religious belief and claim are relative to culture and history and explicable as such. But pluralism takes the fact of relativity not as a reason to revise our account of reality as mind-independent, but rather as a ground for revising our ideas about awarding cognitive success to the details of any particular faith.

The last response to the fact of religious diversity on my list is neutralism. I coin this label to bring into the debate a variety of approaches to the fact of religious diversity which see it as reason to set aside the question of cognitive success and failure in the religions. Unlike naturalism, confessionalism and pluralism, neutralism refuses to say which religions correspond to reality and which not. We might imagine a practical neutralism which simply concludes from diversity and cognitive conflict that complete agnosticism about the cognitive pretensions of any and every religion is appropriate. Pluralism joins in some of this agnosticism, and links between it and facets of neutralism will emerge in later chapters. However, neutralism as I have set it up affirms that, contrary to pluralism, we do not have the grounds for awarding even the most minimal cognitive success to the traditions.

Neutralism based on agnosticism must have some reasons for saying that the uncertainty in religion shown by its diversity is not a ground for a naturalist rejection of the existence of sacred, transcendent reality. Naturalism must be held to be as equally uncertain as any confessional interpretation of religion. There are arguments for saying that religious agnosticism inevitably leads to a proof of a form of atheism (see Schellenberg 1993). Neutralism has to have a response to these. A full defence of pluralism would need such a response too.

A more subtle form of neutralism could hold that diversity shows us something about the unintelligibility of making global judgements and comparisons as to truth and reality in this area. This line of thought is one that suggests itself to some writers on religion influenced by the later Wittgenstein and can be seen, with this lineage, in the concluding parts of Glyn Richards' study of religious diversity (1989). Again this might look like relativism, but it need not be. The relativist does after all make a global judgement about religions, using a philosophical theory about the character of knowledge and reality to award an easy first prize to all conceptual schemas. It is more in keeping with a Wittgenstein-inspired approach to religions to reject such theorising about epistemology and ontology and instead see the religions as primarily rule-governed forms of social life, regarding which it is not proper to raise questions about their relation to reality, be reality conceived relativistically or not.

Neutralism having now been mentioned departs from the scene until Chapters 6 and 7 where it re-emerges in connection with discussions of the nature of religious language and of the aims and ambitions of the philosophy of religion.

This completes our initial survey of possible responses to the fact of religious diversity. We can see from it that the distinctions between these responses are not hard and fast, and indeed that one response can borrow from another. Thus pluralism borrows features from naturalism (agreeing that much in religion is not the outcome of cognitive contact with genuine sacred), and has affinities with facets of relativism, inclusivism and neutralism. It even agrees with one important strand in exclusivism, namely that the relation between religion and a non-human reality is the key to interpreting its character. As this study develops, I shall have occasion to note that pluralism's commitment to realism means that the lines between it and inclusivism in particular become blared.

Of the making of '-isms' there is no end and two more need to be considered before a more precise refinement of the pluralist stance can be given. They are essentialism and syncretism.

Critics of pluralism perennially accuse it of being essentialist in its approach to aspects of religion. So, whatever essentialism is, it is a bad thing. Further clarification of essentialism is however hard to come by. It is properly a kind of approach to the definition of religion, and so more precise discussion of its character will be found at the start of Chapter 3. Suffice it to say for the moment that essentialism in religious studies is an approach to religion, or aspects of religion, which see it (them) as expressions of an underlying, common core. Essentialism regards differences between religions as unimportant for the purposes of explaining and interpreting them, because they are fundamentally alike in their core – be this core located in doctrine, experience, ethics or where you will. So essentialism wants to assimilate religions and play down their differences. Thus it commits cardinal sins in contemporary eyes by setting aside unique features of religions and their contexts and fitting them into a homogeneous mould. We will see later that the rhetoric of some post-modernist writing on religion rails against these grievous errors.

Now at a superficial glance pluralism might invite the conclusion that it is committed to the logic of essentialism. For pluralism makes a global judgement about many, if not all, major religions to the effect that they achieve a minimal cognitive and salvific success. To do that pluralism must set aside or ignore differences between religions. This might look like downgrading or dismissing these differences. But it is not. The logic of pluralism is not that of essentialism. As I shall show in relation to a number of themes (for example, religious experience and salvation), all the pluralist need do is contend that *for certain purposes* differences between religions can be ignored. This is not at all tantamount to saying that they do not exist or that they are not important in other contexts. We can bring a variety of explanatory and interpretative concerns to religion and religions. Pluralism embodies only one such type of concern. In pursuit of it, it will abstract relevant from irrelevant features of religions in the light of its purposes. Other concerns will cut the cake differently. Pluralism abstracts commonalities and overlaps in facets of religion for certain limited purposes. It need not at all deny that the reality is richer than the abstraction.

Pluralists are also accused of committing the sin of syncretism. Syncretism can be understood as the attempt to harmonise religious diversity by taking elements from each religion in order to create a common form of religion acceptable to all. So it is another tactic for coping with and setting aside differences between religions and thus it might appear to be entailed by pluralism on a superficial view. But pluralism is not outwardly syncretistic. First, pluralism is a doctrine in the philosophy of religion, so it is not a religion or a proposal to construct a new, superior brand of religion. It is a second-order enterprise (more on what this is in this chapter and in Chapter 8). Second, pluralism can readily accept that differences between religions and unique features of religions matter for some purposes, such as their ability to function as living systems of faith. Third, pluralism is a thesis about existing traditions and concludes from their features that they all achieve a minimal cognitive and salvific success. The possibility of creating a religious synthesis out of them by joining some of their elements cannot tell us how religions succeed cognitively in the present unless that synthesis is already to be found in the religions, underlying their manifest differences. The synthesis of all religions must be the underlying essence of them. So for syncretism to be of any interest for the purposes in hand it must be reducible to essentialism, in which case it is subject to the same criticisms as essentialism and is distinguishable from pluralism in the same way.

The pluralist is like an observer of human languages who notes that, despite their many differences, they are alike in certain respects, in so far as all are successful in allowing a range of tasks to be performed. But this is not to propose that we should abstract from human languages and construct a new, philosophical Esperanto out of them. It may turn out on inspection that it is only in and through their unique features that they achieve, in common, these successes. The pluralist will argue in similar fashion in the case of religion.

As we proceed we shall see that pluralism does have some modest syncretistic implications. At various points, a plausible pluralism may suggest that insights from different faiths can be compared and conjoined. But I trust that we can agree that pluralism does not have to establish a synthesis of religion in order to prove its main contentions, or that it promises to construct a new, syncretistic religion to replace the old ones.

REFINING PLURALISM

So far then we have in pluralism three minimal elements: a fundamental realist commitment arising out of the faiths to the existence of a transcendent, sacred reality; a basic cognitive equality between faiths in putting human beings in contact with this reality and enabling them to be vehicles of salvation; and finally agnosticism toward, and therefore disengagement from, the specifics of any confessional stance toward religion. This definition now needs some refinement.

Pluralism is realist in its understanding religion. It thereby attributes a minimal cognitive success to religions. This is sufficient to enable them to be seen as salvific, while it denies sufficient cognitive success to any one religion to enable that to be the means of interpreting the others. The language of cognitive success and failure and the realist commitment of pluralism are best cashed in terms of the notion of reference. Reference is a form of cognitive contact between subject and object. As we shall define it in Chapter 2, it is a minimal form of epistemic access to real things. It is one that is compatible with considerable error and ignorance as to the detailed character of things. According to our argument, reference can be made to the transcendent sacred in the absence of correct, full or detailed descriptions of its character. The language of reference is ideal therefore for expressing a minimal realism and a minimal shared cognitive achievement in all major religions. Successful reference might be possible from them despite scepticism about their other cognitive achievements, and particularly about the truth of their dogmatic structures. Reference can be made and survive intact despite the revisable, limited and mistaken character of descriptions of the referent.

The notion of reference then becomes the set-aside mechanism pluralism needs. Given this common achievement, differences and conflicts between the traditions covered by the pluralist hypothesis do not matter for the establishment of the pluralist thesis. They exist and are no doubt important in other contexts, but they do not matter here. Successful reference might also be seen as sufficient for salvific success if it gets each tradition access to the sacred and if the basic orientation of a tradition toward the sacred is what matters in judging salvation (as we shall implicitly argue in Chapter 4). Pluralism then hitches its cart to the epistemological and semantic doctrine of referential realism as applied to religion.

Thus refining pluralism we get a viewpoint on religions defined by three propositions. (1) All major religious traditions are equal in respect of making common reference to a single transcendent, sacred reality. (2) All major traditions are likewise equal in respect of offering some means or other to human salvation. (3) All traditions are to be seen as containing revisable, limited accounts of the nature of the sacred: none is certain enough in its particular dogmatic formulations to provide the norm for interpreting the others.

How do these three theses hang together? This question cannot be answered properly until the main reasons for advancing religious pluralism are set out. A preliminary account, however, can be given. Central to pluralism as we have defined it is the view of religious traditions as connected, overlapping attempts on the part of human beings to understand and orient themselves towards the sacred. All these attempts are limited to some degree (by the historical and cultural basis of human understanding) and hence none is likely a priori to be more than a stepping stone in the human journey toward full understanding of the sacred. Despite their partial and limited character, pluralism maintains, and *must* maintain, that they provide cognitive contact with transcendent reality and enough relational and practical knowledge about it to offer overlapping, connecting ways of living rightly toward it. So pluralism must be built around a conception of reference and a notion of right practice which allows both to proceed in circumstances of partial theoretical understanding of the focus of the human religious quest. This entire strategy can be seen as a means of neutralising the conflicts between religions which the facts of religious diversity throw up: they are to be expected, given the pluralist's reading of the human religious condition and they do not necessarily deprive at least a range of traditions from achieving, in common, their objects.

So far we have spoken vaguely of 'the major traditions' as being linked in common success according to pluralism. 'How many?' and 'Which precisely?' are questions which the pluralist need not answer in advance. If pluralism can be articulated in a convincing manner, then its account of successful religious reference in conditions of partial understanding should enable answers to these questions to be given (upon application of this articulation to the facts of religious life).

The three defining theses of pluralism and the outlook on religion that underlies them are not theological claims but philosophical ones. Their provenance is philosophical reflection on the character of religion. It is important to see what it means to say that they are theses arising out of the philosophy of religion. That discipline is but one form of human reflection on religion. Since its emergence in the Europe of the eighteenth and nineteenth centuries, one of its chief defining features has been its separation from the dogmatic claims of a particular faith. That is not to say that it is based on the premise that all such claims are false, but rather that it regards all such claims as open to argument. Philosophers of religion who are committed to the dogmas of a faith are then bound to use those dogmas in drawing conclusions *in the subject* only in so far as they can be grounded or supported within it. The same goes for philosophers who are naturalists. In this limited respect philosophy of religion is a form of neutral, detached reflection on religion. It does not claim to be the only or the most important form of reflection on religion, but merely something that is worthwhile as offering some insights at least into the character and foundations of religion.

Let us note what the above account of pluralism and the philosophy of religion does *not* say. It does not say that philosophy of religion is as such committed to the truth of pluralism. The interpretation of religion is properly a subject of debate within the subject and one can find philosophical arguments for naturalist, confessional, relativist and neutralist interpretations too. This study is not, as already indicated, committed to thinking that philosophy of religion can prove the truth of pluralism. Philosophers prove very few things. It contends that this is one viable interpretation of religion fit to stand alongside others and that it is an interpretation which contains a good deal of plausibility as a means of organising a research programme in the theory of religion. Nor are we affirming that philosophy of religion is presuppositionless or without a history. No mode of reflection lacks these things. We note indeed below the opinion that it is a wicked offshoot of Enlightenment liberalism with a heavy weight of bad ideology behind it. While we disagree with this view, the debts our version of pluralism owes to Enlightenment epistemology are admitted in Chapter 5 and held up for scrutiny.

The defining theses of pluralism should thus be separated from Christian (or any other) attempts to work out a theology to encompass the fact of other religions. Being the product of reflection which stands back from the dogmas of any particular faith, pluralism of a philosophical kind can reply to a range of objections commonly levelled against it. For example, some authors note that pluralism entails the non-unique status of Christ, but then argue that nothing that can be recognised as Christianity can survive the abandonment of belief in the ultimate, qualitative uniqueness of Christ (Hastings 1990, 235). If pluralism is a philosophical thesis then it has no prior commitment to dogmatic

Christian claims about the status of Jesus. Such an objection there-fore loses much of its force, though it does signal a problem for those Christian theologians who are persuaded of the truth of pluralism on philosophical grounds and then wish to incorpor-ate it into their theology. It might also indicate, if it could be upheld and generalised, that pluralism was in general too close to a species of philosophical scepticism about first order reli-gious claims to be compatible with religious belief. Pluralism is not naturalism but its agnosticism with regard to the truth and normativity of traditional dogma could signal this problem, in which case it might be grounds for revisionary proposals in religion. (How to distinguish and relate first and second order levels of reflection in religion will be discussed in Chapter 8.) But, even granting all these suggestions for the sake of argu-ment, pluralism could be philosophically defensible for all that.

As a philosophical thesis, pluralism can be discussed and en-tertained by those who have theological and dogmatic commit-ments, and discussed and entertained in a spirit similar to that in which a theologian might go through the philosophical argu-ments on the problem of evil, suspending for the purposes of the exercise dogmatic assumptions which may be under review in the arguments considered. The cogency of any conclusions reached in the philosophical exercise will then have to be weighed in the light of any dogmatic claims they disturbed.

A similar spirit of detachment will enable someone who is committed to the falsity of religion as a whole to enter into the merits and demerits of pluralism. The leading question behind arguments for and against pluralism might then be seen in this light: 'Suppose there is some cognitive success in religion, that at least some religious notions make a reference to non-human reality, what is the best account we can give of the relations between the religions?' The religious sceptic might be convinced that pluralism offers the best answer to that conditional ques-tion. Because the religious sceptic can be a party to the debate about the merits of pluralism, it must be wrong to suppose that we must know certain first-order religious dogmas to be true in order to be able to state or defend pluralism. D'Costa is one who appears to argue in this fashion, though his immediate target is some specific claims of Hick. This would leave pluralism as hopelessly inconsistent. He claims that in order to reason that

God's justice demands that all religions be equal in offering a path to salvation we must know – through revelation – that God is lovingly just (1986, 200ff). But the pluralist no more needs to know this than a philosopher of religion needs to know that God is good in working out the implications of the problem of evil. It is enough in the former case, as in the latter, that traditional formulations assume that God is good and just and that certain general religious requirements (such as the demands created by the logic of worship) reinforce such assumptions. (Hick has his own forceful reply to D'Costa's point: 1990, 198–90.)

That pluralism can be advanced by the religious sceptic – albeit in limited, conditional fashion – should also teach us to separate pluralism's merits and demerits from debates about which theological views best promote inter-religious dialogue. It is a proper concern of religious thinkers to consider the practical relations between their own confession and the confessions of others. Some claim that pluralism's implicit attack on the absolute, normative nature of any first-order religious dogmas makes it unfit to provide a basis for dialogue between one confession and another (Griffiths 1990 is an example). The problem with such an objection is simple: pluralism's three theses and its underlying outlook may be true for all that it makes the task of dialogue difficult. Once more we have a problem about the relation between accepting the truth of pluralism as a philosophical thesis and continuing with allegiance to the dogmas of a particular confession. We should not make light of this difficulty: we would certainly have produced a significant paradox if we had shown that pluralism was incompatible with important aspects of first-order religious life. However, we must insist that the demands of inter-faith dialogue are not normative in a discussion of pluralism. It is possible to debate the cogency of pluralism while having no interest in inter-faith dialogue.

ARGUMENTS FOR PLURALISM

The aim of this section is to give a brief indication of how one can argue for the form of pluralism outlined so far.

The nature of that case made for pluralism depends on what opponents pluralism sees itself as facing. In its battle with naturalism (and to a lesser extent neutralism) pluralism of an unconditional kind has to contend for a minimal realist as opposed to an anti-realist reading of religion. This means finding in the epistemology and semantics of religious discourse signs that it is best interpreted in realist fashion. This is the task of Chapters 5 to 7. Something similar is true of pluralism's battle with relativism. This is a particularly important combat, because as already noted, pluralism uses the alleged relativity of religious cognition in its struggle with confessionalism, so must have reasons not to go the whole hog with relativism. This section concludes by trying to separate pluralist relativity from relativism pure and simple.

Pluralism shares realism with confessional interpretations of religion, but whereas their realism is partial (favouring some one tradition above others), pluralism's is not. Fundamental to the debate with confessionalism is the critique of its divisive view of human religious reality. Exclusivism and inclusivism are alike in this respect: they wish to view the theoretical and practical structures of all religions in the light of one religion's claim to have the definitive, normative account of the nature of the sacred and of salvation. There are 'other religions' but the religion for which the exclusivist or inclusivist makes normative claims is not simply one religion amongst others. It either contains the only truth in the whole array of human religious life (exclusivism), or is the final interpreter and summation of such religious truth as human beings can grasp (inclusivism). Any such view must contend that the favoured tradition plays a decisive role in discovering the true nature of the sacred and the right way in which human beings are to be oriented toward it.

Such a divisive view poses a particular problem for those confessionalists who are also theists – the problem of divine justice. Since much of the contemporary debate about pluralism has taken place in the context of the adequacy of Christianity's traditional theologies of world religion, the justice problem has loomed large. Assuming the truth of theism, God – a personal being – uses one favoured religious tradition as the means of relating (if only finally, definitively) to the whole of humanity, but does so in the full knowledge that only a portion of humanity can ever come to a real knowledge of that tradition – in this life at least. This can seem to be an odd way for a deity to behave and it is the source of the traditional argument from divine justice against inclusivist and exclusivist positions.

Thinkers sceptical of the truth of the traditional theistic religions of the West have long seen the problem of divine justice in the face of religious diversity as a major objection to these traditions (see Byrne 1989 for the historical use of the argument). However there are two reasons why this study leaves it largely behind. One is that it is important only in the context of arguing for pluralism against theistic confessionalism. It makes no sense to complain against a Buddhist interpretation of religion that it makes the dharma out to be 'unjust' in only 'revealing' itself to one favoured tradition amongst others. The categories used don't fit the Buddhist scenario. The second reason for leaving it behind is that its cogency remains hotly disputed and space does not permit us to unscramble the debate about it. Defenders of confessionalism will see it as essentially a version of the problem of evil, one which asks how a good and just God could leave some without salvation, or at best delayed salvation, through no fault of their own. As such it is open to similar replies to those offered for other forms of the problem of evil – appeals to: free will, compensating after-life and so on. Moreover, one could add that there is no question of justice to raise in relation to salvation. God has no obligation to save any one: salvation is a gift on any sensible account. Therefore he cannot be blamed if he offers means to salvation to some but not to others. On the other hand, the justice objection could be represented as a separate, and more forceful, objection to theism. Proponents of it will contend that what is in question is how we perceive the relation between the God of theism and humanity. Religion is the seat of that relationship. While human beings may not deserve salvation, once God has decided to enter into a relationship with humanity and answer humanity's deepest needs by granting a means of salvation to some folk, then he is bound to act impartially. Any account of his dealings with humanity that represents God as partial or arbitrary in his behaviour represents him as unjust and less than perfect. What human beings can demand is not salvation but impartial forms of relationship with the divine. Confessional accounts of religion cannot portray God acting impartially. So the debate goes on.

Leaving these arguments behind, we shall see that, in arguing with confessionalism, pluralism must stress the implausibility in the divisive accounts of the human condition that confessionalism offers. Divisiveness of this sort is particularly prominent when we consider the epistemological doctrines behind confessional accounts. These must represent some portions of humanity as capable of a doctrinal accuracy and certainty, and as possessing a corresponding freedom from relativity in understanding the transcendent, a freedom which escapes major parts of the human race. Pluralism's main assault on confessional accounts will thus stress the epistemological implausibilities in exclusivism and inclusivism. These are shared by versions of these stances in both theistic and non-theistic traditions. The epistemological problems surrounding the selection of any one faith as definitive and normative can be simply put. We are asked to believe that one religious tradition has attained a normative, albeit not absolutely final, account of the sacred. A major task of Chapter 5 will be to present an account of the epistemology of religious belief which makes such claims to certainty seem implausible.

Presumably any tradition, theistic or not, can defend its own claims for normativity by contending that, while it had the definitive views about the transcendent, other traditions are blind on this score because they are limited by the forms of understanding available in their host cultures. Thus a Buddhist thinker might claim that the forms of Islamic, Jewish and Christian culture did not allow the truths about the dharma to be appreciated properly at the birth of these religions. And proponents of other faiths can make corresponding claims about Buddhism.

Exlusivism and inclusivism posit an epistemological divide between parts of humanity, but the problem with appealing to the cultural basis of human thinking to justify this divide is that *all* religions seem to be historically and culturally conditioned in their forms of understanding. Forms of confessionalism will contend that one normative tradition escapes such conditioning to the extent that it can produce a dogmatic structure which is detailed and certain enough to be the means of interpreting religion as a whole. Its key concepts and claims perhaps sum up and complete the insights contained in other religions. Now we must put this question: if human beings are able to discover definitive truths about the transcendent, and if one tradition has such truths, why do not representatives of the other traditions

recognise the definitive truths of the normative tradition on being confronted with them? Inclusivism postulates forms of relationship between the normative tradition and the rest which
should make this question seem an important one. For, after all,
according to inclusivism definitive truths about the transcendent
are knowable and known. The other traditions prepare for, or
implicitly teach, those truths, so should we not expect them to
recognise them when presented with knowledge of the normative tradition? As Knitter notes, claims for the normativity of a
particular revelation or tradition should be capable of being supported by reasons which are universally available to all peoples
(Knitter 1985, 143).

It should be a problem that such reasons are not generally
forthcoming. Of course, traditions are not slow in producing
reasons which are meant to convince those of other faiths. Christianity has long appealed to Jews to accept that Christ fulfils the
prophecies and claims about the Messiah contained in ancient
Judaism. The problem, of course, is that such reasons seem to
have little neutral weight and tend to be convincing only after
conversion. They are another expression of the favoured tradition's dogmatics. (For a recent attempt to provide reasons of an
allegedly neutral, universal kind for Christianity's normative
status, see Netland 1991.)

The apparent inability of the major religious traditions to recognise one among them as normative brings us back to the problem of the cultural basis of human and religious understanding.
Claiming the normativity of any one of the major traditions involves drawing a distinction between it and the rest. They – the
'other religions' – contain illusion or partial understanding. The
normative tradition can be admitted to have its share of human
error and limited ideas, but by contrast to the rest it contains a
reliable, detailed account of the sacred. It is easy to make this
distinction appear hard to swallow and one of the major merits
of inclusivist over exclusivist positions is that the distinction is
softened. We have already noted that inclusivists might plausi-
bly appeal to the fact that forms of human understanding, including religious understanding, are culturally based and limited
as a way of accounting for partial, only tacit, insight in many of
the traditions. But this very fact is much more a reason for accepting pluralism's claim that no tradition can reasonably be

expected to have definitive knowledge of the transcendent. For it indicates the likelihood that *all* attempts to envision the sacred are going to be limited and ultimately provisional – if any are true at all. Surveying the history of human religious life and the human, cultural factors that have influenced the beliefs and practices produced by that life, the pluralist is convinced that they suggest the improbability (at the very least) that definitive truths about the sacred have yet been achieved in any of the religions.

The human, cultural basis of religious understanding and development is the detailed theme of the various branches of the historical, scientific study of religion. Hick is surely right to see pluralism and such study as in natural alliance (Hick 1989, 7–9). The scientific study of religion, in enforcing a sense of the human basis of religion, provides two particular ways of supporting the pluralist outlook. One is through an implicit attack on the idea of revelation or decisive religious enlightenment. Non-pluralist stances require the epistemological elevation of one tradition amongst others. The idea that one is in receipt of a normative and definitive revelation and the others not must be called into question, if we allow the success of the sciences of religion in bringing out the human basis of all sacred scriptures and the origins of all religions. Just because the application of critical, historical methods to sacred texts undermines a 'high' doctrine of revelation, it has been attacked as religiously loaded and biased by defenders of the idea of revealed truth (see Abraham 1982). So we should be aware that the very idea that the techniques of the science of religion can be applied equally to *all* religions is controversial. However, there are arguments of a general kind in favour of their universal application. These can be supported by inductive arguments based upon the success – in bringing illumination upon religion and its developments, in giving rise to research programmes in the study of religion – that has grown out of these methods. (Byrne 1989, 241–55 tries to sum up the debate between proponents and opponents of the universal application of the techniques of historical criticism.)

In addition to scepticism about the idea of revelation needed by its opponents, the very general epistemology of religion required by pluralism is supported by the human basis of religions revealed by their scientific study. The more information we have about the precise historical and cultural circumstances which give rise to religious ideas and developments, the more the pluralist can reflect on the extent to which those ideas and developments are limited and conditioned by their human background and the less likely it appears that they could be normative or definitive.

Enough has been said to indicate the general direction of pluralist thinking about the human and cultural background to religion. But it is important to note that pluralism must define its commitment to the cultural basis of religious thought very carefully. It cannot, on pain of incoherence, ally itself to any doctrine affirming that all thought, or all religious thought, is through and through culturally relative or determined. It needs instead an account of how religious thought is culturally *limited* and hence relative *to a degree*. A more thoroughgoing relativism is out for two reasons. First pluralism says of the major traditions that they make reference to a sacred, transcendent focus. They could not do that if human thought is too radically determined by its cultural background. The notions of reference and cognitive contact required to make sense of this affirmation demand an ability in human cognition to rise to some degree above its cultural background. Second pluralism is a theory about the religions which itself claims to rise above the culturally set bounds of human thought. It would be unstatable and insupportable unless human thinking were capable of being detached to some degree from the restraints of cultural background. Pluralism itself makes global, universal claims. Some such claims must be possible if pluralism is worth discussing.

Pluralism has powerful ammunition in reflecting on the fact of the human, cultural basis of religious traditions. But in drawing conclusions from this it must state them precisely and carefully. Despite an epistemology which partly draws upon the culturally conditioned nature of human thought, pluralism must commit itself to what Hugo Meynell describes as the 'self-transcendence, moral and cognitive' of humankind (Meynell 1981, 67–8). This is our ability to rise above our individual, class and societal interests and perceptions and respond in thought and action to facts and values which transcend all of these. If moral and cognitive self-transcendence is possible then an all-embracing cultural relativism cannot be true. While affirming this cognitive and moral self-transcendence, pluralism must offer a balancing statement of the limits on our understanding of the sacred set by the cultural basis of thought, limits which then provide reasons in favour of the overall view of the relative and partial nature of religious beliefs that is part of pluralism. There is no contradiction in holding to the cultural basis of thought, affirming the possibility of cognitive transcendence and suggesting that such transcendence is limited by the cultural basis from which thought begins.

Pluralism cannot be committed to a thoroughgoing cultural relativism and there are alternatives to this kind of relativism which nonetheless make use of the general fact about the human basis and limits of religious thought that critical scholarship reveals. It follows that critiques of pluralism based on ridiculing the application of thoroughgoing relativism are wide of the mark (for an example see Newbiggen 1990). The precise mitigated and focused relativism the pluralism requires in order to be plausible will be explored below (especially in Chapter 5). Two preliminary points about pluralism's precise relativistic outlook need to be made now.

Part of the way in which the mitigated relativism required can be focused is by stressing the way in which the human and cultural limitations of our thinking affect knowledge of the sacred in particular. While this subject is more properly the topic of later chapters, we can note now the need for pluralism to set up a problem about the definiteness of our knowledge of the sacred that arises from the sacred's own transcendent character. In view of this character it can be argued that the sacred will exceed the ability of human thought to produce definitive, normative statements about its objects and reveal the cultural basis of such thought in a telling manner. Central to this argument is the perception of a common thread in the ascription of a radical transcendence to the foci of the developed, non-polytheistic faiths. This thread is well brought out by David Pailin in his *The Anthropological Character of Theology* (1990), a work which, amongst other things, can be seen to provide a sustained argument for a mitigated, focused relativism in relation to religious affirmations. The notion of God, Pailin contends (1990, 9), is the notion of that '. . . which is ultimate ontologically, rationally and valuatively'.

The pluralist needs to extend some such definition of a sacred focus across the religions. Any object of reference which fulfilled the function of being ontologically, rationally and valuatively ultimate for human beings can be argued to be one which is radically unknowable. It must stand at the limits of human thought (Pailin 1990, 6) because to fulfil this role it must be radically unlike any mundane thing. The degree to which it belongs to any categories to which mundane things belong will be doubtful. It will thus perhaps be something which can only be described positively by models and metaphors (this will be the theme of Chapter 6). The models and metaphors used will draw upon the modes of understanding with which human beings are familiar (and must do so if they are to work) and they will thus root positive, direct descriptions of the transcendent in the thought forms of particular cultures and give a radically human basis to such descriptions. Pailin notes: 'As a result of these factors theology must be seen to be inescapably tentative and changeable' (1990, 3). It is this conclusion that pluralism needs from a mitigated, focused relativism: enough to cast doubt on the normativity of any one tradition's positive, dogmatic, accounts of the sacred, but not yet strong enough to amount to a scepticism capable of defeating the realism pluralism needs.

We must re-affirm the need to see pluralism as turning around the assertion of a mode of limited cognitive and salvific equality between the faiths, which is buttressed by a perception of them as containing revisable, tentative insights into the nature of the transcendent. It should be possible to state this view in a way which clearly distinguishes it from a thoroughgoing relativism or idealism with regard to the sacred. The three component parts of this view just do not hang together unless it can be clearly distinguished from relativism and idealism.

PLURALISM, TOLERANCE AND LIBERAL IDEOLOGY

I have deliberately tried in the first two sections of this chapter to give pluralism as austere a definition and setting as possible. One reason for giving the most minimal account of its essential features is so as to avoid discussion of the merits or otherwise of pluralism being tied up with the ins and outs of the theologies and philosophies of those particularly noted for its advocacy in recent thought. Thus I wish to distinguish between the debate about pluralism and the debate about the writings of John Hick, Wilfred Cantwell Smith and others. Many of the criticisms levelled at such authors (be they fair or not) are irrelevant to pluralism identified in the manner adopted in this study. Pluralism as we have defined it faces many intellectual problems: it is obviously committed to bold, subtle theses in the epistemology of religious belief and in religious language – to name but two areas where it must support its claims. But I wish in concluding this chapter to set aside as misconceived an area of criticism of pluralism which we may call 'ideological' or 'political'. Criticism of this sort is visible in Morris 1990 and in recent papers by Kenneth Surin (1990a and 1990b; my comprehension and criticism of this mode of writing about pluralism is greatly indebted to Donovan 1993).

Morris is one who contends that pluralism wears a false mask of tolerance while in fact offering an oppressive ideological liberalism instead. Pluralism promises tolerant acceptance of the major traditions as equally valid, but only at the cost of transforming the way they are to be seen. Their absolute claims must be abandoned. They must all conform to the supposed universal notion of liberal rationality (Morris 1990, 193). In so doing they are transformed into so many commodities: since none of their elements can claim absolute truth, the aim of pluralism is to make us view them as so many homogeneous entities among which individuals are free to choose (so charges Surin 1990b, 123). What the pluralist cannot tolerate is a tradition (Morris cites Judaism) which insists that religion is not a matter of choice and which has a social expression which would be emptied of meaning if it were seen as something to which folk could choose to ally themselves according to their personal predilections. Pluralism as a philosophical thesis is here linked to liberalism as a social ideology, an ideology whose aim is to free people from traditional allegiances, to teach them that such things are not to be taken seriously and to inculcate a preference for free choice, choice made possible because the differences between the traditions are said not to matter any more. In this vein Surin charges that pluralism 'sedately but ruthlessly domesticates and assimilates the other – *any other* – in the name of world ecumenism' (1990a, 200). He connects it with a dominant ideology which 'declares that nations, cultures, religions, and so forth, are simply obsolete if they are maintained in their old forms as fixed and intractable realities' (1990a, 201). This dominant ideology is linked, according to Surin, to the purposes of advanced capitalism in its desire to reify and privatise human life (1990b, 123). He even connects Hick's aim to see all religions and cultures as parts of a common human history of relations with the transcendent to capitalism's domination of the third world.

If pluralism is primarily a thesis in the analytic philosophy of religion then it principally rests upon and speaks about matters of epistemology. We have seen that in order to make good its claims it needs to assimilate the religious traditions of the world *but only in certain respects*. What pluralism as a philosophical thesis needs to assert is that differences between the traditions do not matter when it comes to considering whether such traditions make reference to a common sacred reality and offer means of orienting human beings' lives toward that reality. Pluralism asks a limited range of questions about religions and in the light of these questions contends that they can be linked together. This is obviously compatible with there being any number of other respects in which religious traditions are different. Because pluralism is a philosophical thesis the question of how it leaves the actual practice of the faiths remains open. If pluralism were plausible it would by no means follow that a policy of abandoning all particular religious allegiances in favour of embracing a homogeneous, global theology was correct.

The consequences of accepting pluralism are to be explored more fully in Chapter 8 below, but we can note now that it is open to the pluralist to insist that, despite its truth, the only way in which a life can be lived in relation to the transcendent is through allegiance to and involvement with a particular, 'positive' form of religion. Pluralism does involve a form of scepticism brought to bear upon the detailed dogmatic claims of particular faiths. It will therefore need to show that it does not entail abandonment of the forms of discourse and life offered in the particular religions. Here is a doubt about its possible reformist consequences which must be met in the conclusion to this work. But as a philosophical thesis about religion, pluralism is not yet an alternative religion nor a programme for transforming existing religions into a common mould. So while Wilfred Cantwell Smith and others might link it to the call to produce a world theology (Smith W.C. 1981), such a programme is not of the essence of pluralism.

Donovan is right, therefore, to protest that pluralism does not of itself entail commitment to 'a "modernist" project whereby the beliefs and practices of others are to be progressively brought into line with a secular, scientific, and humanistic world-view, to form a uniform global culture' (1993, 220). This project he styles 'ideological liberalism'. Pluralism is committed to the raising of critical questions about the faiths and relies (as noted in the previous section) on the results of critical, historical scholarship applied to human religious life. As such it is linked to the Enlightenment and its intellectual inheritance. Indeed the very idea that there is a subject styled 'the philosophy of religion' is a consequence of the Enlightenment. Pluralism may then instantiate 'epistemic liberalism' (Donovan 1993, 220) as a consequence of the questions it raises and of its intellectual roots. But there need be nothing sinister in this. Epistemic liberalism involves regarding human beliefs as one and all fallible, open to question and possible revision.

Pluralism starts with a set of questions about the major religious traditions, questions about the extent of their common cognitive and salvific success. The raising of these questions rests on assumptions and implies that it is worthwhile pursuing a search for some views about religion and culture as a whole. It may be that some of these assumptions are wrong. Thus we will note in Chapter 3 the objection that there is no class of 'religions' which would enable the pluralist's questions to be put properly. Where questionable assumptions of this sort are identified, their merits should be debated. I see no easy way of making out that such assumptions are politically wicked. Someone might object that the very desire to reach an overall view about the relations between faiths and cultures evinces an imperialistic tendency to assimilate 'the other' to a common frame of reference. So Surin contends that 'In the process, the "otherness" of the Other is traduced, and the real possibility of any kind of dialectical confrontation between the different religious traditions is extinguished' (1990b, 123). Yet once we begin to think that there are many cultures in the world we have attained some kind of global view of the human situation. The possibility of then raising certain kinds of questions – such as 'Do their various religions have a common reference?' – arises. The questions may turn out, on argument being offered, to be badly put or unanswerable;

though, even to show something of that sort is to show something global about culture. A thesis that cultures and religions are incommensurable or mutually incomprehensible says something global and significant. Moreover, the particular questions asked by the religious pluralist appear to arise out of the religions themselves. Confessionalism in the interpretation of religion is built on the fact that religions make absolutist claims about salvation and truth for *humanity*. If such claims are impossible to put then they are in trouble. No one from within one of the major traditions should complain if the philosophy of religion takes up these questions for itself.

We should readily accept that the kind of critical thinking (Donovan's 'epistemic liberalism') that created and informs the philosophy of religion is not without its presuppositions. Philosophy of religion should be prepared to defend these when it is relevant to do so. Further, it should be prepared to acknowledge the limited nature of its inquiries. It may be that no pluralist thesis in the philosophy of world religions is remotely provable and that we have in this book raised a series of questions that cannot be answered. But to acknowledge the presupposition-based and limited nature of philosophical inquiry is not yet to concede that it must be ideological in form, while such inquiry is prepared to support its questions and conclusions by reasons. Someone might object that the very commitment to rational inquiry is ideological. Not so. It is rather the consequence of the mere fact of a commitment to *discuss* issues in a public forum. There might be arguments to be offered against discussing the questions raised by pluralism (they are ill-formed, perhaps). Considerations may be raised against the giving and weighing of evidence and reasons on topics of this kind (the truth of religion is to be felt not judged, perhaps). But to contend thus is after all to give reasons why reason should not pursue answers to these questions. The only way to avoid reason here and elsewhere is to refuse to engage in discussion.

Neo-Marxist arguments are available for the conclusion that even seemingly innocent exercises of the capacity for rational enquiry are ideologically loaded. Surin offers one when he contends that religious pluralism is a materially and historically conditioned discourse and thus reflects, like all material facts in the human world, a specific social, political and cultural configuration (1990b, 115–18). Thus, he thinks, it cannot claim political innocence. The problem with Marxising of this kind is that it either proves too little or too much. If we take seriously the point that *all* communication, as a set of material acts, has a socio-economic and thus political context, then it will turn out that the 'discourse' in the pages of a journal of pure mathematics is political. The requisite university departments which support the scholars editing and contributing to such a journal are indeed dependent on advanced capitalism for their existence, and all involved – poor souls – endeavour to use a mathematical language to enunciate truths of global significance. If everything that is spoken is ideological for the reasons cited, then the sense of 'ideological' has become too thin to be of interest. Any thicker sense must surely be discriminating and attach itself to opinions and ways of speaking because of specific facts about the content or presuppositions of what is said. This in turn implies that non-ideological modes of thought and speech are possible. I have tried to indicate in this chapter how we might narrow down the statement of the essence of pluralism so as to make it prima facie ideologically innocent.

We may think the presuppositions of pluralism so wildly false that it must be a non-rationally and perhaps politically motivated view about cultures and religions. Yet such a critique, or 'deconstruction' to use the contemporary jargon, can only work if it is employed in contrast to the idea of questions in this area that rest on more adequate presuppositions, and which are thus not candidates for this kind of critique. Non-ideologically motivated thought in the field must thus be possible. Unless fashionable 'deconstructionist' critique is used in the service of finding more rationally acceptable views, it will lapse into a radical yet rather tired relativism (a fact cogently argued for in Gellner 1992).

What is at issue in confronting post-modernist critiques of pluralism and philosophy of religion is the possibility of the cognitive self-transcendence of human beings described above. The denial of the possibility of such transcendence in the form of a thoroughgoing relativism is of course always liable to be self-refuting. The philosophical enquiry that gives rise to pluralism must be committed to the possibility of cognitive self-transcendence. In order to take seriously the thought that some or all of the religions make genuine reference to a sacred, transcendent reality, cognitive transcendence by human beings must be admitted as a practical possibility. The very endeavour to pursue a reasoned answer to the questions behind pluralism is itself grounded on a commitment to the possibility of cognitive self-transcendence.

If this possibility is after all an illusion, then the enterprise is lost. But if so, the conclusion will not help those who wish to make absolutist claims from within the traditions, claims which the pluralist thinks we have reason to question. Such claims will be no more worthy of respect than the pluralist's if some form of deconstructionist relativism is true. A kind of realism about truth and knowledge is required as much by the religiously conservative and traditional as by the Enlightenment liberal who contends for the truth of pluralism (Donovan 1993, 224). Both may be wrong, but both then go down together: defeated by the contentions of the peddlers of deconstruction and relativism.

2

Reference

The doctrine that all major religious traditions refer to a common sacred, transcendent reality is at the heart of pluralism. To distinguish itself from naturalism, it must affirm that some sacred, non-human reality informs the religions even though no religion ever describes that reality adequately (Martin Soskice 1985, 149).

It is evident that pluralism's thesis of common reference gives rise to major philosophical questions about the nature of reference and hence that pluralism is reliant here, if no-where else, on philosophical argument to succeed. It would be comforting, then, to discover that philosophical analysis could agree on the question of when two or more names of the transcendent referred to the same object, or at least on the methods to use in answering the question. No such agreement can be found. We may contrast those philosophers who think that methods for tackling the reference question are available and can be expected to yield an answer (Gale 1991, 4–11) with those who consider that the question can be answered in all manner of ways depending on which philosophical-cum-religious perspective one brings to bear upon it (Shaw 1992). Moreover there is no agreement in general philosophy on what reference is and on how the references of names are to be determined. Descriptive and opposing causal theories vie with one another and there are different varieties of each to be reckoned with. Differences between descriptive and causal theories of reference will be seen to have important consequences for how the reference question posed by pluralism is to be answered.

The feeling that the reference question is inchoate and perhaps unanswerable in objective terms is something that the pluralist must resist, for it threatens to destroy the sense that there is a real issue between the pluralist and his or her opponents. In order to maintain a sharp idea of what is entailed in the pluralist's

31

reference thesis, it must be thought of in the context of the larger view of religions of which it is a part: each major tradition is to be seen as a revisable, limited, relative but nonetheless valuable attempt to put human beings in contact with a sacred, transcendent reality. The existence and nature of this reality has informed all these major traditions to a degree. When seen in this light pluralism's reference thesis is shown to have analogies with similar ones in the philosophy of science. For example we might ask if, or how far, successive atomic theories in the history of physics can be seen as overlapping, limited and revisable attempts to describe the nature of the *same object* (the atom).

The comfort to be drawn from taking leads from the philosophy of science comes not only from the fact that specific points in the theory of reference can be carried over, but also from the vindication we might thus get for the belief that such questions can be pursued in a non-arbitrary manner. To be sure, there are those who argue that the purported references made by terms in science are inscrutable and opaque, with the consequence that questions about whether two or more theories refer to the same things are always unanswerable, but such arguments have been more than adequately refuted (see Smith P. 1981, 46ff). Judgements to the effect that two or more scientific theories refer to the same realities can be made despite the fact such theories describe those realities in a conflicting manner. At earlier stages of atomic theory atoms may have been believed to be physically indivisible. Modern atomic theory now contradicts this assumption. But some earlier theories may yet be referring to what are now styled 'atoms' nonetheless – if perhaps enough of their other descriptions of atoms are shared with contemporary theory or if the contexts of earlier and later uses of 'atom' are sufficiently similar. This point will even survive recognition that an earlier theory may have regarded a description such as 'physically indivisible' as an essential or definitional truth about atoms. A larger view of the theory in the light of others may yet acknowledge error in prescriptions of essential truth while still making a case for saying that other factors enabled the theory to refer to the same things which a later theory defines differently.

We shall see below that causal and descriptive theories of reference differ on how far and on what basis reference can survive differences in description. All views must maintain that reference to an object across different systems of thought does not require complete agreement on descriptions of that object, otherwise we could not recognise two people as holding different opinions about one and the same object. This means that endeavours to establish a thesis of common reference for the religions need not be initially defeated by the varied list of key features which have been applied to the transcendent in them. Vroom notes over 20 of them: goodness; bliss; omniscience; omnipotence; immutable; omnipresent; creator; ground of being; maker; origin; acting; determining all things; revealer; revealed in some book or person (Jesus, the Koran, the Vedas); incarnate (in a person or persons); judge; righteousness; merciful; forgiving; self-sacrificing; personal; non-personal; the all; distinct from all; non-dual (Vroom 1990, 87 – I have altered the list slightly).

Vroom's list brings home just how different conceptions of the sacred can be. There is a fundamental difference, on the surface, between personal and impersonal conceptions of the sacred and there is room for further differences within each of these two families. And we can go beyond this list and think of more specifications of the transcendent that will create divergences. Vroom's list does not bring out, for example, the differences between monistic and Trinitarian accounts of the essence of a God conceived in personal terms. Yet we should also note a fact which Vroom's list throws up: that there is considerable overlap between different traditions' descriptions of the transcendent. Even traditions that differ over whether the transcendent is personal or non-personal may use similar epithets of it (such as: bliss, ground of being, origin). The overlaps between items in the list bring out the apparent major point of agreement across many traditions that there is a transcendent ground of reality which is the sum and source of value, as Pailin's notion of the ultimate brought home to us in the previous chapter.

Since the pluralist is not a naive essentialist, he or she need not suppose that divergences in conception can be dismissed as unimportant in the light of an esoteric doctrine of the sacred which all religions share. Common reference has to be maintained in the light of frank acceptance of genuine divergences alongside such overlap as is present. The pluralist thesis is not that such divergences don't exist or matter, but that *they do not count decisively when reference is judged*. In beginning the task of mounting a case for common reference the pluralist can draw comfort from the fact that opponents of pluralism from within the traditions are already committed to a tolerance about reference similar, at least in some respects, to his or her own. Consider the traditions we are most familiar with. There are many communities and theologies considered alike Christian despite differences between them on the nature of the Christian God. Frequently these differences are profound. Yet no theologian will say that only his or her particular school succeeds in referring to the God of Christianity. Faced with the choice of declaring that rivals past and present either speak wrongly of God or speak of nothing at all, he or she is more than likely to opt for the former alternative. Furthermore, it is essential to Christianity as we know it now to claim that its God is the same God as that of Hebrew religion. Reflection on the intellectual and spiritual need to see a particular theological endeavour as part of a continuing tradition, and on what is involved in so seeing it, should reveal the force of this last point. Where the option of declaring that others speak of nothing at all is chosen, it will be connected with a concern to mark the outer limits of the continuing tradition.

Of course it would be wrong to over-emphasise the extent to which existing dogmatic systems are already committed to something like a pluralist's notion of continuity of reference. There will be specific continuities which link references in different parts of the one tradition. In Christianity it is no doubt the figure of Jesus that provides such continuities. Granted the common, defining item of Christian belief that Jesus is the prime means for gaining access to God, then different strands of Christian thinking about God are still different strands of thought about the same God. Perhaps a similar thing could be said of diverse forms of Indian tradition in relation to the common thread of Vedic ways of identifying the transcendent. Pluralism demands a genuine extension of such judgements of sameness-with-difference across traditions or, as it were, the postulation of a 'super-tradition' of intellectual, moral and spiritual endeavour of which the varied traditions are component parts. This is why we can associate pluralism with Cantwell Smith's affirmation of 'the unity or coherence of humankind's religious history' (Smith W.C. 1981, 3), provided that the unity and coherence in question is specified in the manner suggested so far in this study.

HOW NOT TO REFER TO THE TRANSCENDENT

In the philosophical tradition that comes down from Frege the reference of a name depends on what information, what descriptions, a community associates with the name. The information conveyed in the descriptions associated with a name both give the sense of the name and thereby fix its reference. Reference is a function of sense. A sufficient amount of descriptive information, a suitable number of these descriptions, must be true of the referent to enable reference to succeed. On this descriptive theory a name denotes an object only if its user believes truly a number of descriptions which serve to identify it, and thus distinguish it from other things. Reference on this account is a function of descriptive knowledge of objects.

If this account is at least somewhere near the truth about the nature of reference, then any pluralist has to be worried about the fact that so many of the fundamental descriptions of the transcendent across the traditions are incompatible with one another. An account of reference in terms of sense and successful description may make it harder to suggest that if any one religious tradition successfully refers, they all do. The descriptive theory would have to rely on finding a description of the alleged, common focus to the religions which was both rich enough to be clearly identifying and yet shared by all the traditions included in the thesis of common referential success. Something like Pailin's 'that which is ultimate ontologically, valuatively and rationally' would have to be capable of doing these two jobs. Moreover, from the descriptive theory of reference a particular view of the nature of realism follows, which can be styled 'truth realism' (Harré 1986, 58–9).

If we ask the question whether science is to be interpreted realistically, the descriptive theory will encourage us to see that question as one about whether science has built up a stock of descriptions of items in the physical world which are known to be true and identifying. Realism in regard to human religion will similarly be a matter of finding sufficient identifying descriptions of the transcendent across traditions. Even in the scientific case, it takes only a modest degree of scepticism about the cognitive achievements of science to cast doubt on realism so understood. It goes without saying that similar scepticism about religious knowledge, understood as issuing in stock of assured descriptions of transcendent reality, will deal a similar blow to religious realism. Since pluralism's rejection of confessional interpretations of religion is built on a degree of scepticism, it looks as if it will have overwhelming motive for rejecting truth-realism. Given that it wants to maintain realism in some guise, it ought to reject descriptive accounts of reference since these bring truth-realism with them.

Pluralism then has two motives for developing a non-descriptive account of reference. Such an account will better accommodate divergences in description of the sacred across the traditions and it promises a different version of realism which does not tie it too far to descriptive knowledge of religious reality. Pluralism's agnosticism gives the second motive its power. But how can a convincing non-descriptive account of reference for religion be worked out?

Short cuts in dealing with the problem will not do.

A first short cut to be identified and set aside is John Hick's suggestion that Frege's distinction between sense and reference is after all able to solve these difficulties of itself. If this were so, we might make pluralism work without abandoning a descriptive theory of reference. We are quite happy with the thought that different names or descriptions, containing different types of information, may nonetheless refer to the same thing: for one thing may be identified in many ways. 'The evening star' and 'the morning star' both refer to Venus, the second planet in the solar system. Hick has offered this suggestion – that one and the same object can be known in quite different ways – as at least a first step to answering objections to his pluralism which stem from lack of agreement about how the transcendent is to be described (Hick 1985b, 106–7). The fact that two traditions use quite different descriptions to refer to the same thing should not then be initially puzzling.

It can be argued that the analogy behind Hick's point will not help us very much for two reasons. In the first place we know that the two bodies of information contained in the different ways of referring to Venus do so refer only because we have other information about the object of reference in terms of which we can trace the connection between the two ways of describing it. In the religious case we surely cannot trace differing names of the sacred back to the sacred itself and thus back to each other via a third body of information. To claim as much as this we should need a sure body of religious information which told us what the sacred definitively is and how the religions were aware of aspects of it (so argues Netland 1986, 260). Perhaps Hick's suggestion can be saved from this objection. It still faces a second objection. Our problem in attributing common reference arises because competing names for the transcendent have apparently *conflicting*, and not merely, *different* descriptive, information-bearing content attached to them. This puts the possibility of the names of the transcendent having a common reference but different senses in a new light, as Hick now acknowledges (1993a, 153).

Hick's more developed ideas in *An Interpretation of Religion* try to overcome these problems by employing the distinction between the sacred as it appears in the various religions and as it is in itself. The fact that the sacred in its former guise is named in incompatible ways does not stop all traditions making a common reference to the sacred in its latter guise. This approach to the problem of reference is part and parcel of an entire theory of religion. Treatment of Hick's solution to the reference problem at this stage in our argument must inevitably be partial and incomplete but some points about Hick's solution in abstraction from its total context can be made.

While the appearance/thing in itself distinction relativises and hence neutralises the incompatibilities in conceptions of the transcendent, it does so only at a cost of suggesting a barrier to reference to the sacred as it is in itself which we cannot get across. Reference is fundamentally a mode of cognitive contact between speaker and object, yet it is very easy to read Hick's account as giving us only cognitive contact with the appearances of the transcendent. It is not merely that we do not know this side of eternity whether the transcendent as it is in itself is like our culture-bound descriptions of it, but that it is ineffable, so that no humanly-devised predicate applies literally to it: 'In Buddhist terms it is "sunya" or empty – that is, empty of all that human thought projects as it seeks to grasp reality' (Hick 1991, 26). So Hick is telling us that there are good grounds of a general kind for saying that our descriptions of the real are not true of it. (He does of course distinguish literal and mythological truth in this context: our descriptions of the sacred may be mythologically true. More on this in Chapter 6.) This looks like an account of something with which we can have no cognitive contact, if we define cognitive contact in terms of the descriptive view of reference. A name or description refers on that account if it is associated with or conveys some true information about its referent. But from Hick's use of the appearance/thing in itself distinction, true beliefs about the sacred as it appears and as it is defined by my culture do not carry over into true beliefs about the sacred itself. Sense in this case does not appear to be connected with reference.

What Hick would have to say in reply to this is that the negative descriptions of the transcendent explicit or implicit in the religions are sufficient to enable sense to determine reference. It would not be enough for him to contend that reference to a common focus for the traditions could be secured simply through the description 'whatever reality is manifest in the experiences of the various traditions', for that description does not yield the required result that this reality is single, sacred and transcendent – it could be a natural or human reality that is experienced in the traditions. He must instead rely on a two-fold suggestion: that the traditions are agreed that there is an ineffable transcendent reality, and that this description, with further negative or non-substantive supplement, is sufficient of itself for saying that they speak of one and the same thing. Some commentators, be it justly or unjustly, have criticised him precisely for maintaining these two assertions on the ground that both are manifestly false (as does Ward 1990, 8–9).

It is notable that Hick denies that the transcendent in itself is or can be the object of a cult or of worship. What is worshipped is a phenomenal focus, e.g. Krishna (1993a, 197–8). This implies that the religions worship different things and have different foci for their cults. Is not this dangerously close to admitting that there is no common reference across the traditions?

In this study (see Chapters 3 and 7 in particular), we shall argue that Hick's distinction between the transcendent as it is in itself and as it appears leaves too little in the way of human cognitive responses in the religion to be caused by the transcendent, and too much to be caused by human social and historical factors, to enable us to posit cognitive contact with religious reality. For Hick stresses throughout his discussion that it is to our culture that we owe the specific beliefs and experiences relating to the transcendent that we have. We experience it in the way our culture allows us to. Determinate beliefs and experiences of the sacred require concepts and these come from cultural background. But then it looks very much as if we could have those beliefs, those experiences, regardless of how the transcendent in itself acts or of whether it exists at all. In other words: culture and religious tradition play too great a causal role in generating the means of referring to the sacred (compare Stoeber 1992, 110). Hick might maintain that what was due to cognitive contact with the sacred was the fact *that* we had religious experience, even though *how* we had it was down to our culture and tradition. I confess to finding this hard to understand. An appropriate analogy might be: imagine different people looking at a common light source through different prisms or glasses. In virtue of the differences in the medium, they see the light as having different colours, but that they see a light at all is due to contact with a common source. But this will not do: for the properties of the *perceived* light are not wholly down to the medium. A white light source will produce different perceptions from a red light even though they are seen through the same medium. Genuine cognitive contact with an object surely entails that *something* of how that object is perceived is down to its character.

This anticipation of later criticism of Hick points us toward a causal account of realism and reference. This causal account introduces one more alleged short-cut in solving the reference problem. It comes from those who argue that a simple causal theory offers a way of cutting reference to the transcendent free of any descriptions used of it and therefore dissolves at a stroke the problem created by conflicting ways of describing it. This approach to reference and God has been advocated by Miller (1986) and Alston (1989c).

Alston and Miller take over the causal theory of reference advocated by Kripke and Putnam and apply it to the reference of 'God'. According to the causal theory, names refer to their referents by way of their causal-historical connections to those referents. For a name to refer successfully to an object two conditions are normally held to be sufficient by those proposing the theory: (1) that there should have been an initial baptising or dubbing of the referent by someone making use of the name in question; (2) that later users of the name are causally indebted to that initial dubbing, such that they intend to refer to whatever it is that was dubbed with the name. Miller and Alston apply this account to 'God' through the supposition that the reference of 'God' is initially fixed by using it to dub *whatever it is* that is encountered in communal activities such as prayer and worship and in religious experience in general. Thereafter the faithful intend to use it to pick out the same object that was initially encountered in these contexts. From both Alston's and Miller's accounts it follows that the beliefs about God and the descriptions of God are unimportant in fixing the reference of 'God'. Thus Alston hypothesises that something quite other than God as traditionally described (say the devil or a Freudian internalised father figure) might be the real object encountered at the initial introduction of the word and was the real causal origin of its use. In that case, he affirms, it would turn out that what the religious community had been referring to all along was that unknown source of their referential practices: it would be that unknown source they were in fact addressing in their worship, prayer and theology, despite the fact that it satisfied none of the typical beliefs they hold about the object of their faith (Alston 1989c, 110–11).

As Miller (1986, 13–14) and Alston (1989c, 115) both note, this theory of reference *appears to* transform the problems of religious diversity at a stroke. For the fact that different traditions hold different beliefs about the object of worship, prayer and religious devotion will not now tend at all to show they refer to different things. On the contrary, the beliefs about the sacred in all traditions might be false but yet they successfully refer to one and the same thing, if that thing lies at the origin of the causal-historical process which the theory alleges reference to consist in.

One way of putting the causal theory as applied to references to the sacred in perspective is by using a distinction between referential and attributive uses of definite descriptions made famous by Donnellan (1977, 46–7). On the Fregean account of reference names refer because they are associated with descriptions which their referents are found to satisfy. But Donnellan notes that we may use a description to refer to an item even though the description is false and quite dispensable. Thus at a party I might make quite clear who I am speaking about by saying 'The lady with the whisky on the rocks is a famous philosopher' even though she has coke in her glass. Here the identifying description is used referentially, in Donnellan's terms. It serves to help to pick out something in context while being false. If, in contrast, I use a description attributively I use it to refer to *whatever it may be* that matches it, perhaps having no specific thing in mind that will fit that bill. Now Alston and Miller are in effect claiming that descriptions of the sacred are used referentially by the various religious traditions. Adherents have 'something in mind' when they refer to the sacred: the thing encountered in religious devotion and practice. The means they employ to describe it are quite dispensable in this task. So when Christians refer to their God as 'omnipotent, omniscient, three-in-one' and so on, they do not intend to mention *whatever it may be* that has these attributes. Rather these descriptions are used referentially to help pick out something which is fundamentally the being that is encountered in worship and was encountered at the start of the tradition. If all descriptions of the sacred are used referentially in the faiths, then they are all in like manner dispensable. If there is reason to suppose that there is but one reality causally responsible for the referential practices of these traditions, then that thing would be referred to by all of them, regardless of how they described it.

We must be wary of this seductively easy solution to our problems. The causal theory in so crude a form is too simple an account of the sufficient conditions of reference. This can easily be seen by considering Evans' refutation of the sufficiency of the two criteria for successful reference offered by simple versions of the theory. On reflection we can see that even if a group of speakers is historically and causally connected to the original baptisers of an object and intend to refer to what the originators of a name intended to pick out, they can still fail to refer to the same thing. Europeans now use the name 'Madagascar' of an island off the African coast. The name was picked up from native speakers who used it to refer to part of the continent itself. Later Europeans are historically and causally indebted to the inventors of the name for their use of it. But a misunderstanding of the original use and the occurrence of a false belief about the intended object of reference means that we do not refer to the same thing as the originators of the name (Evans 1977, 202).

Miller's and Alston's account of the reference of 'God' cannot guarantee that the existence of historical and causal connections back to some original source of reference allows reference to succeed. We must allow the possibility that a radical enough change of belief about the character of the referent will change one object of reference for another or make later uses of a name empty. We can argue further that the implicit attempt to cast all descriptions of the transcendent as referential rather than attributive can be questioned. It might be argued that some of the descriptions used of God in, for example, the Christian community are to be understood attributively. It has been maintained that there is a 'hard core' of Christian descriptions of God which have to be true of something if Christians are to refer to anything at all. Thus we might say that if we discover the thing causally responsible for Christian language of God but find nonetheless that it is not a being worthy of worship, or not that than which no greater can be conceived, then it is not God after all and Christians just have not been referring to anything at all. Between communities historically or geographically divided there must be some links in the hard core properties they ascribe to their God for them to be referring to the same God (so argues Gale 1991, 7–8). In the light of this it is surely incorrect, *contra* Alston (1989c, 110–11), to assert confidently that if we discover that the being causally responsible for a community's experiences shares none of the hard-core properties of the God that community thinks it worships, then it is still worshipping that thing. We would in such a case have a good ground for saying that it turned out they were worshipping nothing at all.

RECONSTRUCTING REFERENCE

The discussion so far has been negative in its implications but out of it can emerge a positive account of how sameness of reference to the sacred can be judged.

It looks as if pluralism must detach itself from a descriptive theory of reference, both because it does not provide an easy way of securing common reference in the face of cognitive conflicts between religions and because it promises an unfavourable account of the character of realism. If we review arguments against the descriptive theory from its opponents (as in Devitt 1981, 14–20), we find the contention that correct description is neither a necessary nor a sufficient account of successful reference. It is not a necessary condition because it fails to take account of the many examples where folk use a name to refer but have mistaken ideas, or no very clear ideas at all, as to how to identify the object of reference. In other words the theory posits a degree of identifying knowledge of objects of speech which the majority of users of a language do not possess. For the majority of speakers, it seems that using a name to refer depends on relying on some few who are experts on, or are acquainted with, the referent. Perhaps this division of linguistic labour means that the few on whom the rest rely must have identifying, descriptive knowledge of the referent. Donnellan's points contend against this conclusion. Moreover, this is where the point that successful description is not a sufficient condition of reference comes in. We can see how this might come about when we reflect that reference must at heart be a mode of contact, epistemic and cognitive, with things. Yet I might believe a set of descriptions to be true and these descriptions might be uniquely true of something in the real world without those descriptions thereby establishing cognitive contact between me and that object. It might just happen that I have come to these beliefs which happen to be uniquely true of this thing. If they do not arise out of contact with the referent or lead to further contact with it, it is implausible to say that I refer to it. We are here supposing that there has to be a causal element in the notions of cognitive contact and reference. Reference has to be grounded in some way in the referent and the notion of true description does not suffice to explain that grounding. In other words, we point through the notion of reference to the fact that our language hooks on to the world at some points. There must be semantic and epistemological links between human subjects and reality if there is successful reference. Yet 'believing true descriptions' does not suffice for establishing semantic and epistemological links – 'hooks' – to reality. True beliefs can arise in all manner of ways and if they arise in a way which is not related, however loosely, to the existence and character of the object of reference, then they do not constitute semantic and epistemological links between speaker and reality.

So far a reconstructed causal account of reference for a given name seems to involve two things. First, some speakers or other are able initially to ground use of the name in the existence and character of the referent. Second, later, or other, speakers are indebted to these original users for a tradition of so using the name, without too many hitches of the kind we noted from Evans in the previous section. But more needs to be said.

One reason why the causal theory needs supplementing is that the notion of an initial ground of a name in some contact with the referent needs expanding. Not just any confrontation of a causal kind between speaker and object resulting in the speaker coining a name will mean that the speaker subsequently refers to that object by using the name coined. We have argued that, if Freud was right, and religious folk originally encountered repressed memories of a father figure in coining names like 'Jahweh', they would not refer to that father figure by the name 'Jahweh'. An initial *cognitive* contact between speaker and object is required to ground later uses, and that implies that there be some identification of the object by the speaker. This identification may not be wholly correct. It is certainly not tantamount to having a stock of true descriptions about the object. But it does imply that the speaker is able to locate the object in some rough category or kind. (This is to agree with Devitt 1981, 64 and disagree with Gellman 1993, 201.) In our Freudian story, religious folk just did not make an initial cognitive contact with a repressed image of a father figure if they identified it by way of the notions of a transcendent object of awe and worship, for all that they were causally in contact with that repressed image when they first spoke of the numinous.

The notions of the initial grounding of a name being dependent on some very roughly correct identification and of involving placing the referent in some broad ontological category are vague. They incorporate an element of the descriptive theory back into the explication of reference. In particular they get *some* of the sense of the contention that there must be some elements in common in the different clusters of descriptions two or more speakers associate with a name for them to be using that name to refer to the same thing (as argued by Smith P. 1981). The notion will be made a little clearer below when we expand on Harré's idea of reference as involving material practices (1986, 105). Referring as a mode of cognitive contact goes along with (supports and is supported by) other exemplifications of such contact with the referent, such as patterns of investigation into, and manipulation of, the referent. Evidently, the material practices associated with speaking of a transcendent, sacred reality, such as worship and prayer, do not fit with the character of the Freudian repressed father image. Hence, they could not survive recognition that encounter with this object is what prompted use of the names for God. A more or less wholly different set of material practices would be invoked by putative recognition that *this* is what the faithful were really talking about. This kind of judgement, then, might flesh out what is meant by saying that some minimal identification of the referent had not taken place or had been so misplaced as to destroy reference.

In the above we are conceding that the notion of material practices in reference has some descriptive implications. To be engaged in a material practice with regard to a referent is implicitly to be committed to the appropriateness of some, however general, categorisation or description of that referent. Yet this is not to say that the material-practices approach collapses into descriptivism. For stress on practices as an important part of reference helps to cement the idea that reference involves causal contact with the referent. Moreover, general descriptions implicit in material practices with regard to a referent need not be entertained or drawn out by those involved in successful reference.

The notion, then, of an initial grounding of a name in a referent is complex. In the case of religions and their names for the sacred, it is obvious that we have different groundings of a set of names for, allegedly and according to the pluralist, the same referent. Numerically different occasions of initial contact and encounter prompt use of the names for the transcendent. Many ordinary names are grounded in multiple contacts by many people with the objects they name (Devitt 1981, 20–1). According to a causal theory of reference, it looks as if we should say there are multiple groundings of names for the one sacred reality if we found reason to say that the same object was behind these groundings and the right, rough and ready modes of identification were present in the many occasions of grounding. If we construe names for the sacred on the model of proper nouns, the situation would be illustrated by the following parallel. Let us suppose we have a unique object such as Halley's Comet. English speakers refer to it via that name. But it will have manifested itself in many localities and to many cultures and so have other names in different languages. All these names are names for the same thing if causal connections of the right kind trace each of these names back to one and the same object. Or we might construe names for the sacred on the model of names for natural kinds (as does Senor 1991). In which case our parallel for names of the sacred would be this. There is natural stuff – say, gold – known about in many cultures. A whole host of names in a myriad of languages are used to pick out this stuff. They do indeed pick out one and the same stuff if and only if the practices of using them descend from appropriate causal contacts with samples of the same natural kind. Whether names for the transcendent are to be assimilated to proper nouns or to the names for natural kinds is not an issue that need be decided here, though in Chapter 6 I note an important alleged advantage some versions of pluralism might see in following Senor's account and in thinking of the transcendent as a kind.

In the nature of the case, we are not going to have direct evidence that all or most names for the sacred causally descend in the right way from grounding in contact with one and the same referent. We are not going to be able to trace directly the causal link back to the one transcendent object. Our reasons for postulating such a link will have to be indirect. We will have to look for indications that it is plausible to suppose that the causal pathways trace back to the same referent via very roughly similar forms of identification. Similar material practices will again be important here, as will larger programmatic considerations (such as economy). The insight the causal theory helps us to is that we are looking to give a best guess about the history of cognitive contact with a referent and that agreement in detailed descriptions is not necessary to judge that history to exist. Successful reference establishes a cognitive tie between speaker and object. That tie is not made through the sheer fact that the speaker's descriptions happen through chance to best fit the object and does not depend on descriptive success in any detail. Referring is a material practice which entails a causal link between cognitive subject and referent (Harré 1986, 68–9). The truth that the causal theory grasps is that reference is a relation between people and things: speakers refer, whilst terms denote (Harré 1986, 69).

We have seen reason, however, to supplement the causal theory of reference with insights from the descriptive theory. The root errors of an unmodified causal theory stem from its undiluted extensionalism. It seems to portray the meaning of names as flowing from objects up to referring expressions. But in science and in religion the idea that we are confronted with given objects for which we then simply have to find names is naive. Rich and complex processes of interpreting and inferring from experience are required for the object of knowledge to be made available. Hence, reference depends to some extent on our descriptive resources and on the way in which we use these to divide up and anticipate experience (see Harré 1986, 68).

One way in which a causal theory needs supplementing is through the idea that we can use conceptual and linguistic resources to anticipate grounding references. Science abounds with examples that illustrate this possibility. The name 'virus' was coined before researchers had the ability to observe viruses with the aid of the electron microscope. The word was coined to refer to the cause of a range of effects – symptoms of disease. 'Virus' referred to whatever it was that was the explanation of these effects. This is still causal grounding in a referent. The name is anchored in what it names by virtue of a causal link, running via observed effects of the referent. It is also important to note that this causal link is a cognitive tie because coiners of the term had some rough and ready notion of what kind of thing it was, the effects of which they were observing. They were looking for something in the category of 'micro-organism', something analogous in some respects to bacteria, only – to put it crudely – smaller. So, through naming by way of a thing's effects and some classificatory ideas that were roughly right, experience was anticipated. Reference was made to that which was not yet directly encountered. For all that early ideas about what a virus was underwent change as explorations to fix the precise character of the referent of 'virus' proceeded, we can say that later researchers discovered what was true and false of the thing that earlier biologists referred to. In the process of discovery some of the earlier sense of 'virus' would have been altered. Yet the reference of the word did not change with changes of its sense. Sense does not determine reference, but rather the possibility of reference (Harré 1986, 33).

It is one of the great merits of Donnellan's account that it brings home the extent to which the establishing of the tie between human subject and referent can be maintained through the discovery of gross error in some of the speaker's identifying descriptions. The *context* in which a speaker endeavours to identify the object of reference may establish that tie despite error, hence at the party it may be obvious that I refer to the philosopher with the coke even though I identify her through a false description. The context in which early talk about viruses became established is sufficiently like that of later talk to enable identity of reference to be preserved.

Knowledge of the causal context of speech can eliminate candidates for reference. Our thoughts about what scientists of an earlier generation might have been referring to by their words will depend crucially on what we think they might have been experimenting on, manipulating and the like. Scientific activities of this kind constitute a range of material practices which establish ties between human subjects and objects. We will ask of earlier scientists 'What could have been the focus of their material practices?' We will identify that focus via what we believe to exist and to be capable of causally entering into cognitive ties with human beings. If we see a continuity between their material practices and ours, and if their descriptions of the objects they investigate are not too widely at odds with ours, we will say they refer to the same things as us.

I am of course suggesting that similarity of context and thoughts about causality will help us set aside differences in the descriptions associated with names of the sacred. This is a strategic thought. It is meant to bear fruit in later discussions of the definition of religion, of salvation and of religious experience. It is open to immediate objection on the grounds that there are no precise similarities in the material practices associated with different names for the transcendent and the sacred. For example, the ritual practices of religions differ markedly. We need not deny this point. The task of later chapters will be to present a plausible case for the pluralist's minimal common reference thesis by suggesting continuities across contexts which ground talk about the transcendent. The strategy employed will not entail denying differences of detail. It will entail finding likeness-in-difference by noting general continuities that cut across differences.

Similarity of context and a sense of continuity in material practices might enable us to tolerate very great differences in how
two or more subjects describe the same referent. As Harré puts
it, 'However, reference to a referent, once secured, can be maintained through massive deletions from and additions to the cor-
pus of beliefs we hold to be true of that referent' (1986, 66). In
judging how diversity of description affects identity of reference
what matters is not whether defining descriptions of referents
are held in common. After all, the way in which common substances and kinds (such as gold, water and acid) have been defined across different ages of science has altered markedly. Yet
we do not wish to say that the reference of words for these
substances and kinds has changed as thoughts about how they
are constituted have developed. Overlap and continuity in material practices and a range of classification are powerful arguments against such a view. What matters more is that changes in
basic category and kind should not disturb such continuities and
overlaps too much. Two examples from Harré will serve to illustrate this point (1986, 105).

In the history of astronomy a planet (Vulcan) was thought to
orbit the Sun inside the track of Mercury. Some observational
evidence of Vulcan's existence at roughly the right place was
found. We now believe there is no such planet. Those observa-
tions were probably of a sunspot. But we would not readily say
that 'Vulcan' was the name for that sunspot. We have a good
idea what caused the experiences said to be of the planet Vulcan,
but the earlier astronomers just did not succeed in making a
successful reference to that thing, so wrong were their ideas about
the basic category of astronomical object to which it belonged.
By contrast, though the 'planet' Pluto, known and investigated
for decades, is now believed not to be a planet but a captured
comet, we want to say that this discovery is a new fact about one
and the same thing as was first observed and identified as Pluto
on 21 January 1930. We might want to save the reference of
'Pluto' to the captured comet now believed to orbit the Sun at
the outer edge of the solar system for a number of good reasons.
Continuity of material practices is one. The efforts to observe this
orbiting heavenly object which commenced in the early decades
of the century are continuous with those undertaken today. The
context of enquiry continues much the same. There is an overlap

in many of the descriptions of Pluto then and Pluto now. Finally we may be moved by a principle of charity in interpreting belief. If we say that what was referred to as Pluto in mid-twentieth century astronomy can no longer be taken to be about Pluto then a great many beliefs which would otherwise be true turn out to be false.

The force of Harré's examples depends on our seeing that there is too great an error in the mode of identifying 'Vulcan' for us to be able to say now 'It did name something; it was their way of referring to a sunspot'. Suppose we are sure that there was a single, unique sunspot, observation of which had led to the coinage of 'Vulcan'. There would then have been a causal chain that takes later use of 'Vulcan' back to a unique object. But we are asked to concede the point that this is not sufficient to give us the grounding of name in object which an amended causal theory requires. Grounding is the first stage in cognitive contact with, epistemic access to, objects. So an amended causal theory has to see grounding as other than a purely extensional link but rather as associated with features of a cognitive context, such as: modes of identification, procedures of investigation and research. We should note, however, that a good theory of reference will not rule that reference is an all or nothing affair. There is no stark choice between referring and failing to refer. In the historiography of science it has been necessary to develop a notion of partial reference (Smith P. 1981, 79; Devitt 1981, 138). So we might say that 'mass' in Newtonian physics partly designates relativistic mass or, more controversially, that 'phlogiston' in eighteenth-century theories of combustion partly designates oxygen. Such partially denoting terms had some links with reality, allowed some cognitive contact with the real. They may not have just been empty names. Yet major hitches, cognitive and causal, in the paths that take these terms back to a grounding in real things lead us to conclude that they did not hook on to reality one-to-one.

From this discussion we can sum up a number of points about reference which may then be taken over into discussion of reference to the sacred. (1) Reference can anticipate encounter with the realities referred to because it is aided by sense and indirect causal links. (2) Reference is dependent upon the establishment of a causal link between speaker and referent. (3) Descriptions of referents are to be interpreted and weighed in the light of contexts of speech and enquiry, contexts being determined in part by material practices (in science such activities as: observing, experimenting, investigating). (4) Identity of descriptions held true by two speakers is not required for sameness of reference, because: (a) referents are identified through very rough and ready classifications and causal contact; and (b) continuity of material practices can discount quite massive divergences in identifying descriptions. (5) Divergences in descriptions which entail too great a gulf in basic classification of a referent can prevent attributing identity of reference to two names or two uses of the same name.

The above points can be applied to referring to the sacred to yield useful points about how sameness of reference can be judged in the religious case. For a start we can see more clearly the limitations in the Alston–Miller account according to which 'God' and similar names are employed to fit whatever it is that believers encounter in prayer, devotion or religious experiences. Janet Martin Soskice *seems* to imply such a view when she hints that a reference for 'God' might be fixed through such statements as 'Whatever appeared to me on the mountain was God', 'Whatever caused me to change my life was God' (Martin Soskice 1985, 151). In the material practices associated with putative attempts to identify the sacred, such as prayer, worship, spiritual discipline and right action, basic characterisations of the 'whatever it is' that lies behind the experiences will be implied. It is only a certain kind of thing that could be an appropriate object of these material practices. So Gale has some grasp of the truth when he insists that some hard-core properties of God are required in one's descriptions of God for one to be referring to him at all. Moreover the sacred is not simply encountered as a bare given, but only as mediated through the concepts and descriptions of a tradition. The religious quest is for an object that will serve as a focus for the material practices of religion. Such a quest presumes a rough ontological classification of the referent while allowing that there is much to be learnt about its precise, detailed character.

Contextualism in reference can be taken further by asking what restraints causality might impose upon interpreting reference. It is tempting from within the philosophy of religion to assume that no polytheistic account of transcendent, sacred reality is a candidate for truth. Philosophers will be inclined to infer from this assumption that what religions refer to, if anything at all, is what philosophical thought in the East and West has identified to be the only plausible candidate for this status, namely the ontologically, valuatively and rationally ultimate reality referred to in Chapter 1 above (see also Clarke 1992, 147). Such an assumption narrows the field to say the least. There can be but one unique referent for the religions if there is any referent at all. If the names of the sacred in a religion do not name the transcendent ultimate postulated by so much philosophy, East and West, we may be unable to assign them any reference whatsoever. Hence we have a powerful motive, resting upon the demands of intellectual economy and charity, to assign all traditions the same referent, provided we find similarities in important material practices and not too dissimilar classifications of sacred focus. It is of course in this kind of light that Vroom's collection of conflicting yet overlapping descriptions of the sacred from various traditions becomes significant.

These last thoughts might appear to make the pluralist's reference thesis too easy to establish. We help ourselves to the assumption that there is but one referent – the ultimate – for religious discourse if there is any at all. We can then go on to say that only those descriptions and predicates in the religions which are cognate with 'ultimate reality' are to be seen as attributive. They fix the nature of the kind of thing referred to. All other descriptions of the transcendent in the traditions which are not cognate with 'ultimate reality' are to be understood referentially, so their truth, and thus their consistency with one another, can be discounted for purposes of fixing a reference for notions of the focus of religions. Pluralism wins hands down. But this is a *reductio* of its ideas about reference. It cannot be as easy as that.

The reply to this objection is that in a way we do wish to show the plausibility of pluralism by making its key theses seem obvious. Defining pluralism in a minimal way helps in this. Producing a modified causal account of reference is meant to allow painless and considerable discounting of doctrinal clashes between religions in judging reference. Yet pluralism's account of reference still has some bite and some work to do. For example, even taking notions connected with ultimacy to be the only attributive ones connected with the transcendent, there is still a problem over whether strands of Buddhism can be included in the minimal referential thesis of pluralism. There are well-founded doubts as to how far systems of thought in the Buddhist traditions are committed to referring to, or engaging with via material practices, an ultimate, absolute reality. This point is taken up in the next chapter and in Chapters 6 and 7.

The thesis that 'if one refers, they all refer' is not obvious to many confessional exclusivists who deny that all religions are in cognitive contact with transcendent reality. For while some exclusivists might say something along the lines of (in the theistic case) 'Other religions worship the one God, but they do so wrongly, superstitiously', others will no doubt balk at this. Against this kind of thinker we shall have to mount arguments (in Chapter 5) to the effect that religious experience across *many* traditions should be taken as veridical if *any* is. We will want to show the exlusivist that it is implausible to suppose that if one religion is referentially successful, the others are grounded in human fancies. We will also want to argue against the inclusivist that referential success does not usher in the possibility of a fully-fledged description of the character of the sacred which will decisively favour one tradition over an other. Against the relativist, we will want to contend that reference is nonetheless best interpreted as being to an extra-mental, extra-mundane reality if it is to anything at all. So there is still argument to be undertaken over the character of the realism implied by the reference thesis. Finally we shall not be able to discuss pluralism's reference thesis in a conditional mode forever. To show that pluralism is a plausible philosophical thesis in the interpretation of religion, we will have to indicate in what follows how there is much to be said in favour of attributing a genuine, unconditional referential success to all the religions.

PLURALISM AND REFERENCE

The preceding section brought us a rough and ready list of criteria which must be satisfied if pluralism's thesis of common reference is to be made good. Pluralism needs a common religious context, and particularly similarity or overlap or continuity in the material practices which might tie religious believers of different traditions to a common religious focus. This appeal to linked contexts must be supported by some means of overcoming such divergences of description of the sacred focus as are found among the traditions. Divergence in description can be overcome via a range of routes. Stress on context might lessen the need to have converging descriptions beyond agreement on a basic category into which the alleged common focus falls. Arguments for the non-literal character of descriptions of the transcendent could provide ways of overcoming seeming contradictions between tradition-based ways of characterising it. In addition, if alleged identifying descriptions could be seen as referential not attributive, because they were facets of a gradual, fallible *process* of epistemic access to the sacred, divergence would not matter to the same degree. Tradition-rooted descriptions would then be valuable but in part dispensable as aids to putting humans in touch with religious reality.

The next five chapters of this study are devoted to setting out and examining these criteria and dimensions of successful reference for names of the transcendent. Chapter 3 will pursue the case for identifying a common context across the religions from which references to a common sacred can be made. It will ask how far the material practices of relating to a sacred focus in the traditions can be likened or linked to one another. Much of this chapter will be concerned with the significance of the category of 'religion' itself, since it is by classifying a range of traditions as 'religions' that the contexts of thought and practice (and thus reference) in these traditions are assimilated to one another. One of the major means of identifying members of any class of 'religions' is via the notion of salvation. The thought that religions are members of a distinct and important common class because they pursue a distinct goal – salvation – will be given some prominence in the argument. So Chapter 4 will consider how far the assimilation of 'religions' under this banner is justified. And since pluralism wishes to link all major religions via a common salvific success, as well as via a common reference, it is vital to investigate what can be said for and against the idea that religions are equal in being means to some kind of commonly defined salvation. How salvation is described in the various traditions will, of course, be found to differ in detail. Difference in detail is also to be found in direct descriptions of the transcendent. Chapter 6 will examine the range of tactics open to the pluralist in coping with such distinct descriptions. Emphasis will be placed on a hermeneutic of metaphor as the appropriate way of reading rich descriptions of the transcendent. The topic of whether and how far the transcendent may be thought of as having a diverse nature will also be explored. That would be another way of saving common reference despite divergence.

Epistemological issues will be to the fore in all these discussions. There are two aspects of the debate about the epistemology of religious faith treated in Chapter 5 which are of particular importance for the exploration of pluralism. One is the establishment of a case for the possibility of sufficient knowledge of the transcendent to enable reference to it to be conceivable. The other is the matching restriction of this knowledge to avoid the possibility that some version of confessionalism is true. Pluralism draws a fine line between knowledge and ignorance about the sacred. To avoid giving way to naturalism, it must avoid the force of such arguments as would make knowledge of non-mundane realities impossible. On the other hand it must itself give arguments for being sceptical of the claims on behalf of any rich, positive account of the transcendent to be normative and definitive. Pluralism, as noted in Chapter 1 above, depends on mitigated relativism when it comes to claims about the sacred. It needs an epistemology appropriate for the conclusion that reference to the transcendent is best secured through minimal, largely negative, descriptions of the transcendent and non-literal, essentially revisable and partial metaphors or models of its character. Such an epistemology will give initial plausibility to the prime element of pluralism as we have defined it here: the view of the major religions as overlapping, limited, revisable attempts to achieve cognitive contact with a common sacred reality.

Pluralism demands a particular type of realism. The closest intellectual analogue to such realism which we can understand appears to be the kind of realism under discussion in interpretations of the history of science. It is this kind of realism – referential realism – we continually invoke in this study when we speak of the various traditions as perhaps overlapping, revisable but successful attempts to refer to sacred reality. Of particular importance in vindicating a realism of this sort in the sphere of religion will be the possibility of detaching realism from strict notions of truth. Exploring kinds of realism and applying them to religion will be the task of Chapter 7.

3

Religion

ESSENCES AND KINDS

In the preceding chapter it was argued that for pluralism to make good its thesis of common reference it had to maintain that religious traditions share common or overlapping contexts of thought, experience and action. This suggests that there must be some substantive similarities between those things we call 'religions' and hence that the category of religion is a genuine one. It cannot be shown to be a genuine one unless in turn it is possible to define 'religion' in some clear and informative way.

Pluralism needs, then, a means of establishing the real similarity or connectedness of those things conventionally labelled 'religions'. This point does not merely follow from the requirements of supporting the reference thesis. The very definition of pluralism entails the same conclusion. Pluralism is of its essence a general thesis about a class of human institutions called 'religions'. It consists of generalisations about members of that class. If that class is not a genuine one, if its members share no similarities or connections, then the generalisations about its exemplifications which pluralism makes will be insupportable. For example, in Chapter 1 we have defined pluralism in terms of three generalisations about the religions: (1) All major religions make a common reference to the transcendent. (2) All major traditions likewise are equal in offering some means to human salvation or other. (3) All major traditions are to be seen as containing revisable, limited accounts of the sacred: none is certain enough in its particular dogmatic formulations to provide the norm for interpreting the others.

These key theses of pluralism of themselves assert similarities between the faiths. We have seen already, and our discussion in subsequent chapters will demonstrate further, that they can only be supported if yet more generalisations, implying other similarities and overlaps between members of the class 'religion', are true.

Pluralism depends on there being certain forms of unity among the putative religions. The questions then arise as to how strong must these kinds of unity be for pluralism to work, and how far, across how many systems of thought and practice, must they extend. The second question takes us back to a matter broached in Chapter 1: just how many, and which, 'major traditions' is pluralism to count as covered by its three defining theses? Would it matter if some traditions commonly counted as religions were excluded from the pluralist fold upon application of its detailed account of what makes common reference and salvation possible? Having aired these questions once more I shall put off answering them again, for it is only when pluralism emerges as a fully articulated theory of the relations between the religions that they can be answered. However we can note one argumentative possibility for pluralism when faced with the difficulties of establishing forms of unity and likeness between traditions: it can narrow the range of traditions united by its generalisations. This is a characteristic move of proponents of pluralism. Hick, for example, excludes the 'pre-Axial' faiths from the direct scope of his pluralist interpretation of religion (see Hick 1989, 36–55). In advance of a detailed working out of pluralism, it does not seem that it must endeavour to include everything that is or has been classed as a religion in the scope of its generalisations. There may indeed be a cost to exclusion of many, or some major, traditions, namely that it becomes more difficult to preserve an intelligible picture of the relation pluralism postulates between humanity and sacred, transcendent reality.

The immediate problems facing pluralism's postulation of a unified category of religion stem from the problems in asserting a common essence to religion and the well-known difficulties in finding any definition of 'religion' at all that would enable us to see it as denoting a clear-cut, *bona fide* class of systems of thought and practice.

Is pluralism committed to the claim that all religions share an essence? In Chapter 1 I noted the criticism levelled at versions of pluralism to the effect that they entail essentialism (as in Cobb 1990, 81). Essentialism cannot merely consist in the notion that there is sufficient in common between, or connecting, the various religions to make them members of a genuine class: for otherwise we could not then explain the particular odium attaching to the word 'essentialism' in the contemporary study of religion. Essentialism is thought bad because it has overtones of a view which regards the differences between the religions as trivial in relation to the common core they all share. Belief in an essence to religion implies that features of religions beyond this essence belong to the surface of the phenomenon of religion only. Religions underneath are everywhere the same, but their common essence manifests itself in different ways in different circumstances.

One way to cash the metaphors behind the characterisation of essentialism is to think of the religious essentialist as someone who has a thesis about how to explain religion and about the relative priority of different factors in the phenomenon of religion (for a fuller account of what follows see Clarke and Byrne 1993, 16–26). The essentialist maintains that in the explanation of religion the common core of religion comes first. There are different religions because this common core (be it of experience, doctrine, ethics or what have you) manifests itself in different guises in different historical and cultural circumstances. But the core remains unaltered in its different manifestations. It is in some such a way as this that the distinguishing features of religions are reduced to trivial status by essentialism. The central, important features of a particular religion, such as Islam, are held to be sufficiently explained by its manifesting the common essence of religion, while its unique, distinguishing characteristics are but reflections of historical, geographical and cultural factors external to religion itself. Essentialism is in part a fictional position invented in debates about the character of religion. It is a straw man set up for refutation. The facts that it downgrades the distinguishing features of religion and that it encourages a priori accounts of the true features of religion make it fit to serve this role. However, it is possible to find writers who come close to the stock figure of the essentialist in some of what they say, as in Otto's well-known accounts of the role of numinous experience as the heart of religion in *The Idea of the Holy* (see for example Otto 1958, 6).

The advantages for pluralism arising from the truth of an essentialist account of religions would be manifold. If all religions are alike in essence and their distinguishing features are of little importance to their character as religions, then the contexts from which folk in different religions endeavour to refer to sacred, transcendent reality are radically alike. The religions form a homogeneous class whose members are strictly comparable. They are not merely variations on the same theme, but the same theme played on different instruments. Hick's account of pluralism comes close to essentialism. For all that he says that religion can only be defined in family resemblance terms (1989, 4), it appears that the family resemblance character of religion's typical features applies only to surface features. He heads one of his chapters with a quotation from Bunyan: 'The soul of religion is the practick part' (1989, 299). This connects with earlier suggestions in *An Interpretation of Religion* that behind all the post-Axial faiths there is a common soteriological core. When described at the right level of abstraction, they have the same soteriology. Soteriology boils down to ethics plus some kind of belief in an after life, it appears, and Chapters 17 and 18 describe a range of respects in which the practical dimensions of all genuine religions are alike. Hence, 'The soul of religion is the practick part'. We appear to have a version of a liberal view of religion which sees it as essentially ethics and sees all religions as having the same ethics.

To avoid giving in to the tendency to essentialism, the pluralist needs a sense in which all religions can be comparable and be counted as members of a distinct and genuine genus yet which does not tend to minimise their individual differences. It may be helpful here to think of other kinds which are distinct and genuine, but whose members cannot be seen as manifestations of the same essence. The class of colours is a genuine one. All the things we count as colours are united by a range of formal and structural properties. Yet individual colours – red, black, green, and so on – can only exist as distinct exemplifications of the class. Colour is a determinable property whose manifestations are particular determinate realisations of the kind.

What offends in essentialist accounts of religion is the selection of some substantive, common feature of religion as the binding feature of the class and the relegation of other features which are variable to the status of secondary, unimportant by-products of this feature. The substantive binding feature might be a shared ethic (as in some liberal views of religion), or a shared religious experience (as in Otto), or some shared beliefs about God (as in Lord Herbert of Cherbury). Binding the class of religions together in this way produces the impression of negating or downgrading the differences between the religions and of propagating a monochrome account of human religious life. A cheap victory is then secured for pluralism: for if the differences between religions are not important will it not follow easily that they are linked in the three-fold way pluralism maintains? Pluralism could be established by appeal to essentialism (so could some form of inclusivism), but only at the cost of defending an essentialist view of religion against the manifold objections to it (explored in Clarke and Byrne 1993, 16–26). More hopeful is the project explored in these pages: of articulating pluralism while accepting fully the differences between the religions. This entails arguing for the genuineness of the genus religion without giving a monochrome picture of its members. It suggests a project of establishing the genuineness of the kind religion on the basis of formal or structural properties its members share. That would allow substantive differences (in ethics, experience, doctrine and the like) to obtain between the religions while it was still true that they form a distinct kind. Thus the pluralist would avoid the charge that his or her interpretation of religion can only be maintained at the cost of fitting all the major religions into a common mould.

An attempt to build the category of religion around common structural and formal properties will be made in the following section. But we must first register a protest against the entire attempt to see religion as a genuine kind. John Milbank asserts:

> The usual construals of religion as a genus ... embody covert Christianizations, and in fact no attempt to define such a genus (or even, perhaps, delineation of an analogical field of 'family' resemblances) will succeed, because no proposed common features can be found, whether in terms of belief or practice (gods, the supernatural, worship, a sacred/secular division, etc.) that are without exceptions. The most viable, because most general definitions ('what binds a society together' and so forth) turn out to be so all-encompassing as to coincide with the definition of culture as such.
>
> (Milbank 1990, 176–7)

Milbank has two charges: first that definitions of religion which might establish religion as a genuine kind are not forthcoming; second that the concept of religion is a Western one, whose use to categorise non-Western forms of belief and behaviour involves interpreting other 'religions' in the light of Christian categories (see the discussion of Cantwell Smith on the category of religion in the Preface, above). The first charge can only be met satisfactorily by producing a definition of religion that does the job the pluralist requires. Milbank's strictures do highlight the difficult choice between specificity and generality in the definition of religion. Specificity is required in any definition if it is to establish genuine likeness between members of the class religion; generality is also required to avoid the class being too narrowly defined. A narrow definition will incur the cost of excluding from the class systems of belief and practice which are commonly regarded as religions and bring the consequence that some important cultures do not have religion. The pluralist needs real comparability between the faiths and the sharing of many cultures in a common human religious quest. This dilemma, then, is a crucial one for the pluralist's project.

The problems highlighted by Milbank's first charge are as yet but warnings of dangers which perhaps a suitable definition of religion might overcome. Milbank in fact thinks that the only content-full yet general definition of religion that works will be one which identifies it via the important feature of most or all cultures, which consists in their offering through symbols and the like a picture of what is real, a picture which in turn directs and undergirds the practices of the culture (1990, 177). This leads him to conclude that

> The commonness that pertains between different religions, is therefore not the commonness of a genus, or of a particular specified *mode* of human existence; instead it is the commonness of Being, or of the fact of cultural – as opposed to natural existence – itself. And there is nothing *necessarily* analogical within the community of cultural being; instead Being . . . or 'what there is', can get construed in sheerly different and incommensurable ways by the many religions.
>
> (Milbank 1990, 177)

Milbank here refers to 'the many religions', so I take it that he thinks the word 'religion' has *some* utility in cultural description.

His main point, presumably, is that there is not sufficient unity among the things called 'religions' to enable us to treat them as members of a genus. They do not form a class about which useful generalisations can be made. In so far as they are objects of generalisation at all, it is only because they are manifestations of cultural being. There is nothing distinctive about the religions as manifestations of culture. I find this conclusion highly counter-intuitive and dependent upon the considerable ambiguity in Milbank's reflections which smoothes his argument along. Granted that all cultures have symbols indicating what is real for the folk who live in them and inculcating practices conforming to such pictures, it may still be the case that there are distinctly *religious* symbols or modes of relating practice to pictures of what there is. This may be so even while it is true that the symbol–practice dimensions of the various religions are incommensurable and distinct to a degree. They could be distinctly *religious* as symbol–practice systems because they share distinct formal and structural qualities which make them religions, while being different, diverse and opposed at the level of substance and content. All this will be explored in the next section.

Milbank's second charge against the genus of religion brings up the thesis, already discussed in this study, that the concept of religion is distinctly Western in origin. Of itself this will not of course show that it is mis-applied when used to pick out aspects of the cultural existence of non-Western societies. Pluralism is rooted in the modern Western tradition of historical and philosophical reflection on the character of religion. It will need therefore to be self-conscious about the possibility that it imports highly ethnocentric assumptions into its interpretations of non-Western forms of belief and practice. Distortions can result. Do they result *necessarily* and on a scale which negates the exercise? That remains to be proved. The business of critical, academic study of human affairs, which is what throws up categories such as religion, is in general Western in origin. By analogy, the notion that cultures have an economic life which is worthy of some separate description and reflection is one with a Western origin. Are we to say then that the thought that non-Westerners engage in actions which are recognisably in the genus 'economic' is therefore spurious? The character of the origin of the terms of cultural classification and description does not of itself refute the thought that these terms have enabled us to describe what was there in other cultures to be seen all along.

Problems with Milbank's suggestion that the so-called religions are Western mental creations out of cultural realities which are absolutely incommensurable arise from the fact that the religions cross boundaries of cultures and are interconnected. Conversions of whole societies to religions which have their origin in different cultures are a persistent feature of religious history. It may be argued that the fact that Buddhism, Islam, Christianity and the rest can be found in diverse cultures suggests that they are not simply identical with the cultural being of particular societies. It rather suggests that there is in such systems something distinct in the way of belief and practice which can be detached from a particular culture and embraced by another. There is Islam in southern Europe and in Malaysia, and while Islam no doubt takes on particular colours in such diverse cultures, we are surely entitled to say that a common system of worship and belief is found across this cultural gulf. This argument stands in need of qualification, for we have conceded earlier that the notion of separate, discrete entities corresponding to labels like 'Buddhism' and 'Islam' is semi-fictional. In reality we are referring to loose families of practice and belief. These may indeed take on very different forms from culture to culture. Yet this is not to agree with Milbank that they offer nothing that is distinctive to cultures. It is surely more plausible to see them as involved in two-way interaction, with a migration of Buddhist ideas, scriptures and institutions across cultures contributing to, while being in part shaped by, the new culture. Milbank could resist this by saying that what contributes to the new culture is not distinctively religious but merely another, new manifestation of cultural being. But this just looks like dogma to me, or at least so it will appear if we can construct a working definition of religion supporting the notion that religion is a distinctive manifestation of cultural being (see below).

The different religions cannot just be incommensurable if, as they do, they see themselves as rivals and as competitors for credence. Such a sense hints that they see themselves as competitive answers to similar questions, or responses to similar needs. This point does not of itself entail that there must be a distinct genus of religion. For the different things we call 'religion' may be rival manifestations of some much broader genus, such as 'world-view'. If Buddhism and Islam provide in part rival answers to the question 'How should I live?' that does not show them to be competing instances of a special genus of religion. Matters will look different if we find some distinctively religious questions to which they provide in part rival answers. Below I will suggest one such question, namely 'How are we to cope with the problems of human finitude?'

Further argument is needed to show that a narrower and distinctively religious category of outlook and practice can be defined. But the thought that the religions might see themselves as rival answers to similar questions is worth pursuing a little more. It would be one fact which would help explain the possibility of conversion from one faith to another. Milbank himself suggests that it is the task of Christianity to convert non-Christians (190). If non-Christians are to be converted, if anyone is to receive revelation, intelligently and with understanding, then something in the general human make-up or condition must enable the grasp of the content of revelation to be possible. And this suggests categories of need, thought or experience which cross cultural boundaries. Milbank acknowledges that there can be such points of connection between two things we call religion, as there is between Christianity and Judaism. But this will be because of 'local common ground between adjacent traditions' (176). This concession is vulnerable to Cantwell Smith's account of how the histories of even 'non-adjacent' traditions intertwine and influence one another (Smith W.C. 1981, see especially 6–14). He illustrates how one religion abuts another in geography and history and how through a chain of such relationships ideas, stories and the like can transfer from one non-adjacent tradition to another. There is an interconnectedness in human cultural history which has to be kept in mind along with a sense of there being discrete cultures. It is worth reflecting as well that the noun 'culture' brings with it no counting principle. The very 'fact' that there are diverse 'traditions' or 'cultures' is in part a product of the commentator's decision to divide human history up thus and so.

A large part of Milbank's animus against pluralism's assumption that the religions form a genuine genus arises from a misconception of what *kind* of genus of religion pluralism requires. He mistakenly links pluralism by definition with the project of dialogue between the faiths (1990, 177) and with the linked assumption that the faiths must agree on a common concrete goal (salvation) and that one then only needs to compare, through dialogue, their routes for getting to this goal. Salvation will be the subject of our next chapter. Suffice it to say now that the way of construing pluralism offered in this study does not entail identification with the project of religious dialogue and it does not entail that the religions' conceptions of salvation are the same in concrete terms. Pluralism must postulate a common salvific success between major religious traditions: they all offer some means or other of living rightly towards sacred, transcendent reality. Such a thesis entails that conceptions of salvation between the traditions covered by the thesis must be comparable. This in turn implies that there must be a general category of conceptions of salvation which can be constructed and into which different notions from the various traditions can, with justice, be placed. But it does not imply that all conceptions of salvation are alike in every substantive respect.

In regard to conceptions of salvation and other typical elements of religion, such as conceptions of the sacred, pluralism does not demand homogeneity or the melting down of all that is unique into a common mould. In the facets of the genus 'religion' and in the genus as a whole, it postulates only comparability-despite-divergence, likeness-in-difference. I suggest that fashionable criticism of such suitably modest aims does not succeed. But how is the pluralist to define religion?

DEFINING RELIGION

We have already seen why pluralism should pursue a definition of religion focusing on common functional and structural properties of the religions. This is the most likely way in which the pluralist can preserve a strong sense of the diversity of religions alongside the desired comparability between them.

Notable efforts to define religion on structural/functional lines are to be found in anthropological theorising about religion. In his *The Interpretation of Culture* Clifford Geertz offers such a definition. A religion is:

(1) a system of symbols which acts to (2) establish powerful, pervasive, and long-lasting moods and motivations in men by (3) formulating conceptions of a general order of existence and (4) clothing these conceptions with such an aura of factuality that (5) the moods and motivations seem uniquely realistic.

(1975, 90)

The fundamental thought behind this definition, as expanded upon in other parts of *The Interpretation of Culture* (notably 127–31), is that a religion integrates two key aspects of a people's culture: its ethos and world view. In its ethos Geertz includes its approved style of life and fundamental values. Its world view includes its picture of the nature of reality, its account of what is fundamentally real. The sense of the reality of its conceptions of what is fundamentally real is strengthened by their association with the values and motives that frame and fuel its ethos. Those aspects of its approved way of life are in turn buttressed by their implicitly reflecting its conceptions of what is truly real. Religions, then, have a common function and structure in serving the purpose of knitting together ethos and world view for human beings and communities.

If such a definition of religion were adequate it would perhaps establish the commonality between religions which pluralism requires while allowing the content with which individual religions clothe this common element to vary widely. But so far Geertz's definition does not do two things which pluralism requires of any definition of religion, particularly with the needs of its reference thesis in mind. It does not indicate in the first place why religions might have a common interest in speaking of a *sacred, transcendent* object of reference. Nor does it, as expounded here, point to common needs and concerns which might animate varying traditions. There are hints that Geertz thinks that all religions do have an interest in reference to a transcendent, as when he comments 'A man can indeed be said to be "religious" about golf, but not merely if he pursues it with passion and plays it on Sundays: he must see it as symbolic of *transcendent* truths' (1975, 98; my emphasis). We need to establish later why the function of religion should demand a relation between human values and a conception of a *transcendent* reality. On the second point, about the relation between religion and human needs, Geertz does indicate that the fundamental concerns animating religion relate to the need for human beings to have a theodicy (in the Weberian sense), that is: a symbol system which provides meaning to human life in the face of suffering and human limitations (1975, 131). The mutually informing harmony between ethos and world view provides such a sense of meaning. This too must be expanded upon below.

As well as needing amplification in the two respects noted, Geertz's definition is vulnerable to the criticism cited from Milbank, namely that it identifies religion through something that is a function of culture itself. Life in a culture is life structured by means of a set of symbols whose function includes that of portraying what is real and what is of value to its members. To avoid the conclusion that religion defined functionally and structurally is identical with culture we must turn to a refined definition of religion offered by J. Stone. He defines it first as belonging to the genus of practices (1991, 337–8). Religions as practices are differentiated from others by the fact that they concern the relation between human beings, the fundamental nature of reality and the highest good. A religion is a set of practices legitimated by a set of beliefs such that there is 'fit' between the practices and the real:

> That is, the beliefs that rationalise the system of practices entail that there is a relation in which a person can, but need not, stand to the rest of what is, which is fundamentally appropriate to the way things are (or the way the reality that underlies the universe is), such that standing in this relation is, in and of itself, the greatest human good.
>
> (Stone 1991, 338)

Stone is keen to point out that the combination of practices plus beliefs which produce harmony between a religious individual and reality should not be thought of as leading to ultimate good in the way that clouds lead to rain. Religions offer systems of practices plus beliefs. The beliefs provide a definition of harmony with reality and of the highest good in terms of which the highest good consists in performing the practices guided by the requisite beliefs. Performing the practices of a religion means that the person of faith *ipso facto* participates in the relation to reality that is the highest good (339).

Stone cannot be accused of identifying religion by means of a definition that reduces it to the fact of culture. Religions are alike in having structurally similar ways of maintaining a quite specific form of portrayal of the human good: good as harmony or fit with reality legitimated by appropriate beliefs. It is a definition with discriminating power. We can ask of some disputed example of religion, such as early Buddhism or Maoism, whether it really is a religion. Our question then pertains to whether the system of belief and practice in question really does identify human good with a relation between adherent and reality, such that to follow a certain set of practices is to be in that relation and to enter into that good (Stone 1991, 350). If, as Stone contends, early Buddhism identifies ultimate good with absence of suffering (and not with some relation to reality) and merely offers directions as to how to attain that good, it is not a religion but a philosophy of life. If, however, the highest good consists in a relation to some reality – be it nirvana or sunyata – which can be entered into through a way of life, and of which suffering is but the sign that it is absent, then Buddhism counts as a religion (1991, 350).

So far Stone's definition has the advantage of having the power to point to a common structural and functional element in all religions without implying that all religions have the same content. Yet as with Geertz it too fails to make any immediate reference to a common concern among religions to make contact with a transcendent, sacred reality. Stone writes sometimes of a religion establishing fit or harmony between believer and the universe (338). Such language will not tend to support the pluralist's reference thesis. The idea of a transcendent reality, harmony with which might constitute the goal of religion, is introduced vaguely in this statement: 'a religion binds together the believer and *that which is most real*, through practices the very performance of which is to assume the relation to that which is taken to be the chief human good' (339; my emphasis). Why 'that which is most real' is a better description of the external pole of the binding relation which religions seek to establish needs further exploration. Further, Stone's account says little about the kinds of needs that might lie behind the religions. He ventures the thought that humankind has a fundamental metaphysical yearning which a religion satisfies through establishing a metaphysical connection which is the chief point of human existence (339–40). Pluralism needs to expand on this if it is to point to common or overlapping human concerns behind all the religions. Such an overlap of concerns is necessary if it is to make good its assumption that there is a common context – a common human religious condition – behind the symbols for the transcendent in the major faiths.

The reason why 'that which is most real' is a better description of the external term of the fit established by a religion than merely 'the universe' stems from the fact that this relationship of fit constitutes the highest good. The practices of a religion do not establish one relative good among others but a good which is the terminus of all striving and which provides a means of measuring the worth of all human activities. Not for nothing have some scholars defined religion in terms of a system of belief and practice which centres around something deemed to be of supreme value and importance (as in Christian 1964, 60–1 and Ferré 1967, 65–9). If the highest good consists in harmony (constituted by the engagement in practices) with some reality or other, there is a logic in making out that reality to be beyond normal conditioned, contingent, limited or mutable things. For harmony achieved with things which are just part of the normal mundane world, or which share its essential contingencies, is thereby vulnerable: if one of the terms of the relationship which grounds fit and harmony is subject to change, decay or destruction, then relationship with it could hardly constitute a final, ultimate good for human beings. So it is natural that, even in reputedly early, 'pragmatic' forms of Buddhism, we should have nirvana described in such terms as deathless, beyond time, unborn, unconditioned, unconstructed (Harvey 1990, 60–1).

We are entitled, on grounds of a workable, theory-inspired definition of religion and a survey of systems typically called 'religions', to assume that all religions have a central concern to refer to, and make accessible for human thought, experience and practice, a transcendent reality. This will be a something or other conceived to be that which is most real among all that exists and which provides an anchor for a relationship which can be thought of as constituting the human good. Hence this most real thing must be thought of as both transcendent when compared with other, mundane realities and as sacred, where 'sacred' refers to that which is, or is the source of, the highest value. Note that this does not as yet entail that the object of religion, the most real, is inevitably thought of in terms of an ultimate, absolute reality in the manner of the philosophical ultimate referred to in Chapters 1 and 2 above. We still need to take on board the suggestion that Buddhism has no conception of an absolute in any of them. What will be at issue in later chapters is how far, if at all, there is any common agreement across things conventionally called 'religions' that the reality which is transcendent and sacred is a metaphysical substratum in some way in the category of 'substance'. This is a matter we shall turn to in the next section of this chapter.

We are well on our way to portraying a common context from which the referential and salvific quests of the religions are launched and thereby establishing the unity-in-diversity that the pluralist viewpoint requires. This portrait can be enriched if common or similar needs can be seen behind the religions and can be associated with the characterisation of religion drawn from Stone. It is helpful at this point to combine Stone's definition of religion with elements from that offered by J.M. Yinger:

> Religion, then, can be defined as a system of beliefs and practices by means of which a group of people struggles with these ultimate problems of human life. It expresses their refusal to capitulate to death, to give up in the face of frustration, to allow hostility to tear apart their human aspirations.
>
> (1970, 7)

At the heart of Yinger's conception is the thought that human beings in all cultures face a range of 'wrenching difficulties' (1970, 7): ultimate problems in human existence which are at once insoluble by ordinary human effort and also threatening to our sense of individual and communal meaning. These difficulties include: the fact of death, the fact of failure in human enterprises, and the fact of human conflict. We might add to this list the cardinal fact of human suffering and frustration which arises out them. Such problems accompany and condition all human efforts and aspirations and for this reason no human efforts can ever remove them. According to Yinger the function of religion is to offer a residual way of coping with the sense of meaning-lessness such problems might give rise to. This is accomplished by invoking a symbol-system which interprets these problems in the light of some larger, transcendent and ultimate value (1970, 15). The values thus invoked are in a manner of speaking super-empirical. While they may be objects of experience, they do not wax and wane, and are not perishable in the manner of ordinary sources and objects of value. The religious adherent can be assured that there are sources of meaning not affected by our meaning-threatening problems and can find these problems relativised in the light of a higher order of values.

We have in Yinger the root thought that each religion presents a theodicy, understood as a way of coping with the fact of human finitude and what grows out of that: frustration, suffering and the like. Elsewhere (Clarke and Byrne 1993, 119–21) I have pointed out how such finitude is revealed in the very fact that human beings are placed in a world in which they have desires and projects but which is, to say the least, never wholly subject to the human will. The source for human religion lies in the gulf between the human ego and the reality in which it is set. The emotional and existential problems which arise out of this gulf are 'solved' by religions through the manner in which they bring the ego's desires and projects before values of transcendent character: in the light of an ultimate, imperishable, non-contingent and immutable good the facts of human finitude are re-valued and lose their power to threaten and disable.

Such a conception of religion fits in neatly with Stone's account. We see now why it might be important to have systems of practice whose function is to establish a harmony and fit between human beings and the ultimate good. Thus can the dissonances and meaning-destructive aspects of the human condition be overcome. The cardinal need for religions to make reference to a focus or foci combining both transcendence and sacredness is supported by another route. We begin to see a common set of needs behind religious expression and thus perhaps a common human religious condition, defined as a compound of facts about human nature and human circumstances which help to account for the existence and nature of functional, structural and substantive similarities in the religions of history (see Byrne 1989, 237).

The definition of religion offered thus far confirms the wisdom behind Hick's distinction between pre-Axial and post-Axial faiths for the purposes of presenting pluralism's main theses. For it is evident that tribal, ethnic religions may not be centrally concerned with ultimate good as 'fit' between individual and reality. They may be as much, or more, concerned with celebration of awe before nature, or with the link between ethos and outlook, or with matters more properly described as magical (because they focus on achieving mundane, utilitarian ends). The definition of 'religion' offered by pluralism is designed to fit a purpose, namely to establish some comparability between major religious traditions. There is an element of stipulation in it, reflecting its theoretical background. As noted above, not everything that has been called a religion need meet its terms perfectly.

We are well on our way to seeing common and overlapping concerns behind the religions which give them a similar quest. All this is quite compatible with agreeing that there are substantive differences between the religions. We must bear in mind our analogy of colours: the colours form a kind but each is a determinate manifestation of the determinable nature of the kind. Not only will there be great diversity in the way in which religions picture the transcendent sacred, but 'the human religious condition' takes on determinate forms from culture to culture. The 'facts of human finitude' may be conceived rather differently across religions. The cardinal fact of death will look different in a culture which believes in a universal cycle of rebirth from how it appears in a culture which regards the natural consequence of death as extinction. In the former case the fact of death feeds into the process of a search for theodicy by massively contributing to the sense of life as accompanied by unconquerable suffering and frustration. Suffering frustrates our purposes and threatens our sense of life's meaning. If life continues in an endless cycle of rebirths then, failing the possibility of liberation and release from this cycle, frustration is endless. In a culture without such beliefs, death provides a more direct limit to human striving and achievement. This kind of diversity is more fully explored in the next chapter, where we ask the question of how far the notion of salvation provides links between the religions.

In the definition of religion and the characterisation of the human religious condition offered in this chapter, I have attempted to draw a judicious line between two extremes. As our discussion of Milbank so clearly shows, contemporary fashions tend toward stressing the point that the so-called 'religions' are incommensurable and radically affected by their unique cultural settings. Pluralism then is seen to commit the sin of traducing 'the "otherness" of the Other' (Surin 1990b, 123), that is, of falsely assimilating systems of belief and practice, of making them fit a common, Western-inspired mould. I have contended that such charges ignore, among other things: the extent to which religions can transcend and cross cultural boundaries, the ability of religions to affect and inter-mingle with one another and the extent to which formal and structural similarities between the religions can be established. From such similarities the pluralist can expect substantive overlaps and interconnections. The pluralist does not have to maintain that all religions are essentially alike in doctrine, experience, soteriology, practice or conception of sacred, merely that in such respects we can make comparisons and draw links between them sufficient to support the three main theses of the pluralist outlook.

In the light of all this the pluralist can happily accept that the category of religion is a Western, if not Christian, invention. This does not entail, however, that it cannot transcend its origins. To suppose that its origins determine its present use is the merest example of the genetic fallacy. The concept of religion began life in the Classical period as meaning the rendering of service and obedience to the gods and came in the pre-modern era to mean offering service and sacrifice to God. But for all that, its meaning has been expanded and altered in the act of discovering that there are non-Western and non-theistic religions. Stone's definition of religion (as a system of practices rationalised by beliefs according to which the performance of the practices constitutes being in harmony with the real and enjoying the chief good) is recognisably an ancestor of the medieval notion of *religio*. Yet it does not on the surface involve any contentious assimilation of non-European traditions to Christianity. It establishes a degree of unity and comparability which respects their variety. Whether it traduces the otherness of the Other I leave readers to judge.

ULTIMATES AND ABSOLUTES

The analysis offered so far is meant to show how religions form a class whose members are genuinely comparable and behind which an overlapping range of human concerns can be detected. What has been argued in the above coheres with the description of the common 'fiduciary structure' which Keith Ward thinks he discerns behind the major religious traditions (1987, 74–80).

According to Ward religions contain an account of the real. They offer a goal to human striving which consists in some kind of relationship to that real. They point to some kind of means by which that goal is to be achieved. They describe the nature of the human limitation which makes activity realising the relationship to the real imperative. And they offer some kind of analysis of the cause of the fundamental limitation they endeavour to overcome. To these elements (of: the real, the goal, the means, the limitation and the cause) Ward adds a further common theme: the dependence of the faiths on some source of authoritative teaching for the source of a religion's account of the human condition and the real. Ward is after unity-in-diversity. Each element of the common fiduciary structure conceals the possibility of diversity. Each contains a 'polarity', allowing for radically different interpretations for each strand. For mainstream Judaism the real is personal. The goal is loving relationship with this real. The means to achieve this relationship is underpinned by grace from the divine. The human condition requires remedy not because the world and self are unreal and must be rejected, but because human responsibility has been misused on account of sin. The entire analysis stems from an authoritative source which is a spoken or written revelation of the divine word. Forms of Hindu and Eastern religious traditions might be found to reverse each of these poles, beginning with an impersonal account of the divine.

So far then we see in Ward a reinforcement of a sense of the *structural* similarity of the major faiths. We should note that Ward argues that in fact each of the major religious traditions (Christianity, Judaism, Islam, Hinduism and Buddhism) recognises and caters for the polarity in each of the elements of the fiduciary structure. To take the example of the real, he finds a dual aspect view 'at the base of each major religious tradition' (1987, 163), whereby each caters for, and holds in tension, the apprehension that the real is both personal Lord and impersonal ground of being.

A radical project like Ward's at once shows how pluralism might develop and deepen its idea of religions as forming a genus, but also how such an attempt raises questions concerning *how many* traditions fall under the scope of pluralism's major theses. Typical forms of pluralism from Western philosophers must face the objection that the assimilation of Buddhism to forms of faith that believe in a transcendent ultimate is illegitimate. We have seen that it is tempting to provide a common reference for religions by saying that what they endeavour to refer to is the ultimate of much Western and Eastern philosophy: a reality that is ultimate ontologically, valuatively and rationally. But we have seen that while the nature of religion as defined above gives all religions a common structural concern to identify a transcendent reality with which human beings can live in relationship, that does not of necessity entail that this reality be thought of as the source of all things. We know from forms of Buddhism that this concern to identify a transcendent good and live in relation to it can be divorced from metaphysical speculation about what the source of all things is. Indeed Buddhism appears to be at root infected with a radical ontological scepticism. What matters in many forms of this tradition is that a liberating good, transcending the limits and defects of ordinary objects, is encountered or realised in certain depth experiences. It does not matter, indeed it may be positively harmful, to speculate about its metaphysical character or categorial status (see Hardy 1994, 182).

As we have described religion, its root lies in a structurally similar existential predicament found in all cultures: how to cope with the problems of human finitude and delineate some good that will rise above them and liberate us from them. This leads to a characteristic concern with a reality that is both sacred and transcendent, both absolutely good and beyond normal conditioned and finite existence. While nirvana seems (to the layman like me) to fit this bill, it seems quite another step to cement the transcendent character of nirvana as the ultimate good by linking it with what is discovered at the end of a metaphysical quest for the source of all things: a something or other which will be the ultimate ground and reason of all that exists. What is crucial about such a metaphysical quest is that it ties in with thoughts about what is the *ground*, *qua* cause, of all things. The reality postulated at the end of the quest may not be at all 'thing-like' if ordinary, material things are our model. But *qua* cause it will fall into the category of substance. So, for example, as sacred it will not merely be supremely good, but act as the source, cause and measure of the value of all else.

So far all we have needed to maintain to keep Buddhist traditions within the scope of pluralism's first thesis is a minimal idea of sacred, transcendent reality. Nirvana and allied notions certainly introduce an object or reality if all we mean by this is 'an object of reference, formal object of intentional attitudes'. It takes a step down a metaphysical road to go further and bring in more determinate ontological categories to characterise nirvana or sunyata and to associate them with the metaphysical notion of the absolute. Some contend that Buddhism never made this step. Von Glasenapp's 'atheistic' interpretation of Buddhism illustrates this denial (see 1970, 50ff). Ward disagrees, arguing that Mahayana schools developed 'Buddhist analogies to God' (1987, 59ff). Smart contends that in such later schools, though there is a teaching about ultimate reality, the fact that this is said to be void, empty – sunyata – means that affirming it to be the basis of mundane reality amounts to a denial that there is an absolute which answers the metaphysical question (1993, 186). It suits Hick's version of pluralism to treat sunyata as another *impersona* of the same ultimate that is also characterised by theists in personal terms (1989, 287–307).

We have here a complex dispute that mixes interpretative and philosophical issues. The interpretative issues surround the understanding of Buddhism, of Mahayana Buddhist philosophy and of the three-bodies doctrine in such philosophy. It is this last which might provide the reason for saying that something like a concept of the ultimate which has both personal and impersonal strands emerges in late Buddhism (see Harvey 1990, 125–7 for a brief survey).

The interpretative question which divides Smart from Ward and Hick is whether Buddhism in any central forms ever developed any worthwhile analogies to the idea of a metaphysical absolute. Fortunately we need not rule on this dispute now (though it resurfaces at the end of Chapter 6). For we can see from the previous chapter that, even if there is no absolute in any important strand of Buddhism, and even if *contra* Ward it has no personal–impersonal, di-polar character, this fact would not entail that forms of Buddhism made no reference to a common religious ultimate. Reference can be made even if those who succeed in reference have no full or accurate idea of the defining properties of the referent. The firm characterisation of nirvana as both an object of experience, belief and reference which is transcendent and sacred in our minimal senses may be enough to say that Buddhism makes reference to the common ultimate reality, or at least partially refers to ultimate reality. This is indeed similar to one facet of Hick's mode of argument (1989, 283–7). He represents nirvana as another *impersona* of the Real that is also known through other images of an impersonal and personal kind. This pluralist assimilation can be conceded to have some strength if the admitted similarities between descriptions of the focus of Buddhism (unborn, unbounded, deathless) are deemed to have some weight and if the nature of Buddhist practices and concerns put it into a working category of religion.

Two final oddities in the pluralist position on this matter must be mentioned. First it seems that pluralists will defend a common reference thesis here even though there is no clear-cut agreement across all traditions on the categorial status of the object of reference. Is it substance, quality, relation or all or none of these? Second the pluralist as I have described him or her is departing from a strict neutrality as between all traditions in presenting the common reference thesis via the notion of an absolute that is ontologically, valuatively and rationally ultimate. For that is to use what are, on many accounts, decidedly non-Buddhist categories to fix the reference of *all* traditions. This departure from neutrality is best admitted. It throws up the intriguing possibility of what a pluralist reference thesis would look like when presented via the ontological, metaphysical agnosticism of much Buddhism.

EXPERIENCES

Appeals to the notions of religious experience have played an important role in debates about the genuineness of the category of religion and about the extent of similarities among its members. Nineteenth century attempts to find an unchanging essence behind the religions frequently took the form of postulating a core religious experience, or generalised form of spirituality. This could be seen as at the heart of all religions while its expression and manifestation differed from one to another (Müller 1893, 13 illustrates this movement of thought clearly). Such proposals for defining an essence to religions presuppose that experience is one thing, its expression and interpretation another: the identity of religious experience can be preserved across cultures and epochs while its interpretation and outward expression in those cultures is historically and culturally variable. This presupposition is supported by the many phenomenological similarities some see between patterns of experience, particularly mystical experience, in the religions. Such common patterns are argued for in Otto's famous analysis of the awareness of *mysterium, tremendum et fascinans* in an allegedly widespread numinous experience (Otto 1958). Recently, claims have been made for an experience of 'pure consciousness' as both vital to and shared between many different religions (see Foreman 1990).

It might seem as if religious pluralism is committed to views about religious experience of this character. It might appear that it is bound to assert an identity of religious experience across cultures and religions. Indeed some of the language in the writings of Cantwell Smith, and in particular the distinction between 'faith' and 'cumulative tradition', suggests that he espouses an experiential essentialism of this kind as the basis of his pluralism (Smith W.C. 1978, 129–31). If pluralism depended on this kind of assumption, then it would fall foul of the fashionable idea that experience is universally culturally conditioned. The counter argument to the assertion of a common core or of significant similarities to experience in all the religions has come from those who insist that experience is not separable from the way in which it is expressed and interpreted. It is identified through the concepts of those who have it. For religious experience, this means that its identity is shaped by the specific concepts of the traditions of religious thought in which it inheres. There is then no generic religious or mystical experience. Religious experience is as diverse as religious traditions. It is constructed and determined by traditions. Such is the case argued by many a recent writer. (The source of this line of thought, 'constructivism', is Katz 1978.)

If pluralism is true it must be the case that in some sense all major religious traditions experience the same thing, just as they must worship, contemplate, praise the same thing. But this does not entail that pluralism is committed to the thesis that all religious experience is identical beneath surface ways of describing and interpreting it. Nor does it entail that pluralism must believe in puzzling pure experiences which have no content and are beyond categorisation and description. The identity that pluralism must assert between all genuine, non-illusory religious experiences is an identity in their *object*. Assuming no polytheistic account of the objects of religious experience is remotely plausible, then they have a real, as opposed to merely notional, internal object only if there is one and only one transcendent encountered in them. But if what is experienced in varieties of mysticism and the like is the same object according to pluralism, it does not follow that what is experienced is exactly the same *phenomenologically*. The traditions could, and no doubt do, experience the common focus of religion differently, just as two observers may have different experiences of the same event because their angles of vision and background expectations and beliefs are different. Object identity does not entail phenomenological identity (see Byrne 1984).

Once we have given it the distinction between object and phenomenological identity pluralism is well on its way to occupying comfortable middle ground in the debate between essentialists and constructivists over the character of religious experience. From this middle ground it becomes important to see overlaps and similarities between different forms and exemplifications of mystical and religious experiences. Yet the phenomenological differences between patterns of experience can also be frankly acknowledged, as can the rootedness of religious experience in specific contexts of thought and action. The simple idea of seeking similarity with difference is at work again. Similarities between experiences become prima facie evidence for pluralism, while differences can be discounted to a degree.

Constructivism is obviously correct in asserting that human subjects form and make sense of their experiences by reference to the stock of concepts and background beliefs they bring to bear on them. Without such a contribution from the subject experiential input would be as nothing to us. We could not make sense of it. Folk from different cultures will then experience a world of common objects in different ways. But it is equally true that in non-illusory experience there is an *input* from the object of experience. (Of course, what on earth this might be in the religious case may be hard to grasp – especially if the object of experience is Buddhist 'emptiness'.) The content of our experiences is not wholly determined by our background beliefs and concepts. If it were, the phenomenon of finding one's existing beliefs and concepts challenged by what one experiences would be impossible. So, of course, we expect folk from different cultures and traditions to be able to recognise each other as experiencing the same world and to have similar experiences of that world.

Why should not these obvious points apply *mutatis mutandis* to religious experience (as argued cogently in Stoeber 1992)?

Many essentialist accounts of religious experience depend on the thought that the contribution to the character of experience from the subject's beliefs and concepts is unimportant, or can be eliminated – as the defenders of experiences of 'pure consciousness' claim (see Foreman 1991, 419). Extreme constructivism depends on the corresponding idea that the object of experience makes no contribution to its content. Pluralism should steer a middle path between both of these assumptions, holding that both subject and object make an ineliminable contribution to the content of experience. Since pluralism espouses a form of realism about religion it should be concerned to avoid extreme constructivism in particular. It is then a paradox that Hick in *An Interpretation of Religion* appears to commit himself to constructivism through his contention that it is the mystic's tradition that determines what kind of transcendent he or she will experience. To this may be added his general argument that the transcendent in itself is not an immediate object of experience, but only its manifestations in particular, tradition-based forms of human consciousness are (compare Stoeber 1992). Hick's argument in favour of our cognitive freedom to interpret the world religiously or not, and in terms of this religious tradition or that, tends in this direction and the result is what might be termed a kind of cultural idealism whereby the object of religion, as known, as experienced, is socially constructed and specific to a particular tradition. For reasons already aired in Chapter 2, I agree with Stoeber in seeing this as implying a religious relativism and not the realism pluralism must espouse (Stoeber 1992, 111).

Stoeber coins the term 'experiential–constructivist' for the view I think pluralism must be committed to (114). There is (by hypothesis) a single object of religious experience (certainly, if there is any object at all, there is only one). How this is experienced is in large measure dependent on the specific categories of particular traditions of religious experience, but if it is real we should expect it to make a contribution to the manner in which it is experienced. Two important consequences of such a contribution should follow. One is that we should expect to find that powerful religious experiences should *challenge* the inherited, background beliefs and concepts of religious traditions in which experiences occur. (Stoeber makes much of this – 112.) Another consequence is that similarities and overlaps between traditions of a real kind should be forthcoming.

How far do we find important similarities within the idiosyncrasies of different traditions of religious experiences? We have already referred to the work of ecumenicalists in religious experience who think they can describe such similarities. Their presence or absence should be an important indicator of the plausibility of pluralism. They are evidence against constructivism. Constructivists who note that they appear to exist argue that their significance is more apparent than real. Overlapping descriptions of the character and object or mystical experience, Katz contends, are misleading: similar epithets used in more than one tradition in characterising experience will be found to have different senses determined by the unique contexts of meaning different traditions supply (1978, 47).

As ever, it is hard to find unambiguous evidence that proves or disproves a large-scale theory. Only in the context of an overall case for pluralism could the value of such similarities between traditions of religious experience as exist, and which cannot easily be explained away, be settled. For the moment it is enough to say that pluralism draws strength from these similarities and is not committed to an implausible essentialism about religious experience. These similarities are further evidence that the category of religion is not a Western fiction but a genuine one.

We shall have to return to the question of the diversity of religious experience in treating of the epistemology of religious belief in Chapter 5. There we shall argue that diversity does not destroy the reliability of experience altogether and that finding similarities between traditions of religious experience is one good way of defending its reliability.

4

Salvation

It is evident that pluralism must assert, at the least, a worthwhile degree of overlap or comparability between religions as systems of salvation. Such an assertion follows directly from the second thesis we have used to define a pluralistic vision of the religions: all major traditions are alike in offering some means or other to human salvation. It also follows indirectly from the primary reference thesis of pluralism. For that reference thesis to be made good, we have seen that it requires us to establish a similarity of contexts from which the major faiths endeavour to speak of an ultimate reality. One of the primary facets of similarity in religious contexts will be a like concern for salvation.

That all religions have a central concern with salvation is something that we have argued for in the previous chapter. Our earlier discussion makes it true by definition that all things which belong to the genus 'religion' have a concern with the highest human good, a concern that is structured in a common way. A religion can be treated as a system of belief and practice which conceives of human good as a harmony with ultimate reality constituted by acting in accordance with the beliefs of that religion. This is as much to say that a religion is a system of salvation. The account of 'fit' between religious individual, ultimate reality and the human good derived from Stone's work shows that it offers the three essentials of any portrayal of salvation according to Grace Jantzen (1984, 580). Our definition asserts that each religion identifies a prior condition (from which we are saved); a means (by which we are saved); and a goal (to what we are saved). The prior condition is human finitude and its essential limitations. The means is by living a life according to certain beliefs, a life which then constitutes being related to ultimate reality. The goal is the highest good conceived of as consisting in being related to this reality. Our definition is also in accord with

83

Jantzen's later account of the essence of salvation as consisting in not so much a future destiny but rather in a present relation to God – in our terms, transcendent, sacred reality (1987, 128).

Up to this point we have noted that the similarities between members of the class 'religion' implied by our definition are fundamentally structural rather than substantive. Such similarities, for all that has been contended so far, allow of wide divergence: between the concrete beliefs which identify for specific faiths the nature of the ills entailed in human finitude; between the characters given to the ultimate reality, relation to which defines the highest good; and hence between the practices which constitute living in that relation. Now this chapter must confront a crucial question for the pluralist which arises out of the argument advanced thus far. The critic of pluralism will ask how much substantive similarity is required in the elements which go to make up the vision of salvation offered by each religion. The critic will contend that for pluralism to make good its case extensive similarities in belief and practice are required and that few in fact are found. Critics of pluralism contend that the theme of salvation offers very little or no opportunity to liken members of the class of religions.

Such scepticism strikes at the heart of much writing in support of a pluralist hypothesis. For example, despite his explicit avowal of a family-resemblance definition of religion, Hick asserts in *An Interpretation of Religion* a substantive similarity in matters soteriological between all post-Axial religions (as in Chapter 4, p. 56) and goes so far as to imply that Buddhist, Christian and other ideas of salvation are expressions of one basic notion. Wilfred Cantwell Smith asserts that there is a common relation, called faith, which each tradition fosters between human beings and the transcendent, albeit it takes different forms in them (1981, 168), and that this relation constitutes salvation (170). Paul Knitter asserts that a common goal for humanity unites all religions (1985, 209), a goal which he later identifies with liberation from oppression (in Knitter 1988, 187). Against these varied assertions of inter-religious solidarity on the substance of salvation, we find many writers affirming that what salvation amounts to differs in substance from one tradition to another, so that the matter of salvation *highlights* rather than smoothes over the dissimilarities which pervade the class of religions. They contend for particularism in interpreting accounts of salvation in opposition to the apparent universalism of pluralists.

It is our task to sum up and adjudicate in the debate between particularists and universalists on the nature of salvation according to the religions. In doing so we shall have to determine how much similarity pluralism requires between accounts of salvation. We must remember as we do so that pluralism does *not* require all religions to offer the *same* account of salvation, merely that all religions must be alike in offering *some* means of relating salvifically to the sacred or other.

PARTICULARISM IN SALVATION

The essential thought behind particularist accounts of salvation can be simply put. What way of life or pattern of action a religion counts as salvific depends on the beliefs of that religion. These will identify both the ills for which relation with the transcendent is the cure and the actions or dispositions to be cultivated by one seeking relation with the transcendent. Since the relevant beliefs identifying and constituting salvific ways of life vary from tradition to tradition, there can be no common way of life that might constitute living in relation to the transcendent in all the major religions.

This argument is forcefully stated in recent papers by J.A. DiNoia (1990a and 1990b, as expanded also in DiNoia 1992). He argues for an intrinsic connection between aims of life and patterns of life (1990a, 123). He cites the example of the Buddhist goal of nirvana. That goal is internally related to a pattern of life laid down in Buddhist doctrine, the Noble Eightfold Path. The substance of Buddhist thought defines the nature of nirvana as a goal. Moreover, only by living according to the Path can one become the sort of person who is able to attain and enjoy the goal. Following the Path entails cultivating certain dispositions laid out in it. It involves becoming a certain sort of person. One cannot attain and enjoy nirvana without cultivating these dispositions and becoming this sort of person. Each religion thus has a distinctive pattern of life. This is directed toward an ultimate goal defined by its account of the transcendent. This goal is further defined by the pattern of life in which the goal figures as the pivot, for it is surrounded by distinctive virtues and dispositions one must have to become the kind of person who can attain and enjoy this goal. After a full account of the Christian, in particular Roman Catholic, pattern of life, he concludes that 'the salvation to which . . . the Christian community bears witness and affords access comprises a highly specified aim, range of dispositions and pattern of transformation' (1990b, 260).

It is possible now to convict the pluralist of simple fallacy and gross error. The fallacy consists in inferring from the fact that what the religions seek can be described under the same general heading ('salvation') the conclusion that they seek in substance the same thing. Since the goals they individually set for humanity only get their shape from within distinct patterns of life and belief systems, what they offer is in each case different in substance. It is even mistaken to take similar-sounding descriptions of the ultimate end out of their contexts as proof that all religions aim at the same thing. Given that definition, attainment and enjoyment of a religious goal is inextricably linked to unique beliefs, patterns of life, virtues and the like, there could be no goal identical in substance across the traditions.

Only formal similarity in religious goals can be found across the traditions: 'To say that religions aim at "ultimacy" or at "reality" is to state an aim of such generality as to fail entirely to describe what actually transpires in religious communities' (DiNoia 1990b, 261). Giving religious life across many traditions a general goal of the kind DiNoia dismisses fails to bring with it any account of the distinct pattern of life in which it might be set, and without which its pursuit will be vain, for the reasons offered.

These arguments about goals, enjoyment and patterns of life can be linked to other points in favour of human diversity and plasticity made by Grace Jantzen (Jantzen 1984). The conclusion that one would have to become a particular kind of person to enjoy the Catholic vision of God or the Buddhist nirvana invites a more general thought. What we are as people, including what we can enjoy and take satisfaction in, is something we ourselves in part create. Human beings are in part self-creating, notes Jantzen (1984, 589), with the result that what may count as happiness, bliss and wholeness differs from place to place and time to time. This self-creating is partly individual and partly social. The social context in which each of us journeys toward happiness defines in some measure the human condition as we experience it and the range of responses to it that are open to us. Thus for Jantzen it will not do to say that what we need to be saved from is the same across all times, cultures and traditions. Nor will it do to affirm that the means or goal of salvation is the same in all these cases. There is no good identical in substance which could be the final goal for a humanity that creates itself in diverse ways.

Kenneth Surin might be taken to be stating the core of the particularistic objection to pluralism on salvation when he affirms that the suggestion that the same salvation scheme can apply to two seemingly incompatible religious traditions is inherently syncretistic (1983, 339). That is to say, it must involve the false assimilation of diverse beliefs and practices. Surin has his own objection to asserting salvation schemes across the traditions to be similar, namely that it ignores the specific Christian claim that salvation cannot be produced by human effort but is dependent on the salvific action of Christ. In particular, the project of Hick and others must run head on against the 'scandal of particularity' (Surin 1983, 336) arising out of the Christian claim that only in and through the life and death of Jesus is salvation made possible. On the contrary, pluralists typically describe and compare the content and efficacy of different *human* recipes for salvation.

Surin's own particularist objection to the pluralist's granting of salvific success to all the major faiths could just be set aside as another instance of the need for pluralism to dismiss the dogmatic claims of each faith about its relative status *vis-à-vis* the rest. This rejection would be part of pluralism's stance as the product of a *philosophical* interpretation of religion, which might thus claim a measure of superiority in its account of human religious life as a whole compared with that offered from *within* the dogmatics of a particular tradition. Grounds for this superiority include the thought that for philosophy of religion the full extent of religious diversity is a first datum for an interpretation of world religions and not an after thought, tacked on to a pre-formed dogmatic scheme, as is the case with the historic traditions (see Prozesky 1984, 3). However, Surin's objection is more important than a simple assertion of confessional superiority. Pluralism must acknowledge that testimony from a number of faiths points to the idea that ultimate human good is not to be attained as a result of human effort alone. Indeed, one of the key elements in the religious perception of human finitude described in Chapter 3 is that its important component evils cannot be removed by human effort alone because they condition that effort. So ultimate good consists in relation to the transcendent and many traditions acknowledge varying degrees of initiative on the part of the sacred in effecting that relationship. This feature of a degree of human powerlessness and of divine initiative is an element of what Ward describes as the fiduciary structure of religion (1987, 77). Part of what is meant, then, by saying that salvation consists in living a certain life according to certain beliefs about the sacred is that such a life may involve the cultivation of kinds of passive, receptive virtues to allow grace from the transcendent to do its work. The danger of over-emphasising within the summary formulae of pluralism the role of the human subject in making his or her own salvation must be acknowledged.

Yet this qualification still does not fully meet the objection from Surin's brand of particularism. For what he wants to say is that a certain philosophy of history is required by any correct account of how human salvation is conceivable. And that philosophy of history is one that acknowledges the necessity of a single, unique and pivotal intervention by the sacred in history. Surin offers what is in effect a general, philosophical argument for the necessity of the Incarnation as it is conceived in Christianity. The argument is general and philosophical in being drawn from an understanding of the concept and character of evil and its place in human life (1983, 331–2). Evil in human beings can only be defeated if God defeats it by assuming the person of a human being. Other Christian philosophers offer different arguments for the same conclusion (compare Swinburne 1989, 148ff). Such efforts are intended to show on a priori grounds that a Christian philosophy of history is true. They help to point to the heart of the difference between pluralism as a philosophy of human history and Christianity, since the latter asserts what the former denies: the pivotal character of a particular historical person's life in the meaning of human history as a whole. This picture of human history as turning around a single event is one that pluralism's gradualist, incremental view of the progress of human thoughts about the good and the transcendent must deny.

So there can be little compromise between one element in

Surin's particularism in regard to salvation and pluralism's universalism. A full defence of pluralism on this score would involve looking at the philosophical arguments in favour of an Incarnation-centred view of moral history and rebutting them. We must pass on, however, noting for the moment that the argument against pluralism just considered is but one attempt to support the dogmatics/revelation of a particular faith on a priori, philosophical grounds. We shall return to the significance of that project in our chapter on epistemology.

PLURALISTS ON SALVATION

It is our task now to see what resources the pluralist standpoint has on offer to deal with the particularist's charge that no common relatedness to the transcendent is or could be found across the world's religions.

Pluralists need to present ways of linking portrayals of salvation across the religions so that we can see the faiths as members of a common enterprise, each of which is likely to achieve sufficient success. These links must be established without creating a false synthesis of the beliefs and patterns of life of the religions – at the cost of falling victim to the justified criticisms mounted by particularist accounts of salvation. What do leading pluralists offer by way of materials for accomplishing this task?

Paul Knitter's distinctive aid to finding convergence in divergence over views of salvation is to outline a common 'liberation theology' for world religions (1988). This endeavours to locate common salvific ground in the fight against the injustice, poverty and oppression that afflicts too much of the world's population today ('right praxis' being the test of the meaning of a soteriological proposal according to Knitter, 192). The best one can say for this proposal is that it is too prescriptive to succeed. It reads more like an injunction to change the soteriological doctrines and practices of the religions than a report on what they actually offer. It is also parochial in an obvious way, magnifying the contemporary liberal's concern with creating justice and plenty on earth into a universal religious demand. Moreover, this account of common ground in salvation is vulnerable to the charge that it fails to pick up what appears to be a common thread in the religions: namely the concern to find some *ultimate, imperishable* good that would be a refuge from human finitude.

Wilfred Cantwell Smith's main contribution to discussion of these points has been to use the notion of faith as a way of referring to human beings' relation to the transcendent and to distinguish faith so defined from belief (as in 1978 and 1979). The distinction between faith and belief allows him to contend that identity in, or correctness of, doctrine is not necessary for us to say of folk in different traditions that they are persons of faith. Faith is a personal quality whose presence in a person does not depend on him or her possessing appropriate beliefs. One can observe over the entire history of human religious history the presence of faith, unaffected by the changing propositional content that might be associated with it. Thus one could use Smith's argument (whose richness and scope has been ignored here) to press the conclusion that one and the same salvation is present in all the traditions.

The anti-propositional, anti-belief part of Smith's case runs its head directly against the points made in this chapter concerning the manner in which the practices and experiences of a religion are embedded in specific patterns of life moulded by specific conceptions of the transcendent – being appropriate to how the transcendent is conceived to be. For all Smith's sometimes-justified strictures on an over-concentration on the propositional content of religion, he appears to have no awareness that the nature and appropriateness of experience, act and attitude are internally related to the perspective on reality held by the human subject (compare Wainwright 1984, 359). This simple fact makes diversity in concrete exemplifications of faith inevitable.

It is not clear that Smith himself would deny the last point since he asserts that there are different forms of faith (openness to the transcendent) in different traditions (for example 1979, 130). But what then becomes of the assertion of the human, generic quality of faith? It loses its force as a support for a pluralist outlook if it merely becomes the assertion that there is a genus into which one can put various instances of living in relation to the transcendent and sacred. For that leaves very much open the question of whether the specific forms of faith are sufficiently alike or linked to enable a pluralist interpretation of them. Matters are not helped by frequent claims that faith is indescribable and that no *two people's* exemplifications of it are the same (1979, 133 and 132). If Smith cannot see the importance of the question of whether items in the genus are truly alike or comparable it is perhaps because of a strong ethical impulse to see no one cut off from salvation. Common salvific success is made true by definition once we are told that faith is a generic quality found in all religions (1979, 6) and that 'Faith is man's participation in God's dealings with humankind' (179, 140). This is hardly to take our problem seriously.

Smith's writings do give us the thought that there might be a genus of 'being related through thought and action to the transcendent' of which different patterns of religious life are properly instances. But we must turn to Hick to see if there is more to be said to overcome the fact of difference between concrete ways of envisioning this relation.

Hick is famous for arguing that there is a common soteriological structure to all the major religions (1981, 452–3). What distinguishes the post-Axial from the pre-Axial faiths is precisely that the former have, while the latter lack, a central concern with salvation/liberation. This concern is defined through a contrast central to all the major post-Axial faiths between the ultimately unsatisfactory nature of ordinary, human existence and the possibility of a transformed state of ultimate happiness or bliss grounded in union with sacred, transcendent reality (1989, 32–3). This leads Hick to his characteristic assertion of the similarity of all major religions in respect of their soteriologies: 'Thus the generic concept of salvation/liberation, which takes a different specific form in each of the great traditions, is that of the transformation of human existence from self-centredness to Reality-centredness' (1989, 36). It is by reference to this generic concept that Hick is enabled in the same place to state of the different accounts of salvation in the faiths that they 'are variations within different conceptual schemes on a single theme'. Part of what Hick means by his definition of salvation as transformation from self-centredness to Reality-centredness is, of course, only intelligible within the larger theory behind his recent work, whereby it is assumed that a putative common object, the Real, stands as the ultimate referent behind all faiths. But we have seen that much of what he has in mind is familiar from our earlier discussions of the contrast between, on the one hand, ordinary existence as containing no ultimate good by virtue of being plagued by the facts of human finitude and, on the other hand, an ultimate good which consists in relationship, constituted by characteristic forms of action, with a transcendent, sacred reality free of the limitations of human finitude.

Having postulated this common soteriological pattern in the faiths, Hick has further moves to make to enforce his assertion that particular soteriologies are but variations on the same theme. One consists in pointing to common virtues or moral norms recognised within different schemes of salvation (as in 1989, 312–25). This emphasis on ethics as the essence of salvation might be seen by the critic as placing Hick firmly in the liberal tradition which jettisons the doctrinal specifics of the religions as unimportant in the light of a common moral core which they all share.

Hick's second strategic move is to point to the presence in an equal degree in all the traditions of the empirical manifestation of escape from finitude and relation to the sacred. This manifestation consists in saintly, self-giving, transformed lives (1989, 307). We can also associate with these two themes the underlying message of *An Interpretation of Religion* to the effect that none of the specific dogmas of the faiths are likely to be true of the sacred as it is in itself. None of the faiths thus defines a way of relating to the sacred which is likely to be *the* true one. Many of the doctrinal beliefs which define specific paths to the transcendent are in fact answers to 'undetermined questions' – ones for which no correct answer this side of eternity could conceivably be given. So Hick is able to conclude that 'different groups can hold incompatible sets of theories all of which constitute intellectual frameworks within which the process of salvation/liberation can proceed' (1983, 490).

It is very tempting indeed to read Hick in the above quotation as asserting that *one and the same* process can proceed despite the different theoretical structures of the religions in which its exemplifications are set. This ties in with his stress on ethics, particularly compassionate behaviour toward fellow human beings, as the route to salvation, and his apparent belief that much of ethics is unaffected by different theories about the sacred. In this light, his points re-enforcing the assertion of some kind of similarity between salvation across the faiths can be seen as propounding the thesis that the differences between the unique patterns of life offered in the religions are unimportant. His account then fails to anticipate the substantial points against universalist accounts of salvation outlined at the start of this chapter. The pursuit of a relationship with the sacred would no longer be intrinsically connected with the distinct pattern of life in which it is embedded. We would then perhaps have to interpret Hick as involved in the syncretism Surin complains of. More generally, he would be allowing worth and success in the faiths' various accounts of salvation only to the extent that their insights were translatable into a language (that which speaks of 'self-centredness', 'Reality-centredness', 'transformation' and the like) which is fixed by a philosophical view external to the religions and pre-given. Moreover the dismissal of the detail and specific features of patterns of life in the religions would seem to be implied by the disregard Hick's account entails for the truth of the concrete beliefs about the transcendent which are at the heart of the faiths' portrayal of salvation. It is these beliefs which will provide the picture of the distinct pattern of life required by one who is to live appropriately in relationship with the transcendent.

Now Hick directly states that such beliefs are true only of the transcendent as it appears and that they constitute attempts to respond to unanswerable, undetermined questions. So their truth and hence their specific content would not seem to matter. How can we attribute a common salvific success to the faiths on the basis of declaring the ideas on which their concrete accounts of salvation rest more likely false than true? Only, perhaps, if we dismiss the relevance of those concrete ideas to the faiths' salvific success. Moreover the emphasis on the *effects* of the religions' accounts of salvation as shown in the spread of saintly, selfless lives across them is bound to have a similar consequence of downgrading the truth and thus the content of specific accounts of salvation. For it is notoriously the case that false claims can have true consequences and illusory ideas have good results. Folk can be inspired by that which is false to noble deeds of self-sacrifice. They may have the experience of being saved and act accordingly while in reality they are not. Experiences of 'being saved' cannot prove that the conceptions of salvation behind them are true (Pailin 1990, 154 and Pentz 1991). So to place such

great emphasis as Hick does on the concrete effects of conceptions of salvation is to downgrade their truth, and thus their
content, drastically, or so a critic would argue.

RESCUING UNIVERSALISM

To this point it might appear as if the topic of salvation is the
Achilles' heel of pluralism in that reflection on it reveals that the
religions cannot be represented as different ways of pursuing a
common quest. Something must be done by way of defending a
universalist perspective on salvation and with it pluralism.

As a start we must note that the problems raised by
particularism in salvation create difficulties for confessional
inclusivism of perhaps an equal kind. Thus Jantzen notes how
odd it is to say that the salvific quest of people of non-Christian
faiths is completed by knowledge of Christ (1984, 589–90). If the
quest associated with following the path toward nirvana is set in
a unique pattern of belief and behaviour, it cannot prepare Bud-
dhists for the goods of the Christian eschaton. Particularism seems
to face those who offer a confessional interpretation of religious
life with two stark alternatives. One is the adoption of the nar-
rowest of exclusivisms – involving the claim that any chance of
relation to the sacred is simply foregone by those unfortunate
enough to be born into cultures where there is no real opportunity of cultivating, say, the Christian pattern of life. The other
option is a heavy reliance on appeal to the after-life. With such
an appeal comes the possibility of 're-educating' folk from non-
Christian religions and cultures into the beliefs and behaviours
which identify relation to the true God. Other confessional viewpoints would need their versions of this story. In this spirit DiNoia
(1990b, 267) appeals to the doctrine of purgatory as vital for a
Christian theology of religions. Indeed, use of that doctrine might
allow a long period of re-education sufficient to overcome the
objection that the identity and self-understanding of many un-
fortunates born out of the Christian fold would otherwise be
destroyed in a crash programme of induction into a Christian
pattern of life.

However, on its own an appeal to after-lives is no solution to the problems aired. If the confessional interpreter of religion leaves different patterns of life in the different faiths sheerly different, if Jantzen's point about the self-createdness of human beings in shaping their understanding of and response to finitude is correct, it is hard to see how any confessional portrayal of salvation can represent its account as giving the end-point of *human* religious striving. The majority of human beings rather have to be re-made and their self-understandings changed if *all* are to find the ultimate good in Christ, nirvana or whatever. So Christianity is not the answer to the religious quest of actual people on this earth. Moreover, if dragging in an after-life can save the bacon for an inclusivist theology of religions, it can surely do so for pluralism. Allowing there to be independent reasons for pluralism elsewhere, one could present the thesis of common salvific success as salvageable in the light of the postulation of a pluralist version of DiNoia's purgatory. The unique, incommensurable character of salvation accounts in the present might then simply be set aside. Indeed, this is one, admittedly crude, way of reading some of Hick's comments in *An Interpretation of Religion*. Hick's speculations on the character of eternal life (1985a) contain their own version of the re-education idea, in so far as they posit further stages of human self-transformation and contact with the transcendent.

Leaving the portrayal of conceptions of salvation to the particularist provides no comfort for any view seeking positive links between the religions, and thus such a policy can be seen as supporting the religious exclusivist, naturalist, relativist or neutralist. It is important therefore for the pluralist to pursue the idea of seeking likeness-in-difference in this area of religious life as well as in others. This entails seeing salvation accounts linked in pluralism's favoured mode: as a series of partial, revisable but connected responses to human dealings with a common sacred, transcendent reality. In the matter of salvation pluralism can draw strength from the fact that the pursuit of likeness-in-difference in salvation accounts is demanded of its opponents as well. This is so not only for the reasons given above (confessional accounts need to postulate likeness between the religions as well), but also because there are substantial differences within any particular confession over what salvation is from, how it is to be achieved and what final state it promises. Yet for good reasons many confessional religious thinkers will assert continuity across the history and present of their confession.

Diversity within a single confession is a point which Jantzen makes much of in the case of Christianity (1984, 581–7). The danger of demons, hell-fire and the glories of deification may have been uppermost in the minds of the early Fathers, but the huge gulf which separates their thoughts about salvation from those of contemporary Christians does not prevent Jantzen from giving a common form to Christian salvation as such: 'Salvation in Christian thought is the transforming experience of God percolating through life'. Such an experience saves, not from hell-fire, 'but from the fragmentation of a life not integrated into the whole-making love of God' (1987, 129). There is an intellectual demand to make sense of any tradition as a genuine tradition by providing an appropriate account of how different belief and practice systems are nonetheless comparable. Too much stress on particularity will destroy the sense of something as a tradition. The particular pattern of life within Catholic Christianity described by DiNoia is different in key respects from that engaged by other branches of the Christian faith. The claim that patterns of religious life define conceptions of salvation should not then be taken to exclude the thought that there can be strong links between these conceptions, perhaps such that, if one is a successful account of salvation, the others are too.

The pluralist must build on this *ad hominem* argument and can begin by making a now familiar point about classification. To say that traditions offer similar accounts of salvation, for example that they all describe a journey from self-centredness to Reality-centredness, need not be to deny that their accounts of salvation are importantly different in detail. It means merely that when we consider the worthwhileness or success of those accounts *these differences do not matter*. To offer a vision of salvation, we may concede, is always to offer a specific vision defined by some beliefs and patterns of life. But in judging the success of these visions their similarities may matter more than what makes them different. By analogy, for something to be an apple is always for it to be one of a particular kind, a cox or a golden delicious or what have you, but for some purposes its being an apple may be all that matters. The pluralist need not deny the idiosyncrasies of portrayals of salvation in existing traditions.

Nor need pluralism be trying to substitute a new, global portrayal of salvation for the extant ones, a portrayal which will be free of idiosyncrasies. The pluralist is merely saying that an overview of the religions suggests that these idiosyncrasies are not necessary for success, while certain similarities are.

This gives us a new way of reading Hick and perhaps Cantwell Smith. The former's account of transformation from self- to Reality-centredness may be seen not as denial of the differences between traditions but as an assertion that what makes them successful in this area is what unites them rather than what divides them. Hick need not intend any belittling of the distinct features of the visions and patterns of life offered by the traditions. It is not *despite* those distinct features that the traditions offer the transformation he describes as common to them all. Similarly it is not despite their distinct features that different varieties of apple succeed in being apples. They could not be members of the general kind except by being apples of a particular variety, but what makes them all instances of applehood is something which does not consist in their variety-specific features, but rather shows through them. So the salvific success of religions for Hick is not constituted by the distinct features of their accounts of salvation but by something that shows through them. But his view might allow the thought that this success-making feature could only be present if tradition-specific features were also present. In other words, we could see Hick as implicitly teaching that salvation – salvific success – is a second-order, supervenient property, whilst the tradition-specific features of distinct patterns of life directed toward the transcendent are the first-order properties on which it is based. Something similar could be read into Cantwell Smith's account. 'Faith', 'openness to and relationship with the transcendent' are names for a supervenient property manifested in and through the lifestyles and beliefs found in the cumulative traditions.

The above manoeuvres show how the pluralist might escape the charge that seeking common salvific success across the traditions ignores the tradition-specific nature of the salvific quest and entails syncretism. But it may be argued that such moves merely serve to shift the argument in another direction. For one can now ask: what *of substance* at a second-order or supervenient level could there be in common between the traditions if it does not consist in any of their specific accounts of salvation or in any syncretistic amalgam of them? In other words, does not salvation or salvific success look as if it must consist in a purely formal property of the traditions? Yes, we might say in caricature of Hick, they all offer some antidote to egoism, but salvific success cannot simply consist in that.

The charge that pluralism entails reduction of salvation to some purely formal feature of the religions as patterns of life can be highlighted if we think why pluralism will want to maintain that salvific success is a property supervenient on the specific patterns of life of the traditions. It is surely because pluralism is by definition agnostic to a degree about the specific, idiosyncratic beliefs the traditions hold about the sacred. Pluralism is rooted in the thought that no particular tradition is certain enough in its dogmatic formulations to be the means of interpreting the others. It preaches that the transcendent is as yet largely unknown. Thus the specific beliefs of a given tradition will inevitably be for the most part radically uncertain. So the specific pattern of life the tradition's beliefs define as the appropriate way of relating to the sacred may in fact be to a large extent misplaced. It will be so misplaced if thought of as informed by an account of the sacred that is known to be strictly true in detail. That is why salvation cannot be judged to consist in any one of these patterns of life taken by itself. But if the content of visions of salvation in the traditions is, almost by definition, unreliable on the pluralist view, this leaves only something formal for them to be right about. How can this be enough? How can common salvific success be predicated on what appears to be common salvific failure?

For pluralism each tradition is a mixture of success and failure. Failure is there in each tradition's implicit claim to give *the* account of the nature of the transcendent. And it must follow that each tradition fails as providing *the* account of how to live appropriately toward the transcendent. The pluralist reasons that what disqualifies a particular tradition as the definitive account of the transcendent and of how to live appropriately toward it does not disqualify it as being a member of a class of traditions which succeed well enough in these respects to be classed together. So it might be argued that what enables members of the class of religions to refer to a common referent does not consist in the specifics of how they describe it, but is at best supervenient on those specifics, which are moreover revisable. What enables them to offer appropriate ways of living toward this referent likewise does not consist in the specifics of the patterns of life they offer but is at best supervenient on those specifics and is revisable. It must follow from this that, in the matter of salvation, what the specifics of the traditions do is contribute to a success-making feature which is in itself non-tradition specific. It does not follow that it is *purely* formal. From the conclusions of the previous chapter this feature must be one that answers the basics of the human religious condition and thus provides an answer to the problems of human finitude. That answer, according to our interpretation of the human religious condition, must consist in achieving some relationship to a transcendent good. Relationships can of course be established though they be imperfect (in respect of knowledge about and appropriate behaviour toward their objects). This is what the pluralist must suppose is effected by each tradition united by the pluralist thesis. We shall now try to show how this might be done, and the answer will point to the significance of moral endeavour in the religions. Our arguments will in the end provide some support for Hick's account of common salvific success.

The factors in the human condition which religions can alleviate include those that reflect human finitude through our bondage to time. They include the fact of death and the fact of frustration of our aims and projects. It is a signal fact that we fail to achieve all our goals and perhaps no project succeeds in every respect. Failing some promise of or path to liberation, death either places a limit on all striving or is the gateway into further rounds of struggle which are in turn marked by failure. Life thus remains bound by frustration and locked into the limitations of time as these are manifested in chance and contingency. Yet the very fact that some of our actions are directed toward a relationship with a transcendent good and are motivated by some conception of the respect that it demands gives them an independence from time. The authenticity and seriousness of the very endeavour to live in a way that constitutes being in a relationship to that which is transcendent and of ultimate value is something which enables human subjects to transcend the limitations of human finitude. Here we are drawing a distinction between practices and acts whose point lies in their achieving an outcome in the

future and those which have a point arising out of their attempt
to relate to or witness to some value which stands free of the
temporal. It is this mode of action which Stewart Sutherland
describes thus:

> some actions do not depend upon future outcome, in so far as
> they are not subject to trivialisation by changing circumstances.
> In such cases, whatever happens, the right thing has been done:
> the demands of justice or integrity and truth have been met.
>   (Sutherland 1979, 119)

There are two points behind this assertion that actions and
practices moved by desire to relate to a transcendent good are
time-transcending. One is that all actions will typically have two
components which jointly answer the question 'Why is it done?'
They are a purpose or objective sought and a motive or reason
for seeking that objective. Actions aim at substantive outcomes
and embody recognition of values, the values that make their
outcomes worth seeking. Further, we can discriminate among
values which make objectives, purposes worthwhile. Some values tell us that purposes are worth pursuing only if we are reasonably successful in attaining them. The actions and the practices
of which they are a part are given only an instrumental value by
the motives and values that inform them. If I value the making
of as much money as I can by the shortest possible route, unsuccessful bids to enrich myself quickly will hardly be redeemed by
the thought 'whatever I did I respected the claims of avarice'.
Avaricious actions are hardly ends in themselves. A practice of
the pursuit of avarice is hardly an intrinsic good the pursuit of
which, regardless of success or failure, is intrinsically worthwhile.

This difference between the goals of goodness and evil was
noted by Aristotle and has been made clear by recent commentators on his ethical writings. As Sherman notes, the point is that
vicious actions do not seem to constitute their own ends in the
way that virtuous ones do (1989, 115–16). Virtuous actions are
capable of becoming ends in themselves because the practice of
the virtues is a means of having one's life informed by goods
which lend value to the very business of their pursuit. They can
be done for the sake of the very activity involved in pursuing
them. Here then we need two thoughts: some values have a

worth which transcends contingency and there are practices which constitute being related to them. These values, being capable of informing practices, are then such as to enable human life to transcend the temporal. (For a fuller exploration of these ideas in relation to a number of contemporary authors see Byrne 1985. Byrne struggles there to show why these values have to be thought of as external to the human subject to do the job.)

The above connects in a natural way with the definition of religion we adapted from Stone in the preceding chapter: a religion is a system of practices that is rationalised by beliefs according to which the performance of the practices constitutes harmony with the ultimately real and good. Religions are endeavours to develop systems of practices which will enable human beings to escape facts of human finitude, the practices themselves constituting the means of gaining contact with the real and good. The interpretation leaves open whether the relationship and good aimed at is attained through practices specially set apart and distinct from normal conduct, or by a transforming vision of the value of ordinary actions and pursuits. Either is allowed. It does however reinforce Stone's distinction (1991, 340) between a religion properly speaking and a spiritual technique. For the latter's practices produce some valuable state, while the former's constitute being in that state. Some further advantages of our interpretation may be mentioned before a major objection is considered.

If our view is correct and the mere participation in an appropriate set of religious practices is constitutive to a great extent of salvation, then we can accept Hick's point about the need for a non-elitist conception of salvation *without* accepting his further appeal to the after-life. Hick contends that unless there is an after-life in which all finish their journey to sainthood, so to speak, beyond the special few who visibly do it in this life, then the idea that religion offers hope for the many is an illusion (1989, 207–8). On our view, an after-life, if we could make its nature sufficiently clear, might be seen as making possible a more perfect relation to the transcendent, but the engagement in appropriate practices with heart and mind of itself effects the decisive self-transformation that Hick seeks. Thereby too we move attention away from Hick's concern with the *effects* of religions on people to the perhaps more relevant matter of the *form* and *content* of religion itself. Further, we confirm Hick's intuition that, in Bunyan's words, 'The soul of religion is the practick part' (Hick 1989, 299). When we consider religions as systems of salvation and liberation our attention is properly directed to a moral transformation they make possible. It is because as systems of practice and belief they enable a new conception of the good to inform our lives, one which involves seeking the ground of the point and worth of action in something transcendent of individual choice and eternal. They make possible a relation with that which is transcendent.

The objection to be considered to the above is the obvious one that it awards the prize of salvific success to all post-Axial, ethically oriented religions only at the cost of cheapening it. All win just by making the attempt. Their very form – something that seems to follow from the mere definition of religion – allows them to win. But this is both to offer a reductive account of what salvation means and to point to no real overlaps, comparisons or similarities between the faiths.

As to reducing the notion of salvation to something unacceptably thin, we must hold out for the idea that salvation *finally* consists in a *perfected* relationship to the sacred and transcendent. Such a perfected relationship may indeed only be possible if a true set of beliefs about its object is present and if perhaps we enjoy an existence where an undiluted, undistracted concentration upon it is feasible. All actual religions are, we have said, going to be partial failures as the means of constituting such a relationship, not least because none will have *the* truth about the transcendent. Yet that does not entail that they are complete failures. Our account of the links between the ethical, the eternal and the transcendent are merely meant to indicate how the presence of a general feature in many forms of faith allows all such forms to be seen as partners in a common quest. Those which have the feature commended can at least be seen as beginning the journey of achieving right relation to the transcendent sacred. Thus such faiths can be seen as all offering a means of living appropriately to the transcendent.

This last point depends on our taking the beginning of the journey to right relationship to the transcendent as a decisive step, because it effects a decisive re-focusing of the self and a drawing upon new sources of meaning in life. Yet it must still remain important for the pluralist to seek overlaps and the like between concrete conceptions of the good in the various traditions. These would cement the presumption that we are viewing partners in a common quest and perhaps also throw up criteria of truth and signs of progress in the journey – agreement in accounts of the good and the virtues being taken as bench marks of genuine discoveries. Hence we see the direct relevance and importance to the pluralist programme of Hick's endeavour in Chapter 18 of *An Interpretation of Religion* to show how such things as generous goodwill, love and compassion are seen as the chief virtues in all major faiths.

Seeing extant religious traditions as various beginnings of the human journey to ultimate, perfect good brings in once more the theme of after-life found in DiNoia and Hick. The traditions' present salvific success is not a consequence of their offering in detail and in the concrete the same pattern of life. Salvific success in the present is a property supervenient on their detailed, concrete patterns of life. Thus, if we want to bring in the thought of eternal life, then we must accept that religions are not preparations for enjoying a form of eternal existence which is in detail the same for all. Further processes of transformation would be required for that possibility to be realised. So, with our eye on the first-order features of religions as paths to salvation, we could say that for pluralism they offer salvific success, because they provide some means to salvation or other, not necessarily the same means. Identity is vital only in reflecting that such diversity as exists in first-order salvific paths makes possible the same supervenient property: constituting human beings in a relation with transcendent good and reality.

Nevertheless it follows from all the above that it must be part of the pluralist programme to demonstrate that a range of overlapping, similar virtues are acknowledged by all the faiths linked by the pluralist thesis. How far such similarities can be established is a matter for detailed survey. But we can note and set aside some general objections to pursuing this survey with optimism. These have to do with particularism and relativism in ethics.

Because the pluralist is concerned with similarity in virtues across religions, he or she can accept the particularity which we have seen attaches to concrete patterns of living in the faiths.

Virtues such as justice and compassion are exemplified in a wide range of acts and practical policies. How they are expressed in the concrete depends on circumstances and on specific ends sought. It is not *despite* but *because of* the particular patterns of life enacted in the religions that common virtues may be found in them.

Common virtues produce different practical policies because their expression in practice is mediated by different beliefs about the world. Particularists can take their view that there is no common moral or salvific vision across the traditions to the extreme of arguing that, where theological ideas differ, so *must* moral ones. Such a view is defended by Alasdair MacIntyre for whom there is no such thing as justice, but only justice as interpreted by this or that tradition (1988, 346). The argument for this trades yet again on the embeddedness of conduct and motive in a tradition and hence in a surrounding mesh of beliefs. This entails that there will be a unique rational and motivational background to, for example, the Christian virtue of charity. Though Christian and Buddhist may preach and practice selfless giving to others, only the Christian will be moved to act and think thus by thoughts about the Sermon on the Mount, the imitation of Christ, and the like. Hence the Christian virtue of charity cannot be another version of a common virtue of compassionate love which could also be manifested in quite other traditions.

This kind of moral particularism has in fact quite marked counter-intuitive consequences, as has been demonstrated in a recent paper by Bonnie Kent (1994). It forces us to say, for example, of two doctors of different religions who faithfully attend the sick, that if one manifests the virtue of compassion, the other may not. It is aligned with movements of thought in general philosophy which would have us believe that when any part of a theory in which a notion is embedded undergoes change so that notion changes. On the whole it seems reasonable to resist the claims of this form of particularism, in favour of saying that, in our example, Christian and Buddhist have from within their dogmatic schemes different reasons for displaying an overlapping virtue. (Damien Keown's account of the nature of the virtues in Buddhist thought can be read as confirmation of this, see Keown 1992.)

The points that defeat an extreme particularism about the

virtues also dispose of some of the major grounds for an extreme relativism about them. Common virtues may survive both differences in detailed practice and differences in theoretical underpinning. Yet both of these facts have been cited by moral relativists as proving the conclusion that there can be no tradition-neutral ideas of right and wrong and that all such notions are relative to specific cultural and religious traditions.

Gavin D'Costa illustrates these lines of argument well. In the following, differences in specific practices are cited as supporting the notion that there are no agreements on basic values:

> There are no sets of basic moral values which are neutral and acceptable to all people, and as soon as one tries to specify some their historical and tradition-specific nature becomes evident. Prohibition on suicide in one tradition amounts to martyrdom in another, avoiding meat only on a Friday in one tradition amounts to a six-day species genocide in the eyes of another.
>
> (D'Costa 1993, 88)

The disagreements cited look less like ones on basic values and more like ones over which particular things are prescribed or forbidden. If religious traditions differ over the way in which animal life is to be regarded, it is much more likely to be because they have different views about the relationship of animal to human life, than because some think that cruelty and murder are permissible and some do not. They will agree on the appropriate virtues forbidding cruelty and killing but disagree on whether the instance of animals is one where they should be properly invoked.

Here D'Costa apparently cites differences in theology as grounds for thinking that ethical content must differ from one tradition to another:

> the Christian's entire morality and pursuit of supreme value is based on difference and participation, difference from God but finally participation in his love, charity and goodness . . . The Advaitin on the other hand is entirely oriented towards unity without difference and oneness without duality . . . Not only is

the goal different, but so is the entire basis of morality and what counts as ultimate truth for the Christian and the Advaitin.

(D'Costa 1993, 94)

Such reasoning reminds us that each developed tradition places morality in its own theoretical context, surrounding it with a rich web of theological notions. But it only follows that 'the entire basis' of morality differs from tradition to tradition *if* the basis of morality is through-and-through theoretical. There can be other, non-tradition-specific and non-theoretic sources of morality and it just does not follow that morality's content changes from tradition to tradition if *part* of its basis so changes. (I have argued for this at length in Byrne 1992; see p. 157 for a summary.) Even the most ardent of relativists on paper will do what most reflective people are capable of doing: use what shape a tradition or outlook gives to moral ideas to judge the adequacy of its theoretical baggage. Thus can we know that the racial theories of Nazism are wrong by the violence they do to any discussible ideas of justified homicide. We judge theory by reference to moral realities which are to some extent independent of theorising.

The precise extent to which, and at what level of abstraction, one can find common moral values across traditions is something that scholars continue to debate. (The material in Outka and Reeder 1992 provides a good survey of contemporary discussion.) The upshot of this chapter is that some suitably qualified notion of a common morality is one of the masts to which pluralism must pin its flag. Orientation to the good is the key mark of the presence of a common salvific quest because such orientation is a token of turning to the transcendent and the eternal. Points of agreement on the content of that good strengthen the idea of a common quest and may provide criteria for judging progress in the quest.

In all of this we have seen that pluralism must set its face against an out-and-out relativism. Its reasons for rejecting relativism will emerge more clearly in the epistemological discussions that follow.

5

Epistemology

HOW TO GET PLURALISM STARTED

The epistemological path pluralism must tread is a narrow and rocky one. One of its three defining theses states that none of the faiths has a doctrinal system certain enough to serve as the means of interpreting religion as a whole. To assert this thesis is to avow a large measure of scepticism toward extant religious convictions. Yet pluralists are not just religious sceptics. For they wish to assert that most traditions do succeed in referring to a transcendent sacred. For this thesis, and the corresponding one about salvation, to be plausible, there must be a real possibility of cognitive contact between human beings and a transcendent reality. So pluralism's scepticism about the certainty of particular confessions, and in particular their absolute claims, cannot be based on the epistemology of naturalism, and its agnosticism cannot lead to neutralism. Despite the fact that pluralists affirm that much of what has been believed about the sacred in actual traditions cannot be known to be true, at least when strictly and literally interpreted, they must offer an epistemology which allows human contact with the sacred.

So far I have pointed to one sketchy means of solving this conundrum. It is the position that the religions should be seen as limited, partial but somehow cumulative attempts to put humankind in touch with the transcendent. The overall view suggested in that formula is of the *possibility* of cognitive outreach to the sacred, while the *reality* is of a series of very imperfect attempts to realise it. This points to an epistemology which preaches a fundamental agnosticism about the transcendent while allowing that this can be breached by the cumulative efforts of the evolving religious traditions.

This epistemology can obviously be related to the 'epistemic liberalism' discussed in the last section of Chapter 1. There we endorsed the view that pluralism was the heir of the

107

Enlightenment in at least one respect – that of regarding all beliefs as fallible and open to question and possible revision. This epistemic liberalism, we shall see, can be an agent in questioning the absolutist claims of the various traditions and, in particular, the source of those claims in revelation.

The theory of knowledge to be associated with epistemic liberalism is gradualist and fallibilist. Its gradualist character is easy to understand. Gradualism is simply a way of referring to the expectation that reliable religious beliefs should have been built up slowly and cumulatively during the long course of religious history. Gradualism contains a tendency to question the existence of definitive revelations of religious truth. Fallibilism reinforces that tendency. Fallibilism in this study refers to the epistemological thesis which says human cognitive powers are fallible. It does not deny that we can be certain of or know some things. It says, however, that we are always prone to error; that, even where we know, we could have been wrong; that our cognitive claims are always open to challenge. It teaches, therefore, a due caution about the use of our cognitive powers, especially where we use those powers in areas beyond common observation or in which disagreement is rife. It is not equivalent to the doctrine associated with Popper to the effect that rational enquiry demands the production of hypotheses which can be easily tested and falsified. Many of our cognitive commitments cannot be easily falsified, not least because we lack a body of certain, unshakeable and absolute basic beliefs against which they could be tested. Fallibilism is therefore compatible with the recognition that enquiry is structured by our allegiance to canons and traditions which have to be taken for granted for the time being even as we question other parts of our cognitive world. It affirms, however, that nothing should be given the status of absolute certainty and that nothing is immune from questioning in the appropriate context.

Two further complications need to be entered on the record.

Not only must pluralism balance scepticism and cognitive contact with regard to the transcendent, its overall epistemology must indicate how *its own* formulation and defence as a theory about the religions is possible. If particular confessions are full of uncertainty in their dogmatic statements, how is it possible to know that? If the answer is that we know because we know we must be agnostic about the sacred, then we can't be so agnostic as to rule out knowing that pluralism is the right account of divine–human relationships. Pluralism is in the prima facie difficult position of being sceptical about much traditional religious belief while making bold claims about the focus of religion itself.

We must also address at the start the question of the scope of the pluralism thesis. In earlier chapters I have suggested that one way of understanding the scope of pluralism is as a conditional thesis, that is, it affirms that if *any* of the religions refer to a transcendent focus, if *any* offer a salvific path, then most do. On the other hand, it could make these key affirmations unconditionally. This scope question must be disambiguated before we proceed. It should be evident in fact that a purely conditional reading of pluralism is epistemologically uninteresting. It is compatible – so long as it affirms conditional equality between the faiths – with the most severe religious scepticism, one which leaves the actual chances of any religion achieving cognitive and salvific success very, very remote. It is right, in my view, for an initial outline of pluralism, such as is offered here, to fall short of a categorical affirmation that there is a transcendent sacred to which all major religions are related in the manner proposed. It better fits the limited nature of this undertaking and the present state of human reflection on the religions to see pluralism as the affirmation of a research programme with some promise but no guarantee of success. For it to have that status it must be read as affirming of itself: 'This is a plausible way of looking at the religions'. So then its epistemology must not be merely agnostic about confessional claims. It must also give a portrait of the human epistemic situation which enables us to see promise and plausibility in the idea that human beings have as such the ability, albeit limited and faltering in execution, to gain cognitive contact with the transcendent.

There are some tall orders awaiting fulfilment here and we must begin by addressing objections to the entire epistemological enterprise of pluralism.

TRADITIONS, PLURALISM AND RELATIVITY

John Hick's epistemology in *An Interpretation of Religion* represents in outline, if not in detail, the kind of programme pluralism must offer in this area. On the one hand, he has arguments aimed at questioning the authority and certainty of the specific claims of the confessions, while, on the other hand, he offers grounds, allegedly untouched by this scepticism, for thinking that there is an ultimate ontological anchor for the faiths whose existence is a reasonable postulate (compare Twiss 1990, 537–8). He thereby affirms the possibility and plausibility of a broader view of religious reality than is contained in any one confession. Much of the sceptical work on the traditions is done via reflection on their historically limited and conditioned character. It is this, worked out in detail to give critiques of claims to revelation and the like, which shows the traditions to be unlikely to offer propositions possessing absolute truth. The critique in Hick's writings of the traditions' absolutist claims contends that they are relative to historical and social circumstances, but Hick's version of the pluralist thesis must, of course, be thought of as escaping from a similar relativity.

Critics of pluralism will want to know at this point how this specific kind of scepticism directed at the confessions can make headway without devouring the pluralism that it is supposed to support. It may be asked, 'How can the traditions be targets for sceptical critique while pluralism as an intellectual enterprise remains untouched by the same critique?' We are back to the intellectual territory briefly explored in the last section of Chapter 1. We noted there that pluralism self-destructs if it rests on a *universal relativity* of human thought to circumstance. It must find a large measure of relativity in extant traditions, but one that is redeemed by a partial, limited escape toward cognition of an object of knowledge which not only transcends circumstance but the human altogether. Human cognition is thus relative-but-transcendent of circumstance and it is this which allows pluralism as a reflection on the religious aspect of that cognition to be possible.

Such neat formulae are challenged by those who assert that *all* cognition is tradition-based, that all reasoning is thus dependent on the forms and criteria of a tradition. This perspective offers to rob pluralism of its key epistemic contrast: the contrast between, on the one hand, the faiths whose modes of understanding the sacred are partial and limited on account of their relativity and, on the other, pluralism, whose philosophical credentials enable it to transcend that relativity. On this view, epistemic liberalism reveals itself to be just another tradition of thought amongst others. Like others it makes absolute claims (such as 'All human thought is fallible and open to questioning'), and like others it makes them from a basis which is relative to a particular phase of intellectual history. Critique along these lines flows from the recent writings of Alasdair MacIntyre (MacIntyre 1988 and 1990) and their conception of 'tradition constituted enquiry'.

In his attempted refutation of Hick's epistemological programme, J.V. Apczynski contends that 'the very project of offering philosophical foundations for a field theory of religion from a religious point of view is a mistake' (1992, 40). That is to say, one cannot offer both to respect a general epistemological and ontological claim that arises out of the religious traditions and endeavour to transcend their limitations by giving a non-tradition, non-relative and non-conditioned account of the focus of those claims. The major premise of the argument for Apczysnksi's conclusion is derived from MacIntyre: 'All enquiry, rationality and justification is tradition specific'. The pluralist is represented as searching for a standpoint for a theory of religion which is in fact unattainable. It would be one free from the epistemological limitations of any specific tradition of describing the sacred while culling elements from a whole range of them. Two specific things are wrong with this. First it falsely assumes that specific parts of the traditions can be understood and compared independent of their home contexts. Second it ignores the revelation from MacIntyre about rationality and tradition which entails that pluralism can only be another tradition (itself specific, historical and so on) like any other and so incapable of taking a view of the territory of religion superior to any other tradition.

The first of Apczynski's objections embodies thoughts that have been extensively considered in the previous chapter in discussing the debate between particularism and universalism. We shall therefore leave it aside. The second objection contends that the endeavour in pluralism to achieve a view of religion independent of particular traditions and cultures is doomed to failure. In fact, the epistemology of pluralism arises out of a highly specific tradition. This is the tradition of post-Enlightenment, liberal rationality, so that pluralism uses the reason 'espoused by the tradition of modern liberal culture' (Apczynski 1992, 42). Hick's interpretation of religion is thus seen as being parochial in the same manner and to the same extent as that offered by any confession (Apczynski, 47). It too tries to assimilate opinions and concepts in other traditions to the language of itself. It too allows cognitive success only to those parts of other traditions that cohere with its own conclusions. The fact that pluralism has an epistemology which makes few, if any, substantive claims about the transcendent is no mark of its tradition-independent status. It is but another reflection of its dependence on the liberal intellectual tradition (Apczynski, 48). Hence, epistemic liberalism may turn out to have an ideological load after all.

As noted above, with the major premise from MacIntyre to the effect that all enquiry is tradition constituted, there appears to be no room for the fundamental contrast on which pluralist epistemology rests. That is the contrast between limited, conditioned, confession-based traditions and pluralism, as containing a surview of them which somehow avoids the limitations of their absolutism. What follows from MacIntyre is thought that all large-scale theories and their accompanying epistemologies embody a particularised universality. They all make claims to universal truth from a basis which is particular to a given mode of understanding and which in turn claims to be superior to its rivals. One tradition can be judged superior to another, but only with the benefit of hindsight, when it may be seen that an earlier tradition reached an epistemological crisis which was only satisfactorily resolved by its giving way to another tradition (MacIntyre 1990, 150). Despite the possibility of such retrospective judgements, the general truth remains that 'We, whoever we are, can only begin enquiry from the vantage point afforded by our relationship to some specific social and intellectual past through which we have affiliated ourselves to some particular tradition of enquiry' (MacIntyre 1988, 401).

The target in pluralism's response to the MacIntyre-based critique of its epistemological aims must be the major premise 'All enquiry, justification and rationality is tradition specific'. What is true in this proposition is the unquestionable fact that any enquiry and any enquirer starts from somewhere – a point in intellectual history and space which gives that enquiry a set of given background beliefs and assumptions about method and the like. No one inhabits an absolute conception of the kind enabling escape from the limitations of a particular intellectual inheritance. Also contained within the MacIntyre premise is the truth that to a large extent what individual enquirers will regard as plausible depends on their prior background beliefs. So to that extent what is and is not rational *will* depend on which prior system of thought, if any, we occupy.

Pluralism need not constitute a denial of the first thought about the rootedness of the starting point of any enquiry. It need not claim for itself independence of such a starting point. But then it should not admit that its critique of the specific claims of the religious traditions amounts to attacking them for merely being forms of cognition with roots in time and history. Rather, pluralism must see its critique as depending on the thought that *in relation to this particular topic* the claims of the traditions are worthy of scepticism. The specific character of their claims is such that the pluralist can and must reinterpret them in the light of facts indicative of their relativity. So to argue is not to make a sceptical point about relativity *per se* but to make a specific, focused use of this point. There will be more about this below. The second thought about background beliefs can also be acknowledged and it does entail a limitation on the extent to which pluralism is provable. Since enquirers come to the field of religion with a vast array of background beliefs, there may be little pluralists can do but offer their interpretation of religion as an hypothesis backed by suasions which make it initially plausible and worth exploring. Theories of religions with such limited ambitions may nonetheless be interesting and worthwhile.

If so much is true in epistemology-according-to-MacIntyre, then what is questionable is the elevation of these thoughts to generalisations about all enquiry taking place within traditions. This immediately transforms the truism (albeit a truism with profound implications) that all thinking is someone's thinking to the philosophical thesis that there is a range of things called intellectual traditions, that they are distinct and that every enquirer is in one or another. But such a thesis is plausible only to the extent that we can demarcate these entities and find that to each there corresponds a unique set of 'criteria of rationality'. Consider the way in which the point about background beliefs and probability is thereby transformed. With the MacIntyre generalisation behind it, it becomes the thought that there are sets of these background beliefs that constitute something close to exhaustive and exclusive pictures of rationality. This is intellectual apartheid with a vengeance and no more plausible, in my view, than a relativism which hypothesises a range of distinct world-views or conceptual schemas to be the sharply demarcated prison of every knower. The reality is surely that there are intellectual traditions but they are loose families. Individual thinkers differ in background beliefs, and traditions have loose, fluid boundaries so that the background beliefs of those 'inside' and those 'outside' these rough groupings merge at the edges – with the result that intellectual exchange and the development of new ideas that results from such merging is easily conceivable.

One of the advantages claimed for the MacIntyre epistemology is that it steers an acceptable middle path between a reductive relativism and false view of enquiry as contextless and unrooted (MacIntyre 1988, 390). While preaching his doctrine that all rationality and justification is internal to traditions, MacIntyre does teach that truth transcends tradition (1990, 201–2) and that faced with crises traditions can and should reflect on and develop their fundamental doctrines. Thus with hindsight one can see a rational evolution in and across traditions. It has been persuasively argued (see Markham 1991) that MacIntyre's internalism about rationality and justification gives those inside a tradition no obligation to respond to awkward facts and the challenge of rival traditions by a process of open development. Those observing a tradition from the outside can have no expectation that this is the way it will go if its enquiries remain tradition constituted. For MacIntyre's own internalism about rationality grants to a tradition the power to respond to challenges in a closed manner, that is by keeping itself unaltered through employing internal resources to explain away challenge. Only if traditions are already infected with a liberal openness to challenge and to possibilities for revision typical of 'post-Enlightenment rationality' (our epistemic liberalism) will MacIntyre's more optimistic scenario be realised (Markham 1991, 266). The fact then that traditions of enquiry have evolved or been given up in the face of challenge by rivals and recalcitrant facts suggests, contra MacIntyre, that not all rationality is tradition constituted.

Post-Enlightenment ideals of enquiry do inform at least in part the pluralist's epistemology. And it is these which make pluralists question whether any past tradition can claim absolute truth about the religious field and which encourage them to offer pluralism as a tentative, fallible re-interpretation of religion. It is these ideals, further, which should make the pluralist reinforce the opposition to relativistic epistemology at this point.

In Chapter 1 relativism was set aside because it appeared to deny the cognitive and moral self-transcendence of human beings, something that in turn was said to be required by the pluralist outlook. So if this commitment is maintained then the alleged fact of the relativity of particular religious traditions should not be seen as support for relativism. We noted how relativism allows human subjects to live in a pluriform world. Plurality in all these things exists because relativism partakes of idealism: the human mind through conceptual schemas in part creates the world it engages with. The working out of these themes for the plurality of religions is spelled out in Runzo when he claims that the relativist can allow each separate religious tradition to refer to the sacred because there are as many foci of the religions as there are religions. Each has its real focus but each is phenomenal (Runzo 1993, 209). The merit claimed for this conclusion is that truth and certainty in the traditions remains undisturbed (Runzo 1993, 210). There is no need for the implied scepticism towards the claims of all positive traditions that flows from pluralism and the ideals of enquiry that lie behind it.

We shall advert to general problems in relativism below, but there is a crucial reason for resisting its tempting offers in the interpretation of religion. This reason derives from David Pailin's point that conceptions of the sacred must combine both salvific relevance *and* ultimacy (Pailin 1990, 159–60). Salvific relevance is needed through the fundamental feature of religions that requires their conceptions of the transcendent to provide the seat of the human good and the means of a definitive, secure answer to the problems of human finitude. Ultimacy is argued for by Pailin on the grounds that the focus of religion should serve as the end point in being and in explanation, an object that is the final regulator and goal of all thinking. Whether this is what all conceptions of the sacred must do I leave others to judge. It does appear, however, that if relation to the transcendent is the ultimate good, then the external term to this relationship cannot be thought of as a mere human product, whose precise characteristics depend, in some manner or other, on how a particular socially and historically limited tradition conceives of it. If the focus of religion is to serve as the final goal and sure anchor for the human struggle for well-being, its nature cannot be thought of as a human creation.

Religious truth looks, then, as if it has to be a human-transcending goal of enquiry, both practical and theoretical. There are very well-worn arguments for saying that relativism lacks coherence as a point of view because it must implicitly use system-transcending notions of truth and rationality in its own statement and defence (see Putnam 1990 139–41). It certainly looks as if pluralism is committed to such notions. Hence it opposes the implicit denial of such notions in the MacIntyre epistemology. It can accept what Runzo styles as 'the dependency principle of relativism', namely the view that religion is in large measure a social product, leading in turn to divergent and incompatible forms of religion across cultures (1986, 13). But it must draw different consequences from this principle from those favoured by the relativist. It takes this principle of dependency and divergence to be a ground for fallibilism and agnosticism in the field of religion, to be something that, in short, dissolves substantive, detailed absolutist claims about the transcendent. It will accept that this principle applies across the board, so leading it to be fallibilist and agnostic about its own theses. But, surely, someone might object, this is to erect a methodological scepticism and fallibilism into a new absolute. We can't avoid making absolute claims somewhere and the pluralist is making them about his own commitments to fallibilism. Well not exactly: there may be some things we ought not to apply fallibilism to, but we need to be given specific reasons why not. And we could always be mistaken about those.

How can pluralism be fallibilist about its own theses? If it adheres to a strong version of fallibilism, that will of itself serve to undermine the dogmas on which confessional interpretations of religion rest and thereby serve to argue for pluralism's interpretation. So, it will be contended, fallibilism cannot be even-handed. In reply the pluralist must say that it is in the spirit of pluralist fallibilism to be alive to the possibility that convincing arguments for the detailed, dogmatic scheme of any one tradition will be forthcoming. Apologetic arguments of this sort will in effect be arguments against the application of the dependency principle to the specific dogmatic scheme they favour. The importance of pluralism confronting apologetic endeavours of this kind is stressed below. Pluralism rests upon a number of considerations, such as the dependency principle. Within its epistemological foundations, fallibilism is the outcome of those considerations. But this fallibilism should be reflective enough to allow us to see pluralism as something capable of challenge. Some kinds of challenge will, paradoxically, question the application of fallibilism to some religious beliefs.

We are back to the position of Chapter 1 and the need for pluralism to adopt a mitigated form of relativism. There is relativity in the dogmas of the particular confessions, but it is tempered by the human struggle for cognitive and moral self-transcendence. This entails that, within the relative and fallible conceptions of those confessions, a move will be discernible toward forms of cognition which escape relativity and contribute to a human-wide search for cognitive contact with that which transcends all relativities. So the whole truth about these confessions is not given by Runzo's dependency principle. The fact that relativity is mitigated means that reflection on the traditions can lead to discernment of an overall meaning in them such as pluralism finds. The scepticism which grounds this reflection and arises out of awareness of relativity means that this reflective thesis must confine itself to minimal claims about the transcendent and recognise that it too is conditioned by fallibility.

The facts that religious notions arise out of particular historical and social circumstances and that their origin can be explained in large measure by reference to these circumstances should be taken by the pluralist to be evidence against the certainty and authority of detailed dogmas about the sacred and not against the possibility of truth in religion altogether. What is wrong with confessional interpretations of human religious life from the standpoint of pluralism and its epistemic liberalism is that they are ultimately based upon traditional affirmations about the transcendent and humanity which allegedly have an absolute, privileged status and/or which derive from sources for which such status is claimed. Thus we noted in Chapter 1 how, in the case of Christian interpretations of religion, for all the talk of inclusivists about seeing dialogue with other religions as a means of adding to and correcting traditional Christian perceptions in the light of other religions, there remains a list of key dogmas about Christ and incarnation which are held to be definitively and absolutely known. In many ways the identity of such traditions is bound up with giving definitive and absolute status to such affirmations and sources (but not, it is sometimes alleged, in the case of Buddhism; see Williams 1991).

It must be the contention of pluralism that such definitiveness and absoluteness in religious affirmations and sources is inappropriate for a reflective account of the general meaning of religion. (It may be appropriate in first-order religious life – but that is a matter we shall return to in our concluding chapter.) Pluralism as a research programme needs to point to some general considerations for rejecting definitiveness and absoluteness in religious sources and affirmations. These considerations will be ones supporting the mitigated agnosticism and relativism on which pluralism rests. Arguments for this agnosticism are offered in Pailin's *The Anthropological Character of Theology*. They turn around the interaction between, on the one hand, the character of the transcendent as unknowable, as providing a limit to human enquiry which is always sought but never reached, and, on the other, the rootedness of human enquiries in specific historical and cultural circumstances. Since Pailin's arguments have been given an airing in Chapter 1 already there is no need to adumbrate them further save to underscore two of his points. The first is that transcendence plus relativity are powerful reasons for doubting the idea of a definitive self-disclosure of the sacred. There is no word or action of the transcendent in history free of human interpretation. So we can doubt the thought that we might escape relativity through appeal to such disclosure (Pailin 1990, 117ff). The second point is that relativity plus transcendence do not entail scepticism as such, for that would be to give up as vain the *effort* to refer to and grasp the transcendent.

Human religious thought has been moved by an attempt to transcend the human condition. In this effort the notion of a transcendent sacred reality has played an important regulative role. In Kantian fashion we may say that definitive and absolute knowledge of the sacred has not been given, but knowledge of the sacred has been set as a task (compare Pailin 1990, 81). When Pailin asserts of theologians that 'Their judgements, consequently, are to be seen as only tentative insights perceived from relative standpoints' (30), this should not be seen as the prelude to either a full-blown relativism or an unmitigated religious scepticism. Rather we can take it as invitation to view extant religious thought as contributing to a process which has no absolute stopping points or achievements, but which has a realist intent and a regulative goal of genuine understanding.

If anything marks pluralism's indebtedness to 'post-Enlightenment' forms of thought it is this commitment to gradualism and fallibilism in enquiry, two facets of epistemic liberalism. It need not entail commitment to classical foundationalism and its view that there is once and for all a set of incorrigible propositions which we use to test others. (In Chapter 7 it is argued that classical foundationalism is incompatible with realism.) We can be fallibilist about some things only while other things are taken for granted, but what we take for granted shifts from context to context. There may be some things which at one moment we just cannot question, concerning which we cannot then apply fallibilism. But we have to say why we should not – and those reasons are themselves open to discussion. The epistemic liberalism avowed here is implicitly expanded upon by Ernest Gellner when he appeals to the intellectual ethic derived from post-Enlightenment thought to decry the idea of a unique and final Message, delivered at one place and time, exempt from scrutiny, from the dissection into its constitutive claims, and from the need to subject those claims to question (1992, 84–5). He preaches a post-Enlightenment 'ethic of cognition' whose first principles are that there are no privileged sources of cognition and that all supposed data are in principle open to analysis and question (83–4). This epistemic ethic is compatible with the thought, familiar from Polanyi, that scientific enquiry is itself constituted by traditions of thought and enquiry in which personal judgement and authority play their full part (as is fully explained in Harré 1986). What characterises the ethic of scientific enquiry is that its authorities and methods have been found to be capable of transcending national and ethnic traditions. Moreover, to accompany its passional and personal elements, it has developed an ethic of enquiry which makes intellectual authority temporary and subject to fallibilist questioning.

Let me sum up how I think pluralism stands with regard to the idea of traditions of enquiry.

Pluralism need not deny that all enquiry is rooted in historical and social circumstance and dependent on traditions of thought and understanding. It need not present itself as untainted by historical and social circumstance and the influence of tradition. However, it must reject any strong claims to the effect that there are a range of discrete intellectual traditions to one or other of which all thought, understanding and rationality is internal. Further to this, and in consequence of its affirmation of the possibility of cognitive and moral self-transcendence and of the ultimacy of the focus of religion, it must contend against a relativistic view of reason and of reality. It draws gradualist and fallibilist morals for knowledge and reason out of the tradition-based and relative character of human enquiry. Its quarrel with confessionalism in the interpretation of religion is not with tradition as such, but with the inappropriate absolutism which it sees in confessionalism. In all this pluralism acknowledges its debts to a particular epistemic tradition deriving from the Enlightenment. Its claim is not that this tradition is self-evidently true, but rather that its mitigated scepticism and mitigated relativism are both inherently plausible and appropriate to a reflective interpretation of religious belief. One of the reasons for regarding them as appropriate in this context is the fact of inter-religious disagreement, which figures largely in the next section.

APOLOGETICS, DISAGREEMENT AND THE CASE FOR PLURALISM

As part of its fundamental epistemological stance pluralism must admit that some confessional account of the religious life of humankind could conceivably be true. What it must insist on is that any such account be supported by appropriate apologetic arguments for the fundamental claims of the confession which drives that interpretation of the religious. Pluralism concludes that such apologetic arguments are absent and that reasons can then be offered for favouring its interpretation of religion over the remaining rivals, such as naturalism and relativism.

There are two planks to this stance: the necessity of apologetics for confessionalism and the judgement that, in the absence of a successful apologetics for a confessional outlook, pluralism is the most plausible choice.

Pluralism need not commit itself to saying that first-order religious life in the traditions requires the buttress of apologetics, but it should insist that reflective conclusions about the meaning of religion as a whole must be supported by appropriate argument. Appeal to the authority sources or fundamental dogmas of a given tradition is not appropriate in supporting such conclusions in the context of reflection on the meaning of religion as a whole. Reflective thought on this matter can only begin once we recognise religious diversity and thus a measure of conflict between traditions. One thing traditions conflict over is authority sources and fundamental dogmas. Hence, that this or that tradition's sources are definitive and absolute is unquestionably moot in this context. So no reflective interpretation of religion can appeal to the definitiveness of such sources or dogmas unless they have the support of appropriate apologetic argument. (See Griffiths 1991, 82–4 for the basis of this argument.)

From within the thought-world of religious traditions it is frequently a matter of dispute how far the fundamentals of faith can be and should be supported by apologetic arguments. But there are many examples of enterprises of this kind and readers will be familiar with at least some mounted on behalf of Christianity. In contemporary philosophy of religion Richard Swinburne's version of the attempt is perhaps the best known, beginning with the basics of belief in a personal God and ending with an as-yet-incomplete defence of the details of the specifically Christian account of that God's doings in history. How is pluralism to respond to such attempts? Is it simply to combat them one by one (as Byrne 1993 offers to do in relation to part of Swinburne's vast scheme)? Or does it have some general arguments which show that this kind of endeavour must fail?

If pluralism is true, endeavours of this kind should prove unsuccessful in backing up any rich kind of traditional dogmatics about the transcendent. So far as I can see there is no a priori proof that they are unworkable, but rather some general considerations can be offered which cast suspicions upon them. These considerations are just those outlined above arguing for the appropriateness of a mitigated agnosticism about the transcendent. They depend on its presumed ultimacy, suggesting its relative hiddenness as an object of knowledge, and upon the relative and fallible character of human enquiry. Such considerations are, however, hardly sufficient to discharge pluralism of the obligation to treat each and every apologetic enterprise on its merits, which is one reason why pluralism remains a tentative hypothesis resting on suasions not proofs.

The above provides another point at which this study can be compared with the approach of John Hick. The epistemology he derives from Kant gives him reason to be confident that no apologetic programme will work. His account of human knowing gives the human subject a heavy input into all cognition, one which increases as we move upward from physical to moral to religious elements of reality. The amount of freedom the human subject has to experience the world as having this or that character increases in proportion. We in part make the world we know, because it is known only as phenomenon not noumenon. Different cultures know it differently, for the further we move up the cognitive spectrum away from simple physical object judgements the more different cultures constitute it through different interpretative categories. If this story were true, then we could know in advance that, for example, no proof of the existence of a personal God from facts about the world could work, still less could detailed salvation stories be established from independent facts about this God's intentions and about human history. All such apologetics would fall foul of the religious ambiguity of the universe. To do him full justice, we should note that Hick also offers detailed criticisms of apologetic enterprises like Swinburne's (Hick 1989, 104–9).

Criticisms of Hick's epistemology are legion; in particular it faces powerful objections if seen as an attempt to show that apologetic proof is an impossibility (see for example Penelhum 1971). I have already noted why I reject it in this study: its quasi-Kantian, quasi-social idealism appears to me to devalue the referential commitment at the heart of pluralism as I define it. I shall have occasion to refer to what I view as its inadequacies in later chapters. For the moment I trust it is clear how it is different in fundamental respects (despite real similarities) from the fallibilist, gradualist epistemology outlined here.

The negative epistemological case for pluralism has now been set out. Negatively, pluralism rejects as too much open to doubt the dogmatic bases of confessional interpretations of religion. Positively it must maintain at least the prima facie plausibility of the minimal ontological commitment to a sacred, transcendent reality. The fact that it employs only a mitigated scepticism and relativism to question the bases for confessional interpretations of religion at once allows this positive thesis to be stateable and supports its minimalism. But its epistemological judgements need further support and this it can draw from two sources: reflection on the requirements of seeing a due order in human religious life and reflection on certain fundamental religious experiences.

Fortunately for this study, the first of these sources is largely a matter for the working out and application of pluralism rather than something to be demonstrated in a mere prolegomenon. What distinguishes a pluralist view of the religious field from a naturalist view (or a relativist one) is three things: seeing religious history as one important phase of human being where cognitive and moral self-transcendence has displayed itself (albeit imperfectly); postulating a minimally described anchor point for that self-transcendence; and supposing that there is present in the religions cognitive contact with that anchor point. These elements help constitute the realism that is at the heart of pluralism. If pluralism is worth discussing, these elements will provide a means of exploring and ordering human religious life that is at least initially plausible. Its plausibility would have to be borne out by it proving fruitful when applied to actual religions. It should define or guide a research programme which is found to yield insights into, and connections between, religious phenomena – insights that are not otherwise available. Without the fundamental ontological commitment of pluralism and its attendant theses the wrong kind of sense, or not enough sense, will be made of the phenomena of religion. (More on this in Chapter 7.)

Those who are convinced that all justification and the like is theory-relative will see this area as not providing any evidence for pluralism at all. Against whose background beliefs or 'criteria of rationality' is the fruitfulness of the pluralist interpretation to be judged? If we can rid our minds of this relativistic cant for a moment, we shall see that the question boils down to: do studies of religious history, sociology of religion, religious experience and the like yield insight and profit under the pluralist paradigm or not? A brief illustration of the thrust of this kind of question will be given during the course of the discussion of religious experience that follows.

Reflection on fundamental experiences will provide support for a pluralist interpretation of religion if such experiences can make pluralism's basic ontological commitment initially plausible while at the same time not being evidence for any specific confession. Pluralism appeals to the ubiquity of kinds of human experience to argue against naturalism and to the diversity of these experiences to defeat confessionalism. First we can appeal to certain moral experiences for support for pluralism.

Religion as defined in this study is bound up with apprehension of and desire for relationship with transcendent good. It is a common feature of moral experience that we feel ourselves bound to respect a range of values that we do not ourselves seem to create. We feel the demands of justice and truth and the like as constraints on the human will which bid us to act in ways which counter our own preferences. So much is a commonplace of the moral life. This experience has a properly religious dimension. For it is natural for us to think of the values to which we give our ultimate allegiance as uncreated and eternal. In this way we distinguish between those activities whose point derives from our personal desires and those which do not. Of the former we may say that their point lies in the fact that they will secure something independent of them which we want. Of the latter we can say that their point lies in their pursuit being called for by values which transcend us and our personal concerns. The good in this way has a claim on us bound up with the thought that it is uncreated, unchanging and transcendent. And this connects with points made in the last chapter. The thought that such values wait to be acknowledged in action enables some of our actions to have a point and worth regardless of whether the concrete goals they seek are realised. That worth and point rests on their being acknowledgements of the claims of the good.

The readiness of human beings down the ages to associate religious language and notions with the apprehension of the good is well documented (see Taylor 1989, 73ff and Byrne 1985). The apprehension would seem delusive if it is not an apprehension of something 'out there', discovered rather than invented. The apprehension carries with it a peculiar sense of responsibility and, as we have seen, associated ideas of relation to the eternal and the ultimate as the means of escaping the meaning-threatening aspects of human finitude. Such moral experience predisposes folk to believe in the sacred. This belief is one crucial way in which they have made sense of human finitude and its paradoxical fusion of meaning-threatening and meaning-enhancing elements (Clarke and Byrne 1993, 120–1). Such forms of moral experience do not constitute a proof of pluralism's fundamental ontological commitment as against a naturalistic view of the reality and its associated interpretation of religion as the history of mere delusion and error. But they should be seen as a substantial consideration in favour of pluralism's ontological commitment. They are so if we accept the force of what Charles Taylor describes as the 'best account principle' (1989, 58). The terms for describing our most fundamental experiences have to be ones which make best sense of them. We have no other access to reality than these experiences. If reflection should show that these can best be explained by making an ontological claim about the uncreatedness, eternity and transcendence of value, then so be it. As Taylor says, we should treat our deepest moral instincts as our mode of access to the world in which ontological claims are discernible (1989, 8).

Such arguments will cut no ice with the naturalist. Naturalists will claim that experiences of this kind cannot be true because they cannot be accommodated in a world view which sees reality as described fully and adequately by the natural sciences. In this world view value must be explained as a human projection. Morality is not a source for ontology, rather the result and seat of illusion. Of course, *if* there were a proof that the natural scientific description of the world was exhaustive and thus normative for our understanding of reality, then the best account principle would not yield an ontological claim of a religious kind. Any prima facie plausibility pluralism had thereby gained would go. The argument to this point indicates where debate needs to focus. Yet we should note that there is a strong case for saying on principle that value scepticism based on the grounds of the exhaustive and exclusive character of the scientific description of the universe must be flawed. The flaw lies in this: such a view leaves totally out of account the fact that the scientific view of reality is created by human selves and must be guided by norms of understanding and reason. It is itself the product and embodiment of a form of value-experience. We cannot, if this be true, pretend that the scientific view of the world shows that values are not part of it or not indicators of its real character. I suggest Putnam may be right in saying 'without *values* we could not have a *world*' (1990, 141).

As is the case with religious experience more narrowly defined, moral apprehensions of transcendent, ultimate good exist in many diverse forms. Some of this experience exists unrelated to the dogmatics of any particular religion; other manifestations of it are registered in the specific terms of a religious tradition – as when the phenomena of conscience are interpreted as the promptings of the Holy Spirit. Since such experience does have ramified, confession-influenced manifestations, those manifestations could be taken as evidence for confessional views and thus as against pluralism's basic postulates. Pluralism's strategy for dealing with this problem has to be as follows. The fact that confession-specific forms of moral experience differ is ground for concluding that collectively these forms point to no precise ontological commitments about the character of the sacred, but merely a minimal commitment which can be gleaned from them all, a commitment sufficient to support a pluralist interpretation of religion. The adequacy of this strategy is best discussed by turning to religious experience proper.

Religious experience looms large in John Hick's epistemological case for pluralism in Part III of *An Interpretation of Religion*. It is not difficult to see why. Arguments for the fundamental ontological postulate of pluralism which call upon the apologetic tradition familiar to Western philosophy of religion deal in too rich an ontological commitment for pluralism. But for a thinker like Hick religious experience has the merit of having transparent epistemological and ontological significance (by reference to his own version of the 'best account principle' used above) whilst also being something that cannot be taken as clear evidence for one confession rather than another. Hence it supports pluralism's minimal ontological commitment. The anti-confessional part of Hick's use of religious experience depends on balancing its diversity against its ubiquity. Present in all religions, experience provides evidence for no specific one against another when viewed in the light of an epistemological version of the Golden Rule: weigh similar evidence in other people's traditions as you would weigh its counterpart in yours (Hick 1989, 235). Divergence calls into play Hick's version of Kantian idealism. Divergence is best explained by concluding that the specific character of religious experience is derived from the input of the human subject and his or her tradition-derived categories of understanding. The specific characteristics of experiences are thus constructed by human beings out of the different conceptual resources they bring to an encounter with a Real that is beyond all their conceptual resources. So divergent experiences are not evidence at all for divergent confessions. They can be neatly explained away.

I have given reasons in Chapter 3 (drawing upon Stoeber 1992) for not taking up this neat way of coping with diversity. It embodies too extreme a form of constructivism in relation to religious experience. It is so extreme as to threaten directly the presumption that religious experience points to contact with a human independent reality. This is yet another point in this study where I find that Hick's Kantianism too idealist in its thrust and too ready to undermine pluralism's fundamental claim for human cognitive contact with the transcendent.

Yet Hick's fundamental strategy of using the ubiquity and diversity of religious experience as an argument for pluralism is right. A better way in detail of using diversity in religious experience to support a distinctly pluralist use of it can be derived from Caroline Franks Davis (1989, particularly Chapter 7, 166–92). This approach can be seen as an application to religious experience of a common sense response to divergences and conflicts in perceptual experience. If we find a number of observers giving divergent and conflicting accounts of one part of our world, we should conclude, in the absence of special reasons to the contrary, that none of them was giving an utterly reliable account. *Our* account of what they *really* observed should be cast in terms that favour none but captures something minimal that is confirmed by all. The special reasons that might cause us to set this procedure aside would be proof on independent grounds that one of these accounts was correct or that one of these observers was more reliable than the others. In the absence of such grounds we must remain agnostic about much of the detail of conflicting experiential reports.

Applied to diverse forms of religious experience, this model can be given substance by noting that to some degree or other all such experiences are informed by beliefs and concepts, and that they thus come with an interpretative load that links them with some confession or other. There is every reason in this context to avoid tedious debates about the possibility and extent of pure, unmediated experiences or about how far prior concepts and beliefs create experiences. Kant's famous dictum that intuitions, that is, experiences, without concepts are blind has one certain message for us: unless religious experience can at some point, albeit *post facto*, be given an interpretation it is useless as a contributor to religious knowledge since it cannot then engage with beliefs. Most religious experience appears to come with a clear interpretative load. Some, perhaps that which challenges existing notions, seeks one. Experiences should be taken on trust and this implies that their component interpretations should be accorded prima facie plausibility. This means further that, other things being equal, they should be taken as giving some support to the doctrines with which their interpretations enmesh them. But circumstances can remove that prima facie plausibility, in which case we shall need to support them via their enmeshing doctrines or whatever independent grounds they rest on. One circumstance which takes away that prima facie plausibility is the existence of experiences of contrary traditions which enmesh with contrary doctrines. This is a case where we surely need to see if there are independent arguments in favour of one of those doctrinal schemes. If not, then what these divergent experiences are prima facie evidence for cannot be doctrinally, confessionally specific. It must, if it is anything, be a minimal picture of a religious object that might be behind all, or as many as is reasonably possible, of these divergent experiences.

We are back here once more to a familiar choice: either there are successful apologetic arguments for the veridicality of one tradition and against that of others, or pluralist interpretations of the many traditions should be favoured over confessional interpretations, presuming naturalistic interpretations to be discounted. The minimalist, pluralist interpretation of the object of religious experience would have to be one which allowed us to see varied forms of experience as latching on to facets of the one ultimate reality that is sacred and transcendent. At the end of her survey of numinous and mystical experiences Franks Davis lists six conclusions which diverse forms of religious experiences can provide good evidence for (1989, 191). They are as follows. (1) Reality is not exhausted by mundane, physical things. (2) There is a deeper, truer self than that apparent to normal self-consciousness and which somehow participates in ultimate reality. (3) Ultimate reality is holy, eternal, of supreme value and finally real. (4) This reality can be experienced in personal terms as a loving power. (5) The focus of even introvertive mystical experiences can be seen as having connections with numinous experiences of an awesome power. (6) The chief good consists in a union or harmony with ultimate reality.

Franks Davis' list is geared to showing that there is some common testimony to theism in forms of religious experience. Her six conclusions would have to be adapted to remove their bias in that direction if they were to serve precisely the needs of pluralism. In particular (4) would have to be balanced by recognition that: (7) The ultimate can also be experienced as impersonal law or principle (often as the deepest layer in the self). It would then be for a pluralist account of religious language to reconcile (4) and (7). I do not think that is impossible.

Let us get clear as to the exact character of the pluralist response to religious diversity described above. It is not, despite Franks Davis' language to the contrary (1989, 190), the assertion of a common core to all religious experience. That is to say, it does not amount to the claim that all religious experiences within and without the historical confessions are alike. It is not the affirmation that the common testimony drawn from diverse forms of experience is also their common phenomenological content, as if the tradition-specific descriptions they have are added on to the same experience underneath. The assimilation pluralism wants to make with regard to diverse forms of religious experience is not a descriptive one but an explanatory one (Proudfoot 1985, 196–8). At the level of explaining their epistemological import, experiences can be considered as offering a common testimony. At the level of describing their phenomenological content, we must rely on their grammatical objects: they are of Brahman, of the risen Christ, of sunyata and so on. But we can't, for the reasons favouring agnosticism about such specific objects given above, reasonably say that they are grounds for believing in things so specified. As I have tried to explain at some length elsewhere, epistemic identity is not the same as phenomenological identity

(Byrne 1984). We are back to a familiar point in this study: pluralism is not predicated on the denial of differences between traditions but on the thought that for some purposes they can be ignored.

Included within the seven facets of common experiential testimony in the religions is experience of harmony with the transcendent as the ultimate human good. In the previous chapter we noted and criticised Hick's use of these experiences of salvific transformation as strong evidence of common salvific success in the religions. Experiences of salvific transformation get their due place in our argument as part of the epistemological testimony religious experience provides for pluralism's minimal affirmations. Their ubiquity and divergent specific content means their epistemic status can be treated in the same fashion as other religious experiences. They also point to the possibility of a pragmatic form of justification of minimal pluralist ontological claims that is close to the heart of Hick's own version of the pluralist project. Hick cannot be accused, as he so often is, of swapping pragmatic concerns for truth concerns in appealing to this kind of religious experience. As Twiss notes (1990, 563ff), one way in which cognitive claims in this area can be justified is through their consequences for personal being, consequences borne out in experience of personal fulfilment, transformation and the like. Such experiences are not proof of pluralism but take their place as part of the cumulative weight given to pluralism by a variety of religious experiences and other facets of evidence. Moreover this could be one way of seeing something sober behind the basis for pluralism in Cantwell Smith's writings. The sharp and questionable distinctions between propositional truth and personal truth in works such as *Faith and Belief* can be replaced with thoughts along these lines: if we judge that the traditions lack sufficient apologetic support for the specifics of their creeds, we may for our purposes set those creeds aside in favour of concentrating on the common, experienced relation to the sacred they point to. In the light of certain interests, the testimonies to personal living in relation to the transcendent they provide may be of special importance.

The argument in favour of a pluralist reading of religious epistemology offered so far has depended on the ubiquity of religious experience to suggest a case against naturalism and the divergence of religious experience to suggest a case against confessionalism. The case against naturalism would collapse if some proof of naturalistic metaphysics were on offer and in particular if a naturalist account of religious and moral experience were demonstrated. The case against confessionalism has been acknowledged to collapse if a successful apologetic for the background beliefs of a particular tradition became available. Even these modest claims on behalf of pluralism would be threatened if a certain contemporary understanding of the epistemic status of religious experience were left to go unchallenged. This understanding can be found in writers in the school of Reformed Epistemology such as Alvin Plantinga and William Alston. It is to Alston's presentation of the potential objection to pluralism that we shall now turn.

In *Perceiving God* (1991) Alston argues that Christian religious experience, particularly mystical experience, retains its prima facie power to support specifically Christian doctrinal beliefs even in the context of a reflective awareness of divergent and conflicting forms of religious experience. His argument on this score, like so much in his book, depends on finding parallels between the epistemic practice of Christian experience and that of ordinary perceptual experience. As epistemic practices both of these function to convert an appropriate kind of experiential input into an outcome of beliefs. They are both socially established and in neither case can any independent, non-circular justification be given for their participants relying on them as generating reliable beliefs. Their socially established character and high degree of internal coherence means that participants in them just have to take their reliability on trust.

So far we need not dissent from Alston's picture. We too have appealed to the notion that experiences have to be taken on trust in the absence of reasons to the contrary and have contended that religious experiences can add to the warrant of religious beliefs, as well as receiving warrant from them. But Alston contends that even the reflective and real awareness that other religions have parallel epistemic practices based on experiences and yet produce conflicting beliefs about roughly the same subject matter does not take away the prima facie reliability of a specifically Christian epistemic practice based on experience. He draws upon his analogy with normal sense experience: if we came across people with a completely different form of sense experience which generated beliefs about the material world conflicting with ours, we would still be warranted in sticking with our established practice. Without being a relativist about truth, Alston sees no need to interpret the discovery of diverse epistemic practices on the same subject matter as calling for scepticism or apologetic argument (1991, 274–5).

Crucial to Alston's case is his distinction between intra- and inter-practice disagreements (1991, 271). When we find folk disagreeing over perceptual judgements concerning specific matters of fact *within* ordinary perceptual practice, agnostic conclusions can follow. We expect to find criteria to sort out who is right and who is wrong in such an intra-practice disagreement. If we cannot sort out who is right using those criteria, we may justifiably suspend judgement. But a clash between the judgements of ordinary perceptual practice and some perceptual practice directed toward the material world employing an entirely different conceptual scheme would not be settleable by agreed criteria. If one lacks criteria to settle an intra-practice disagreement, one lacks something one could reasonably expect to have. So the absence of criteria tells against the warrant one should place in the competing judgements on offer. The absence of means to settle the epistemic conflict shows the practice is not reliable in this instance. But one cannot reasonably expect to have criteria to settle disputes between wholly different but competing belief-forming practices. So our inability to adjudicate on such clashes should not lead us to suspend judgement as to which is reliable. Disagreements between the experiential claims of different religious traditions are inter-practice disagreements.

It is clear what the pluralist reply to these contentions must be (in putting it together I draw upon Forgie 1994 and McLeod 1993). Alston has neglected the extent to which the form of religious experience belonging to a particular tradition is enmeshed in and dependent upon background beliefs. Of course it is not news to Alston that background beliefs are involved in Christian religious experience. Yet one can argue that he has neglected their true role by failing to appreciate that Christian religious experience is putatively of a *unique object*. The same is true of other forms of religious experience. The epistemology of religious experience is thus to be thought of in the light of what it is like to learn about unique objects in perceptual experience. Reflection on that shows us that we rely heavily on background information in identifying unique items and thus on taking our experience to give us information about the items identified with the help of those background beliefs. To be aware that one is looking at the table inherited from Uncle Henry or the twin Polly rather than Molly is not just a matter of applying general concepts to one's perceptual experience. Such experiences are mediated, albeit often unconsciously and without inference, by substantive beliefs. Our perception will generate mis-information not information unless those substantive beliefs are warranted.

These points apply to the epistemic practice of Christian (or Buddhist or Advaitin or any) religious experience. It is a practice apparently yielding information about a unique object. It may be non-inferential but it is what McLeod styles a 'mediated practice' (1993, 158). It is mediated by background beliefs and warranted to the extent those beliefs are warranted. These points gain extra force in the light of the much-aired contention that nothing purely phenomenological or given in an experience could identify it as, say, the God of Christianity. For the identifying features of this God do not appear to be discriminable items of experience (compare Kenny 1992, 41–2 but contrast Alston 1991, 96–8, who swims against this tide as well). Such features include the 'omni' properties of philosophical theism and the properties implied by Trinitarianism. This does not entail the sceptical conclusion of Kenny and others that nothing could count as an experience of the Christian God (or of any other specific confessional focus), but merely that such experience is heavily mediated by tacit background beliefs. It is not a simple matter of an experience structured and objectified by a straightforward application of the concepts contained in a perceptual vocabulary. There lies the difference between saying of the thing I see 'It is a chair' and 'It's Uncle Henry's chair'.

The pluralist will welcome with open arms McLeod's conclusion (1993, 157–8) that Christian religious experience should not be compared as an epistemic practice with perceptual experience itself but with the sub-class of that latter practice concerned with perceptual beliefs about unique objects. The apt comparison, says McLeod, with perceptual practice is a general religious experience practice whereby beliefs about the numinous are generated (in our terms: about the transcendent sacred). Within that practice the mediation of confession-based background beliefs allows sub-practices to be formed concerned with identifying and learning about specific, unique manifestations of the numinous. In the light of this account, the disagreement between the experiential claims of different traditions looks more like an intra- than an inter-practice disagreement. So Alston's crucial distinction between forms of epistemic disagreement is weakened by recognising the consequences of the fact that the experiential belief-forming practice of a given tradition is directed toward a unique object.

Massive disagreement is found between the sub-practices that make up human religious experiences but some overlaps between them are found as well. The pluralist's response for those who are reflectively aware of such disagreements seems eminently reasonable: failing independent, cogent argument in favour of the background beliefs of any one of these sub-practices, suspend judgement about the reliability of any one, but presume that the more general, vaguer beliefs that can be gleaned from the entire practice have some warrant.

CONCLUSION

The narrow and rocky epistemological path pluralism must tread has now been sketched.

Pluralism mixes scepticism and affirmation. Its scepticism about the truth claims of particular confessions is based on their divergence and upon the ease with which much that is in them can be explained as the result of historical and social circumstance. In particular it uses divergence and relativity to question the status of authoritative sources of beliefs in the traditions.

Affirmation of minimal ontological claims is possible by finding a remaining warrant in moral and religious experience for those claims, while moral and religious experience also point to the pluralist picture of human nature as capable of cognitive outreach to the transcendent.

The possibility of that outreach is also defended by way of the rejection of relativist accounts of truth and knowledge. Instead a fallibilist, gradualist account of knowledge is affirmed which can concede the fact of relativity in much human cognition while retaining hope that some genuine knowledge is slowly accumulated in the course of human experience.

Fallibilism and gradualism are conceded to be part of the intellectual inheritance of the Enlightenment, and in particular of epistemic liberalism, but argued to be independent of a strict foundationalism. The Enlightenment inheritance is defended so far as to reject relativism and its near neighbour – the notion that all enquiry is tradition constituted.

The epistemology for pluralism offered shows that pluralism could never rest on more than a suasion as opposed to proof. Its key contentions rest on presumptions that are defeasible. Yet the epistemology offered also explains how we might have room to state pluralism and believe it on the basis of some grounds at least.

6

Language

A THEORY OF RELIGIOUS LANGUAGE

Like many an account of religious language in philosophy of religion, that offered by pluralism must be to some extent prescriptive rather than descriptive. That is to say, it will explain what forms of meaning religious language *can* have given pluralism's overall view of the nature of religion. It will not necessarily be an account of the conscious intentions of religious believers.

Many writers now approach the topic of the character of religious language by employing the three-fold classification of George Lindbeck (1984), which focuses in particular on the doctrinal sentences within religious discourse. According to Lindbeck we can view religious discourse as propositional, in which case it is the fact-stating character of doctrinal statements that is uppermost in our minds. Or we can see religious language as experiential-expressive and therefore as the vehicle for the avowal of important feelings and experiences. Or we can regard doctrinal statements from a cultural-linguistic point of view, seeing them primarily as rules which make possible distinctive ways of thinking and behaving.

There is no need to regard these three models as exclusive and elements of all three are compatible with the overall pluralist view of religion. Religious language as propositional is compatible with pluralism's view of religions as endeavours to describe a reality beyond the human. Important experiences are at the same time given expression in religious statements about the transcendent. Finally, religious statements make possible a relation with the transcendent and define a way of life that is held to constitute living in harmony toward it.

The question arises as to whether there is a means within pluralism of integrating these facets of religious language or of providing an overview of the status of religious discourse. This question must be considered in the light of a serious dilemma

137

facing pluralism. On the one hand, it requires something like a propositional view to be true of some facets of religious language, yet, on the other, it requires a propositional view to be severely modified and limited. The first horn of the dilemma is created because pluralism gives religious discourse a realist intent backed by some referential success. The second horn of the dilemma is created because this intent and success is granted to different religions with conflicting doctrinal structures. Thus, in so far as religious discourses are propositional systems, they are in part successful and in large part manifest failures. What pluralism needs is an interpretation of religious language, particularly doctrinal language, which makes a virtue out of this dilemma of mingled success and failure. I believe that there are two ways of coping with this problem. One solution is via the notion of metaphor. The other is by appeal to the notion of a transcendent with multiple aspects, and thus of religious language as a *partial, aspectival* description of the reality of the transcendent. In this section we explore the metaphorical interpretation, relating it as we proceed both to Hick's claims that fundamental religious assertions are to be seen as mythological (1989, Chapter 19) and to analogical accounts of religious language. In the next section the aspectival approach will be outlined.

It can be argued that a metaphorical interpretation of doctrinal discourse best fits the picture developed here of religions as attempts to make cognitive and personal contact with a reality which we must on reflection be in large measure agnostic about. Different religions with their doctrinal statements constitute efforts, by and large successful if pluralism is right, to gain some epistemic and salvific access to transcendent reality. But they are highly fallible attempts to describe that reality. Much of what they have said about the character of the transcendent can be presumed to be revisable and correctable. In so far as they succeed in referring to the sacred, it is not because they each have a true identifying definition of the nature of their ultimate object or of its relations to us. Their descriptive resources help in giving them access to a real object but so do the contexts in which those resources are employed. Religious adherents refer to the sacred and their descriptions denote. Religious people refer with the aid of doctrinal utterance but its final, literal, detailed truth is not required for reference.

We need a mode of utterance in religious language which is the vehicle of reference but which is exploratory, revisable and fallible. This is just the role that Richard Boyd has claimed metaphorical utterance does play in the advance of scientific theory. Boyd in particular states that in important, successful scientific theories there is a class of metaphors which serve the purpose of catechresis (that is, of enabling us to name what was hitherto indescribable). Their success does not depend on their conveying quite specific resemblances or analogies between the known and the unknown. Indeed their referential value and their use in guiding the development of thought depends on their open-endedness (1979, 357). Boyd refers to these metaphors as 'theory-constitutive' since they provide the means of organising the initial and developing insights of a whole branch of study. They introduce the terminology for future theory construction. They refer to phenomena as yet only partially understood. They are capable of yet further refinement and disambiguation (Boyd 1979, 371). Metaphors of this kind are peculiarly apt to help in the task of making reference in conditions of ignorance mentioned in Chapter 2. We make cognitive contact with things and stuffs in scientific enquiry before knowing their natures properly. We continue in contact with them as we progressively abandon or modify much that we initially thought about them. Open-ended, constitutive metaphors can serve as the vehicles for making reference in conditions of ignorance and preserving it through changing, fallible patterns of thought.

It seems appropriate to adapt Boyd's thoughts to the parallel epistemological situation in religion (compare Martin Soskice 1985 and 1987). We have diverse attempts to make and maintain reference to a reality, in large measure hidden, through patterns of thought which are fallible and changing. Thus we should see each doctrinal scheme in the religions as built around, as adumbrations of, a set of constitutive metaphors. Within that scheme, following the pattern of the metaphors, what appear to be literal statements about the transcendent are made. But they are no more than workings out of the constitutive model. In so far as the constitutive metaphors and their adumbrations are true, they are metaphorically true. They have the aptness and insight of worthwhile metaphor rather than the finality of literal truth. Here the possibility of a strong contrast with scientific knowledge seems possible, for we should surely want to claim that the specific hypotheses in a scientific theory that represent the application of its constitutive metaphors are literally true.

This broad picture has further advantages than the ones claimed so far (referential value under conditions of ignorance and revision, on the one hand, and open-ended guidance for thought on the other). We can endorse some of the advantages claimed for 'metaphorical theology' by McFague (1983 and 1987). A metaphorical approach to religious language will enable a greater appreciation of religious diversity, for we are quite content with the notions that metaphors give us only partial, limited insights, and that different, seemingly conflicting metaphors can be used of one and the same object.

To give a proper account of the implications of the metaphorical view of religious language two issues need to be addressed. They relate to the scope of metaphor in religious language, to how much talk of the transcendent is metaphorical, and to the precise nature of metaphorical description.

The pluralist will wish to state why talk of the sacred is to be interpreted along metaphorical lines. The reason given will be because of the sacred's transcendent character and our resulting agnosticism toward its exact nature. That transcendent character must be capable of being filled out if this reason is to make any sense. But if that character can be filled out then the sacred can after all be described and the description cannot be metaphorical on pain of taking us in a neat and tight circle. The way to solve this conundrum is to recognise that not *all* talk of the transcendent is metaphorical. Indeed the ground of the metaphorical interpretation must be found in a non-metaphorical description of transcendent. This description will not be subject to metaphorical interpretation because it is negative and relational. So the pluralist's thesis becomes that all talk of the transcendent is subject to metaphorical interpretation save that which is negative and relational.

We can see St Thomas Aquinas wrestling with a parallel problem to ours about the scope of metaphor in religious language in his discussion of the grounds for analogical discourse in Part 1, Question 13 of the *Summa* (for discussion of the relation of metaphorical and analogical interpretations of religious discourse, see below). He too has to give reasons, not themselves subject to analogy, to explain the necessity and possibility of analogical discourse about God. He finds them in the characterisation of divine transcendence through negative and relational descriptions. The basic intention behind the use of the word 'God' is, he writes, to speak of something that is above all things, the source of all things and distinct from all things (1964b, 1a, 13, 8 ad. 2). We can ally this with the basic characterisation of the religious ultimate we have used earlier: it is a something that is ultimate rationally, valuatively and ontologically. Aquinas is telling us that we introduce the word 'God' to name something, we initially know not what, but which is at least infinitely more perfect than all things in the world, is also their cause and, because it is these, is radically different in its mode of being from anything in the world. This gives us some negative and relational knowledge about this referent which enables us in turn to realise that there will be vast problems in saying positively what it is like, since that knowledge yields the consequence that any resemblances, and thus sharing of properties, between this object and the ordinary things our language is developed to speak of will be deeply problematic. We use the negative and relational knowledge arising out of the basic intention behind talk of the transcendent to tell us that our intention is to speak about something that is radically unknowable. In fact, Aquinas concludes that transcendent perfection does not resemble anything mundane (1964a, 1a, 4, 3 ad 4), does not belong to any genus (1964a, 1a, 3, 5), and so to no genus which includes a mundane thing, and finally that we cannot know what God is, only what he is not (1964a, 1a, 2, 3). We know enough to know we cannot comprehend the transcendent.

Aquinas' account of positive descriptions of God through analogy does not, in my view, seriously disturb this fundamental agnosticism (see Burrell 1973 and 1986, and Hughes 1987). Regardless of the right way to interpret his account of positive talk of the transcendent, it remains the case that he has shown us how a balanced view of the limited scope of literal, unmodified descriptions of the sacred is both possible and required of anyone who appeals to metaphor (or analogy) in this area. A stock of negative and relational descriptions remains as the ground for appealing to metaphor in the first place and the condition of its continued possibility.

Is there a criterion for distinguishing positive language of the transcendent, on the one hand, from negative and relational language on the other? The question gets its point from the fact that a parallel query has been raised in relation to Hick's similar-looking distinction between *substantive* descriptions of the transcendent which are mythic and *non-substantive, formal* descriptions which can be literal. For example, Keith Ward complains that Hick regards absolute perfection as a formal property of the sacred, whereas perfection entails that the sacred is good – a substantive truth (Ward 1990, 10). There is in fact no criterion or rule neatly to divide up that language of the transcendent which is to be metaphorically interpreted and that which is to be literally interpreted because it is negative and relational in force. It is enough if the general notion behind the distinction is clear and if particular cases can be adjudicated upon satisfactorily. The adequacy of the general notion should be admitted if we can find intelligible the intention Aquinas describes behind the use of the word 'God'. We have to understand the idea that folk wish in speaking of the sacred to refer to a something distinct from all mundane things, and thus whose nature is radically unknowable, yet which is related to us in important ways: it is the source and ground of being and of value, harmony with it is the final human good, and so on. Examples of particular descriptions or predicates which are problematic for the distinction have to be treated on their merits. Ward's example of absolute value and goodness can serve to illustrate how discussion of these might go.

The reference to the transcendent as absolute perfection, as ultimate in value, is largely negative and relational. Such phrases point to the distance between it and anything mundane. It possesses none of those defects and limitations which characterise the mundane. Yet it is also the source of all that is of value in mundane things. On the view defended here, any positive-seeming characterisation of value in the transcendent will be subject to the qualification of metaphor. To say of the transcendent that it is good is not to dent our agnosticism of its character substantially for it does not say what it is for this 'thing' to be good. The goodness that is our model for talking of transcendent goodness will no doubt be human goodness, specifically moral goodness. But it is a commonplace in these discussions that the sacred cannot have anything that unproblematically resembles moral goodness. For this reality is not one person amongst others who acquires or exercises virtues, being subject to temptations and facing, therefore, morally significant choices that could go either way. Language intended to refer to that which is ultimate rationally, valuatively and ontologically which suggests otherwise has to be recognised as anthropomorphic and therefore subject to metaphorical interpretation – just as much as language in the Bible referring to God's right and left hand.

It should be clear from the above that pluralism must be guided by a notion of transcendence markedly different from that which dominates so much contemporary Anglo–American philosophical theology. For according to that notion the transcendent, characterised as the God of theism, *does* belong to a genus: that of persons. He is a person albeit one with some remarkable attributes, such as incorporeality, infinity and eternity. These unusual attributes plus God's role as the first cause which is dependent on nothing are the measure of his transcendence. The problem of positively describing God can look remarkably simple to authors in this tradition. It is simply a matter of conceiving how a person who does not have the nature of a human being can manifest the typical qualities of personhood, in particular cognition, volition and action (the passional qualities of human persons remaining problematic). The way is open to deal with this problem by supposing that some slight modifications to ordinary personal descriptions will do for describing God's personal life. These will be modifications which find a core meaning to talk of knowing, intending, acting and the like shorn of their misleading human associations and thus applicable literally and univocally to God (compare Alston 1989a and Swinburne 1977, Chapters 4 and 5).

Pluralism's fundamental conception of transcendence rejects this way of seeing the problem of describing the sacred and hence the solution offered. Its own conception rules out minor modifications to personalist descriptions as the means of accommodating positive language of the sacred and entails radical agnosticism about it. Here we have highlighted another reason why pluralism must reject philosophical theism in its standard forms as the basis for an interpretation of religion.

We have said something about the scope of metaphorical description of the transcendent according to pluralism. Now we must turn to the precise nature of metaphorical description.

Metaphor can be defined as that trope 'in which we speak about one thing in terms appropriate to another' (Martin Soskice 1981, 55). Metaphors typically, though not invariably, involve a subject and a model. The model is more appropriately used of other things than the subject, yet the model is intended to illuminate our understanding of the subject. So in a good metaphor there is a sense of both strain and aptness in resulting description. The best way to understand the means by which metaphors function so as to combine both descriptive strain and success is that provided by Nelson Goodman (1976, 71–4). Metaphors function to transfer what Goodman styles a 'schema' or network of 'labels' from the familiar, understood realm of the model to the alien realm of the subject. This account depends on the simple idea that the model term in the metaphor has an established use which links it to familiar contexts of employment. In that use and those contexts the term acquires habitual associations, a cluster of relations or attributes brought to mind when it appears. In metaphor the model term is seen to be used in a context quite unlike its normal and habitual context. Yet we are invited through the metaphorical employment of the term to explore the subject through the associations, relations and the like brought to mind by the model. In good metaphors, despite the strangeness of the context, this proves fruitful in generating new insights into the subject or in organising existing insights in interesting ways. The peculiar appropriateness of metaphor for talking of the transcendent is that the transcendent must be recognised as an alien, unknown realm for the purposes of applying any positive descriptive language to it. It follows from the negative and relational placing of the sacred that descriptive language which posits a sharing of properties between the sacred and mundane objects is inappropriate. Any positive descriptions of it must be recognised to 'be more appropriate of another'.

It is part and parcel of this account of the nature of metaphor that it should encourage a distinction between how metaphors function cognitively and what the cognitive results of their use is. Contrary to some portrayals of metaphor, our account does not involve the idea that metaphors invoke straightforward comparisons between subject and model, where comparison entails attributing common properties to the two sides (Yob 1992, 478–9). Metaphors function as invitations to understand a subject in terms of the schema or network provided by a model. The cognitive gain from that invitation may be that shared, but hitherto unobvious, qualities between subject and model are revealed. Such metaphors produce cognitive gain expressible in further literal and positive statements about the alien realm of their subjects. But the cognitive gain from a metaphor may consist in increased knowledge about the subject in other directions (as, maybe, increased negative and relational knowledge about the subject).

The above point about the cognitive function of successful metaphors has been challenged by a number of writers, not least William Alston (1990b). His arguments are worthy of exposition and criticism because they are directed precisely at the kind of interpretation of religious language we have alleged is required for pluralism. For Alston any metaphor that is apt does attribute one or more specific, shared properties to subject and model. Thus a successful metaphor always depends upon a literal core which can in principle be stated independently of the use of metaphor. Metaphor turns out not to be an independent way of describing the transcendent or of characterising religious language, because wherever it is judged appropriate it rides on the back of literal, positive statement.

Alston wants us to believe that unless the transcendent literally resembles mundane things it cannot be spoken of in positive terms at all. He argues that the force of any metaphor which can be said to have a truth value is to assert two kinds of similarity between its model and its subject: a general resemblance in respect of some properties or other and a specific resemblance in respect of at least one identifiable property. The general resemblance is open-ended but also tends to triviality, since any two things can be said to resemble each other in general, unspecified respects. Any metaphor worth describing as true must attribute a specific similarity between subject and model, and part of its meaning must thus be literally translatable. For if the user of the metaphor can understand that similarity, he or she must have in mind the shared property the similarity consists in. The user can then be expected to be capable of expressing that property in a concept and in a corresponding literal predicate. Any properties speakers can conceive of must be capable of being correlated semantically with a predicate term (Alston 1989b, 28–30).

Alston intends his argument to apply only to those metaphors which have a determinate truth value. He sees his main opponents as those who hold a similarity or comparison theory of metaphor but who assert that open-ended, general similarities are enough for successful metaphors. Against such thinkers Alston buttresses his case by saying that if metaphors were assertions of vague similarities then *any* two models could be compatible of the same subject. Metaphorical statements about God would have no precise entailments and would therefore lack any clear predictive or practical consequences. A theology that relied on such vague metaphorical statements would be theoretically and practically useless (Alston 1989b, 31–5).

My initial remarks about the meaning of metaphorical utterance indicate that I think Alston's account confused. In particular, it illustrates the fallacy of running together the results achieved by some cognitively successful metaphors (discovering shared properties between subject and model) and the way in which metaphors function as such. Before going to the heart of this matter of the nature of metaphor's function we must consider Alston's charge that unless metaphors do achieve the cognitive gains he outlines, they are useless. What we have to bear in mind is that, on the Goodman-type view of metaphor defended above, the fundamental logic of metaphorical thought will be analogical, pictorial rather than one controlled by strict entailment and contradiction. If it is right to think that a particular subject can be aptly thought through the associations and schema of understanding provided by a given model, then the rightness found is that of a picture which captures well aspects of our experience or which develops insightfully other, existing pictures. This is why we might employ two contrasting metaphors to capture different aspects of the same subject, but why it is not true that *any* two models could be used of the same subject. For example it will not do to say 'God is the great Hitler in the sky': if we undertake to understand the subject in terms of the pattern of associations attaching to the model, our experience of it is not connected or extended in insightful ways. We must recall the stock of negative and relational understanding of the transcendent our account allows. This stock provides a check in the light of which the cognitive successes and failures of suggested metaphorical accounts of the transcendent can be judged. A metaphorical theology is not, on our understanding of metaphor, capable of anything like final deductive systematisation since its modes of thinking remain essentially pictorial, analogical. Exactly this, of course, is claimed by many recent writers to be true of scientific thinking.

If the sting can be drawn from the tail of Alston's argument in the above way, we have still to deal with his central contention. This amounts to: if a metaphor can be cognitively successful in asking us to understand a subject in terms of the schema provided by a model, it can only do so by pointing to at least one specific similarity they each share which can be described independently of the metaphor. By far the best way to rebut this is to use John Searle's examples of metaphors that function successfully without relying on principles of similarity (1979, 108–10).

Searle cites a number of metaphors, based on spatial models, we use to characterise time: 'time flies', 'the hours crawled by'. Even the obvious paraphrases of these colourful expressions are metaphorical: 'time went rapidly', 'time went slowly'. He also cites taste metaphors used to describe people's dispositions, as in the case of 'sweet temper', 'bitter attitude'. There is no way in which time and space literally resemble each other, or in which tastes on the tongue literally resemble dispositions. There may be some initial connections between model and subject in such cases. Space is a system of coordinates, so is time. Sweet tastes are agreeable, so are sweet tempers. But beyond those initial connections, we just happen to find the further associations invoked apt, illuminating and helpfully suggestive in thinking about the subjects of these metaphors. This is rather like the way in which we just happen to find that one thing reminds us of another (Searle 1979, 113). In the case of time, we discover a close parallel with talk about the transcendent, in that the fourth dimension is in a like manner something strange and hard to comprehend. Our language is rich in metaphors for time drawn from space and spatial things and processes. Many of these metaphors are quite unconscious. The simplest of examples, like 'time passes', illustrates this point. Without drawing upon such metaphors we would stammer for want of a rich vocabulary for describing time and our relation to it. We accept the transferred spatial vocabulary without question. We feel at home with it. One reason for this is that we find that it can be extended: one spatial metaphor for describing time's nature leads on into another, and another.

And it usefully organises our non-metaphorical understanding of time. Knowing that time is flying, we also know that we need to hurry.

The preceding points are intended to give the lie to Alston's claim that successful metaphors attribute specific similarities between subject and model *and* to his linked claim that such metaphors should have a core which is re-phraseable in other, literal terms. What the example of time shows is that some metaphors, often indefinitely extendible, create the very possibility of describing a subject and establishing some link between it and more easily understood realms of object. So much is claimed by pluralism for traditional and varied ways of speaking about the transcendent in the religions.

Before closing this section we must relate the metaphorical theory of language about the transcendent to Hick's mythic account and the more traditional appeal to analogy. In *An Interpretation of Religion* Hick defines mythological language thus:

> A statement or set of statements about X is mythologically true if it is not literally true but nevertheless tends to evoke an appropriate dispositional attitude to X. Thus mythological truth is practical . . . For the conformity of myth to reality does not consist in a literal conformity of what is said to the facts but in the appropriateness to the myth's referent of the behavioural dispositions that it tends to evoke in the hearer.
>
> (Hick 1989, 348)

Hick does recognise a sub-class of expository myths which can be literally true of their objects and which function by dressing up literal claims in mythic language. While some religious claims are expository myths, and therefore have a literal paraphrase, Hick proposes to say that those claims which transcend the historical and purport to describe the sacred real itself have no literal truth but only the pragmatic, dispositional truth of full-blown myth. This is because they are responses to unanswerable questions. For example, since no one can know that the transcendent really is personal, the language of personal theism can bear no literal truth for us and can only be truthful as inculcating or embodying right patterns of response to the transcendent.

Hick has been accused of using his account of myth to deny the cognitive value of claims about the transcendent altogether and of implicitly accepting the empiricist dogma that language that is not literal has no cognitive force (Gillis 1989, 165). His response to this kind of charge has been to point out that his theory accepts that non-expository myths can embody truths, so long as these truths are recognised as practical – there being no substantive, positive theory about the transcendent we can judge to be correct (Hick 1990, 194). We can note that in the above quotation from *An Interpretation of Religion* Hick does not deny that there is a conformity of myth to fact, but merely describes what this conformity consists in, namely appropriate attitudes and dispositions. We could read him as pointing to pragmatic results as the means we have of judging the presence of a truth which in fact transcends our practice.

Hick's mythic interpretation could be seen in the light of the above to be approximating to our appeal to metaphor. However, while he does not assert myth to be cognitively worthless, he appears to draw too sharp a distinction between theoretical and practical truth to enable his account to be accommodated to ours. While he recognises a distinction between appropriate and inappropriate dispositions evoked by mythic claims, the cognitive consequences of this distinction are limited. They leave us with no ground for judging any one of the major traditions to have a better account of the transcendent than any other. Provided that each tradition's myths are set in the context of a faith that embodies a genuine encounter with the transcendent and a means of journeying from self-centredness to Reality-centredness, all would appear to be on a par. All this appears to be an implication of saying that the transcendent in itself is a noumenal reality, that questions about the nature of the real are unanswerable, and that there can be no grading of one religion as cognitively superior to another. This is the sense I can glean from Chapters 19 and 20 of *An Interpretation of Religion* and from Hick's various essays on the grading of religions (Hick 1981 and 1983).

It is part of our metaphorical account of claims about the transcendent that, while we can have conflicting models of it which are referentially successful and also apt, there are better and worse ways of speaking of the transcendent. Successful metaphors will have cognitive consequences which may be used to judge that others are inferior. The agnosticism toward the sacred which our account is based on is not that absolute kind implied in the use of the phenomenal/noumenal distinction. It is dependent on the notion that utterance about the transcendent across the traditions is to be interpreted metaphorically because so doing best enables us to see it as the vehicle for a gradual, fallible attempt to make and increase cognitive contact with the transcendent. This general picture fits in ill with making a sharp distinction between theoretical and practical truth. It is notable in this context that Hick has a view of metaphor which holds as a general truth that 'A metaphor's central thrust can be literally translated' (1993b, 100) even though he admits that a metaphor's suggestive overtones defy translatability. It is a view based on a similarity theory akin to Alston's.

If our account does not have the degree of agnosticism or the sharp contrast between practical and theoretical truth associated with Hick's, need it then be tied to the dogma that no positive statements about the transcendent can be made at all? I suggest it need not. The generalisation about lack of positive statements about the transcendent on which this section has been based should be understood as qualified by 'largely and for the most part'. If we admit that there can be cognitive success and failure in metaphorical statements about the transcendent, and that successful metaphorical statements have cognitive consequences, then surely we can admit that a limited number of positive descriptions of the transcendent can be built up through reflection on human religious experience. What the fundamentals of our account do entail is that any such positive statements will be subject to radical forms of analogical meaning.

If I say metaphorically that X is Y, the normal meaning of 'Y' must remain, so that the customary schema of understanding attaching to the word remains alive to enable the mechanism of transference of schema to do its work. But if I say that X is Y, using 'Y' analogically, I modify its meaning without yet destroying that meaning or making the word straightforwardly ambiguous. Analogical speech about the transcendent, as we have defined the transcendent negatively and relationally, cannot simply involve slight modifications and adjustments to words used to describe mundane things as some suppose (for example, Alston 1989a and Swinburne 1977). Standard, personalist theism produces this result, as noted above, but does not seem to have the measure of the full transcendence of the sacred.

Analogy in talk about the transcendent according to Burrell (1973 and 1986) and Hughes (1987) involves a drastic modification or qualification of a word's normal meaning. This is in turn based on a use of something like a sense/reference distinction: we know that certain words are apt for referring to features of the transcendent. The way they refer to them, however, is recognisably inadequate because we know enough to know that the transcendent cannot have these features in the way ordinary things have them. What it is for the transcendent to have them we just cannot know. This view can be unpacked from Aquinas' comment on the sentence 'God is living': 'the sentence is used to say that life does pre-exist in the source of all things, although in a higher way than we can understand or signify' (1964b, 1a, 13, 2 ad. 2; page 55). That is: saying that God is life is affirming that God does have something in his essence that can be referred to by using this word, but that what this thing is we cannot say, save that it exists in him in an infinitely more perfect way than in us and that therefore our way of referring to it is profoundly inadequate. We can know on this account that God is life and good and so on, but not what it is for him to be these things.

Now it may look as if this reading of analogy will not give us positive statements about the transcendent different in character from metaphorical ones. Analogical words turn out to be apt vehicles for referring to the sacred and its facets but give us no real comprehension of what it is like in itself. At most statements using them will tell us of negative and relational matters. Thus, to know that the transcendent is good, analogically speaking, will tell us that certain attitudes (of trust or worship perhaps) are appropriate. How then can there be an issue in deciding whether some descriptions of the sacred rise beyond metaphorical force to analogical meaning? That Aquinas felt there was an issue is clear from the pains he takes in articles 3 and 6 of Part 1, Question 13 of the *Summa* to deny that all talk of God is metaphorical. In an admitted metaphor of God, such as 'God is our rock', it is part of the meaning of the description employed that the things it is normally true of are mundane and imperfect. It is part of the meaning of 'rock' that it is applied to corporeal things (1964b, 1a, 13, 3 ad. 1). But with some other words this is not so. It is not part of the meaning of 'good' or 'wise' that things so described have the nature of mundane entities. So these words are of themselves capable of pointing beyond the mundane realm to the transcendent, for all that there is no precise sense to hand and comprehended which they take on when used of the transcendent.

The question of whether metaphor can ever give way to analogy then boils down to this: is there a class of words which is specially apt for positive description of the transcendent? If there is, then we can find a range of features of the world, those these words name, which are specially apt as pointers to the existence and nature of the transcendent. This in turn suggests the possibility of natural theology – of reasoning from these features to the sacred. Moreover, if these words are primarily ones naming human perfections (as traditions of analogical theology tend to maintain), then the argumentation from world to God suggested by the existence of this special class of words will be directed toward a God who, whatever else he may be, has aspects of the God of personal theism.

We have raised enough questions in connection with analogical description of the sacred to show the complexity of the task of sorting out its appropriateness. What stake if any does pluralism have in the debate about whether it is finally appropriate? Well, pluralism must look for a compromise or a suitable agnosticism on the matter of whether the transcendent is characterised as personal. But perhaps the deep agnosticism within analogical accounts of the kind discussed can accommodate this point (more on this in the next section). Pluralism's own agnosticism would be mitigated somewhat by the acceptance of analogy. That might be no bad thing given its overall theory of knowledge and its mitigated scepticism about the transcendent. If something like natural theological argument is possible, then there would be more to establishing a religious outlook on the world than reflection on the course human moral and religious experience has happened to take across many cultures and centuries.

All of the above may be to pluralism's advantage, especially if the stock of terms capable of pointing to the transcendent provided testimony to universals in thought and life which transcended any particular culture. It might be possible to conceive of pluralist epistemology being augmented in these ways without its relative and sceptical elements being destroyed.

ASPECTS OF THE TRANSCENDENT

We have used the metaphor theory to make a virtue of what otherwise appears to be a major problem for pluralism: the fact that the traditions offer conflicting accounts of the nature of the transcendent. Conflicting metaphors used of the same thing can still have referential and cognitive worth with regard to it. Another, different approach to this problem is to contend that the different systems of religious discourse are descriptive of one and the same reality because that reality has multiple aspects. There are pluriform religious discourses because there is a pluriform religious reality on to which each latches. This approach must avoid postulating a polytheistic religious ultimate, or the pluriform worlds of relativism. So it must hold that the one transcendent manifests itself in diverse ways. What religious discourses do is provide some direct cognitive contact with one or other of these manifestations, and thus some indirect contact with the transcendent in itself which is displayed in these manifestations. Once more, we have an interpretation of religious language similar in appearance to something in Hick, for have we not got close to his picture of each religion describing the Real as it appears, while a Real as it is in itself lies behind these varied appearances? As with the metaphor account, we must devote some space to showing how our restatement of pluralism relates to Hick. We shall see that it is central to the aspectival view as stated here that it is not directly indebted to an idealist or Kantian epistemology.

Hick thinks that differences in conceptions of the transcendent provide prime evidence for the necessity of employing the terms of his Kantian idealism for a theory of religion. They prompt us to make the distinction between the Real in itself and the Real as reflected and refracted within human thought and experience (1989, 247). The latter, phenomenal Real gives us a set of *personae* and *impersonae* through which the Real in itself is encountered. Their authenticity as models of the Real consists solely in whether the traditions which surround them are in soteriological alignment with the Real itself. So, as noted in the previous section, phenomenal *personae* and *impersonae* have a limited cognitive value.

Granted that the Real in itself is said to be beyond all substantive human concepts by Hick, the scepticism implied by Hick's distinction between the noumenal phenomenal transcendent is severe. Throughout this study we have rejected it as too severe, on the grounds that it makes the common reference thesis of pluralism too problematic (Chapter 2 above) and threatens to destroy its realist thrust (Chapter 7 below). Moreover, Hick's phenomenal/noumenal distinction leaves the status of the phenomenal foci of reverence and worship in the traditions unclear. Hick's typical accounts of these phenomenal foci leaves ambiguous whether they are mere *mental* appearances of the Real or not, as when he says they are 'authentic manifestations, or "faces" or personae, or appearances to human consciousness, of the Real *an sich*' (1993a, 171). Sometimes it appears they have only the ideal existence implied in a relativistic reading of religious epistemology, as when we are told that Krishna or Jahweh are real, historical divine figures 'in the sense that he is part of the experience of a people as they have lived through the centuries' (1989, 268). On other occasions, it is implied that there is only one reality encountered in the traditions, it being merely that this is encountered via a transforming process involving models based on the categories of some tradition or other (1989, 273). This latter view is surely the one that fits best with Hick's overall intent. Jahweh and Krishna are not realities over and above the transcendent in itself. They are tradition-based ways of referring to that transcendent (McKim 1988, 397). But then we have the problem we have aired: the means of referring seem too remote from the reality referred to to make reference successful.

If Hick's way of responding to the conflicts within language about the sacred implies too radical a scepticism, what is the way out? Whatever the way out is, it has to fit in with the gradualist, fallibilist epistemology espoused in these pages. According to an aspectival interpretation of religious language, the proper way to cope with these categorical differences is to see them as pointing to some faltering *insight* into the character of the sacred, and not to its absolute unknowability as implied by Hick. In short, we must see such differences as pointing to the true conclusion that the transcendent has both personal and impersonal aspects to its nature. (The Buddhist idea of ultimate reality as absolute emptiness as a possible third view is ignored for the moment – we shall return to it at the end of the chapter.)

The contention of the aspectival view of religious language must be that for pluralism to remain with a continued grip upon realism, the transcendent must be portrayed as having a plural nature. This is the argument of Robert McKim (1988), who maintains that we must embrace the conclusion that the nature of the transcendent has multiple aspects or facets, something McKim notes Hick himself hinted at in publications prior to *An Interpretation of Religion* (McKim 1988, 381, citing Hick 1985a, 98–9). This will allow us to say that what is incorrect with the personalism of one tradition and impersonalism of another is not that both get it substantially wrong, but rather that particular traditions are *incomplete descriptions* (McKim 1988, 393–4). As pluralism says, they are parts of a faltering but nonetheless partly insightful process of human discovery of the character of the sacred. Major differences between traditions point to the selective, partial and revisable character of tradition-based ways of understanding religious reality. This solution is neat and we may note that it could endorse a form of syncretism: by combining different descriptions of the transcendent from contrasting traditions, we might hope to create a 'composite picture' of it. However, the plausibility of such enterprises depends on how far the transcendent can be seen to be multi-faceted. As McKim notes, it is plausible to say that one thing has two or more natures only to the extent that these natures can be thought of as co-existing in one thing at one and the same time, and only to the extent that the imputing of one nature does not imply the denial of the other (391–2). But how can one thing be both impersonal in its nature and yet also personal?

The question posed above seems daunting, yet we need to remind ourselves straight away that there is a distinguished tradition in the scholarly study of religions that has found both reflections of personal theism within profoundly impersonalist conceptions of the transcendent and echoes of impersonalism within theistic systems. The former possibility is easily seen in the teaching of impersonalists like Shankara that Brahman can manifest itself at a lower level of reality and truth as a fit subject for personal devotion and worship. The multi-faceted character of the transcendent also emerges in some accounts of the God of theism. For example, Rudolph Otto devotes an appendix in his *The Idea of the Holy* (1958, 197–203) to arguing that the experience of the numinous in the theistic traditions shows an underlying awareness of an aspect of the Holy that is impersonal.

Otto's analysis of the numinous experience as *mysterium, tremendum et fascinans* is often taken to be the paradigmatic description of an encounter with a personal deity, an encounter which belongs especially to those traditions which approach the sacred via worship and devotion. However, he contends that the awareness of the numinous as wholly other (*mysterium*) contains an element which transcends personality. As wholly other, the numen is frequently encountered (in mysticism, says Otto) as beyond all predicates, as nothingness and as the 'immeasurable plenitude of being' (197). This is hard to fit with a conception of God as purely a person. So too is the consequent sense of merging with the numen that can go hand in hand with this mode of perception. Persons, says Otto, cannot strictly interpenetrate or become inclusive of one another (200).

Otto is lead by reflection on these aspects of the numinous experience to speak of the numinous object as 'supra-personal', that is: as a wholly-other, infinite object of being it has aspects which transcend the personal and cannot be captured in personalistic categories. Otto does not think that such an apprehension of the numinous is to be found only in certain sophisticated mystical modes of theism. On the contrary, he finds this element in and behind the earliest apprehension of the gods, as in the Old Testament encounter with Jahweh. The god is encountered as a manifestation of numen and as such the personality transcending aspects of numinous mystery and power are registered in the way it is described (200). Interestingly, Otto considers that the forms of religious experience in the theistic traditions associated with recognition of this aspect of deity also point to a truth about the personal itself and thus about the human soul. In the relevant kinds of mysticism what is thrown up is that

In us, too, all that we call person and personal, indeed all that we can know or name in ourselves at all, is but one element in the whole. Beneath it lies, even in us, that 'wholly other', whose profundities, impenetrable to any concept, can yet be grasped in the numinous self-feeling.

(Otto 1958, 203)

Contemporary Christian-based philosophical theology has left behind the notion that God is supra-personal. As noted earlier in the chapter, it has simple solutions to problems of religious language which turn around the view that the transcendent is straightforwardly in the genus 'person', albeit he is a person with some remarkable attributes. It can be argued that this is false to the Christian tradition, which has taught, not that God is a person, but that God is absolute being who exists or is manifested in three persons. On this view the transformation of Christian belief into belief in a personal divine being is a mistake explicable by developments in essentially modern modes of philosophical and religious thought (as argued in Jennings 1985).

So far then, the thought is that both personal and impersonal modes of categorising the sacred have been acknowledged as having some validity even within traditions where one predominates. The need for such acknowledgement arises out of a number of sources. One is the type of religious experience documented by Otto. Another is the requirements of a conception of the God of theism as ultimate reality. We have already pointed out how the vision of God as ultimate valuatively, ontologically and rationally points to radical divine transcendence of the kind that means God cannot be delimited by any genus, not least the genus of person. So it is common to find in classical theistic traditions in Christianity, Islam and Judaism the teaching that the divine is being itself, infinite, unbounded and beyond personhood (as documented fully in Burrell 1986 and Ward 1987). Some non-theistic traditions display a corresponding tendency to allow a place to categories belonging to personal theism. This too arises out of the need to cater for types of religious experience: particularly those of personal devotion and grace. More generally, there is a human need to be met in those religious believers who require an alternative to the active seeking of perfection in enlightenment, an alternative that comes via granting the sacred active desire and power to dispense salvation to those who graciously trust in it. Hence, the use made of theistic categories in strongly impersonalist schools noted above.

Considerations of the kind laid out in this section lead Keith Ward to contend that there is a general tendency toward a supra-personal theism, or as he calls it 'dual aspect theism', in all the major religious traditions. The two main aspects of this theism are, on the one hand, a conception of the sacred as infinite being untouched by time, change and free of the properties of personal agency, and, on the other, the sacred as dynamic creator, manifesting itself in the world through its activity and its personal involvement in human life. This is one theism rather than two, because it is deemed essential that God should be both ultimate, unlimitable being and manifest itself as dynamic creative will (Ward 1987, 156). This dual-aspect conception corresponds to Ward's belief in the manifold nature of the human religious condition, 'the fiduciary structure' which Ward claims underlies all the major faiths. The elements of this fiduciary structure correspond roughly to the aspects of religious experience and devotion described above.

How far this dual-aspect conception of the transcendent is normative and predominant in the major religious traditions I leave others to judge (our familiar caveat on behalf of Buddhist emptiness will be entered later). However, it is clear that the positing of *some* common movement toward underlying, general conceptions of the sacred is an important plank on which any plausible version of pluralism must rest. One reason for this has been set out in our discussion of reference in Chapter 2. While agreement across traditions on detailed descriptions of the transcendent is not at all required for common reference by them to the same ultimate, convergence on the fundamental kind of thing of which they endeavour to speak is.

In Ward, dual-aspect theism swiftly becomes multi-aspect theism (1987, 129). The two elements distinguished so far become three as the active God of creation and grace manifests itself in earthly incarnations. Ward thinks that the implication of the trikaya doctrine in Buddhism that there are earthly Buddhas, who embody the dharma and instruct others in how to realise it, is a further example of how two become three. A possible fourth aspect signalled by Ward is the transcendent as absolutely unknowable, ineffable, lying beyond even the eternal, unlimited source of existence previously distinguished from the personal, creator God. So he distinguishes, by reference to Shankara, Maimonides and others, 'the level of complete unknowability' beyond the level of unlimited existence (129). The necessity of and nature for this fourth aspect to transcendence is, to say the least, puzzling. In Otto, and in parts of Ward's discussion, there is a tendency to deny this aspect and in effect to identify the transcendent as ineffable and unknowable with the sacred-as-unlimited existence which lies alongside the divine as personal creator. There are grounds for this identification, for the transcendent as unlimited existence is one which will tend to lie beyond the reach of positive, mundane (and therefore, personal) descriptions. However, the logic of religious thought also contains elements which resist this identification. For one thing, the transcendent as unlimited existence, ocean of being and so forth, still has many descriptions attaching to it. Many of the typical list of descriptive predicates set out in Chapter 2 used to characterise the sacred apply to it, albeit they will tend to have a negative, relational or metaphorical force when used to characterise a referent that is not a person. Furthermore, identification of the impersonal absolute which is being itself with the putative fourth layer in the sacred tends to suggest the conclusion that this impersonal entity is *primary* in understanding transcendence, with the consequence that the personal God of theism becomes a lower manifestation of sacred reality. In other words, identification of these two aspects may become tantamount to philosophical endorsement of an Advaitin perspective on the absolute. We are moving away from seeing both personal God and infinite ocean of being as equally manifestations of an ultimate reality, which, because of its ultimacy is beyond categorisation but which nonetheless has these two typical manifestations (the personal then manifesting itself in two ways: as Lord of history and incarnate sacredness).

Reflections on what it means to treat the sacred as ultimate reality described by much philosophy East and West can take us toward positing Ward's fourth 'level of complete unknowability'. Moreover the approach to referring to the transcendent employed throughout this study can also take us in this direction. This approach has eschewed the notion that common references to the transcendent are secured through the availability of and agreement on detailed, positive descriptions of its nature. Rather our approach might have more in keeping with the view of divinity (the transcendent) as a 'supernatural kind' (Senor 1991). This view takes as its starting point the abandonment of a strict descriptivism in fixing the reference and meaning of natural kind terms. So one says that the properties manifested in typical circumstances by a kind like gold are not final determinants of the meaning of the term 'gold'. Gold can manifest quite different properties in non-typical circumstances (for example, in molten, fluid form). Rather we use 'gold' to refer to an underlying substantial nature which agreed samples of gold are presumed to share. The real essence of natural kinds of this sort lies beneath their manifest nominal qualities and in the case of many kinds may be quite unknown. So, by parallel reasoning, one can postulate that transcendence, divinity is a supernatural kind. Its real essence is something that underlies its typical manifestations.

On this view the sacred as personal Lord and as unlimited ocean of being or unbounded, numinous wholly other are manifestations of a real essence of transcendence which lies behind them. Particular notions such as God and Brahman are to be understood as referring to whatever substance is manifested in the determinate guises known in the developed religious traditions. But none of those guises exhausts the reality of the transcendent or captures its real essence. Of course, if we follow our natural kinds analogy out, the nominal essence of sacredness will be a genuine manifestation of its real essence. Just as gold, at normal temperatures, really is yellow, lustrous and hard, so the transcendent really is personal Lord and impersonal ground of being in appropriate manifestations of its real essence. Yet, just as the nominal essence of gold does not exhaust its nature but points beyond itself to its real essence, so the nominal essence of the transcendent does not exhaust itself but points beyond itself to its real essence.

Now we are back to what seems close to Hick's distinction between phenomenal conceptions of the transcendent and the noumenal transcendent as it is in itself. However, the route we have followed does not go via Kant but via Locke and is not based on any idealist premises about the construction of known reality out of human categories. It relies instead on a point drawn from philosophy of science rather than idealist epistemology, namely that kinds have manifest natures and real natures. In natural kinds doctrine the sense in which a kind's underlying nature is 'real' and its manifest essence merely 'nominal' has nothing to do with the latter being merely a human construct, while the former is human-independent. It has to do with the real essence being causally primary and unchanging, whereas the nominal essence is relative to circumstances, is subject therefore to change and is first in the order of knowledge. Both essences are, however, as 'objective' as each other.

It must be admitted that the analogy which the aspectival view of religious language draws from natural kind terms is limited in its application to discourse about the sacred. The relationship between essence and manifestation in the case of a natural kind and its outward properties is intelligible in the way the relation between essence and manifestation in the case of the sacred is not. In the scientific case the relationship is causal. One identical substance, identified as such by its underlying causal make up, manifests itself in different ways because that make up causally interacts with different natural environments and stimuli to produce different external properties. How can this model fit the transcendent and its alleged varied manifestations? If the transcendent is to play the formal role of being ultimate in being, value and reason, then it cannot be thought of as one substance with a nature amongst others. It cannot be thought of as being causally affected by its presence in one environment or another. The natural kind analogy thus does not help us to get clear on how the one transcendent can have many manifestations. It helps only in showing that the idea of common essence and plural manifestations is known and understood in other areas and that it need not be tied to Kantian or idealist epistemology. Leaving aside Hick's quasi-idealist rendering of the theme, there are other analogies for the 'one nature, plural manifestations' idea, but they will quickly reveal their limitations in this context. For example, we are familiar with the phenomenon of one and the same person manifesting quite different characteristics in relations with different people. What we are as people is in part constituted by our relations with others and, without deliberate deceit, different and incompatible sides to our characters can be brought out in different relationships. But the idea of a person's nature being formed in relation to others will not take us very far here, for the obvious reason that to apply the analogy to the sacred is to judge it as fundamentally personal and thus opt for a form of theism. By contrast, it should be part of the aspectival view to maintain that the sacred is beyond the categories of personality and impersonality when its real essence is considered.

Despite the efforts above to distinguish the aspectival view of religious language from those of Hick's, the conception of transcendence as a 'supernatural kind' has more than an echo of Hick's phenomenal/noumenal distinction. For it does follow from it that the real essence of transcendence is going to be radically unknowable. It has an epistemological conclusion similar to that embodied in Hick's distinction. Normal kinds are such that their nominal essences are the basis for research into and inference about their real essences. The character of the sacred as a *supernatural* kind tends to block off similar research. We have seen that it looks to be true both that the real essence of transcendence is beyond positive, literal description and categories and that the relationship between the real essence of the transcendent and its manifestations is not intelligible in the manner of natural kinds and their outward properties.

The above paragraph indicates why the aspectival view of religious language retains the scepticism behind pluralism. The aspectival view should deepen the sense of the mystery that is the transcendent reality. For example, though it grants a degree of relative appropriateness to individual traditions' accounts of the sacred, it reinforces the sense that those detailed dogmatic accounts are partial and limited. That in turn should fuel our perception of the inappropriateness of basing a picture of the relations between humankind as a whole and the transcendent on any one such account.

The question now arises as to how far the aspectival view of religious language will stretch in accommodating diverse traditions. For example, does the acknowledgement of a fourth, radically ineffable aspect to transcendence accommodate the thought that ultimate reality is emptiness, as posited in some strands of Buddhism? To some writers it appears to. Hick (1989, 291) interprets Buddhist thinking on ultimate reality as sunyata, absolute emptiness, as a form of belief in an impersonal absolute, but one with the nuance that this absolute is beyond all positive conceptualisation. Thus the theme may be seen as a way of pointing to Ward's fourth aspect of divinity, which we have developed in the light of a real essence doctrine. However, such an interpretation still leaves these strands of Buddhist thought committed to the idea that there is a transcendent substance or nature. It is merely that it is radically ineffable.

In contrast to Hick's interpretation, Abe takes the reality-as-sunyata theme to be a denial of this very limited conclusion. The point of the theme is to deny that there is one substantial infinite reality, even an indescribable substantial reality (1993, 320). While still happy to use language such as 'ultimate reality' and to affirm that what Christians and others call God is present in Buddhism, he interprets the relevant classical Buddhist texts on reality-as-emptiness to be saying that there is no divine substance and to constitute a denial of both personal monotheism and impersonal monism in consequence (1993, 320–1). I do not altogether understand this gloss on reality-as-emptiness, but it connects with those commentators who wish to say that Buddhism, at least in some forms, cannot be fitted into a pluralist paradigm because it denies that there is an absolute and so cannot be taken to refer to the same one as other traditions (see Smart 1993 and recall the discussion in Chapter 3 above).

On our overall view of religion and reference, forms of Buddhism which had the radical implications hinted by Abe would not thereby reject a pluralist thesis or necessarily be excluded from pluralism's general view of human religion. For our version of pluralism does not need the premise that all religions are equally correct and it allows for reference to succeed despite error in conception. And appeal to some mode of error would have to be invoked to accommodate these Buddhist conceptions if Hick's interpretation of them was ruled offside.

AN OVERALL ACCOUNT

Both the metaphorical and aspectival accounts appear on the surface to have the capacity for resolving the dilemma at the heart of pluralism's approach to religious language. They can posit both significant success *and* failure in religious discourse. The can both grant cognitive success to *diverse and incompatible* religious discourses. Can these two accounts be joined together or are they rivals between which a philosophical defence of pluralism must choose?

One could argue that they are rivals along the following lines. If the aspectival account is true, there is no need to appeal to metaphor in explaining the cognitive function of religious language. The transcendent really is pluriform in nature. It has one essence but many manifestations. Different doctrinal discourses literally, and for the most part truly, describe an aspect of its pluriform character. Thus they turn out not to conflict, save where they draw absolutist conclusions about the sacred and its relationship to us from merely aspectival insights. But then the traditions are simply false in drawing those conclusions. Common reference to the sacred turns out to be possible in the manner suggested by the analogy of 'corrosive liquid' and 'bitter liquid' as ways of referring to acids, that is, via one substance having divergent ways of showing itself and thus being named.

This simple picture of aspectivalism's superiority will not do. For one thing, we have seen that the aspectival view is only partly comprehensible. The relationship between essence and manifestation cannot be made altogether clear in this case, either in detail or at a general level. In addition, the alleged real essence of the transcendent remains beyond all human conceptualisation. For both these reasons, the aspectival view does not present an easy solution to the reference problem. Moreover, appeal to aspects or manifestations of a pluriform transcendent will not cope with all the problems arising out of divergent doctrinal systems. It will explain perhaps why general, categorial differences between personalist and impersonalist conceptions of the sacred's nature are mutually compatible. The traditions are, however, built around specific elaborations of these general conceptions. It would be attributing a wholly implausible, chameleon-like character to the sacred to suppose that each of these detailed conceptions was true of a distinct manifestation of the one thing.

I suggest that the two models for religious language according to pluralism should be accommodated as follows. In general, each set of doctrinal statements is to be understood in metaphorical fashion. They are the workings out of divergent but mutually apt models for understanding a reality which is for the most part beyond all literal, positive statement (save, perhaps, for limited, severely agnostic analogical description as noted above). The aspectival view is to be seen as a supplement to this characterisation. First it might help in understanding why metaphor is the appropriate trope for describing the transcendent and why different metaphors should be used of it. The transcendent is an entity or state with a largely hidden essence but something which manifests itself outwardly in divergent ways. So we use models of it and different ones at that. Second the aspectival account might help explain in the most general way why a given model of the transcendent was appropriate: because there were facets of the sacred's manifest nature to which it directly corresponded and thus it might be taken to be an indirect pointer to the transcendent's true nature. Third the aspectival view could be seen as pointing to some very general and largely formal facts about the transcendent's character on which convergence between the traditions could be seen. These could include it having a four-fold structure if we are persuaded by Ward's arguments, but at least it having a nature manifested both personally and impersonally, yet somehow subsuming both. The fact that this convergence was at this general, formal level would leave pluralism unpersuaded of the possibility of producing a syncretism of divergent accounts of the sacred *which could then replace them*. Pluralism would remain convinced that the traditions needed rich, detailed models of the transcendent in order to function. Hence, the religious indispensability of metaphorical accounts of the sacred would remain.

However, it must be admitted that use of the aspectival model to supplement the metaphorical account does lead to one form of syncretism. It suggests that different religions have complementary insights into the one reality and thus that a fuller account of that reality can be provided if these insights are set alongside each other. Further, we must note that use of the aspectival model takes us in the direction of a strain of inclusivism, in so far as it is not neutral toward Buddhist notions of reality-as-emptiness. As was pointed out at the end of Chapter 3, pluralism opts for a fundamental ontological category into which to place sacred, transcendent reality and thereby seems to give a message to some traditions – 'you refer to transcendent reality, but by way of ideas mistaken to a degree'. The discussion in this chapter confirms that move away from strict neutrality. If scholars like Abe are correct in their reading of forms of Buddhism, the aspectival account has to be *read into* these strands of tradition from an external philosophical and religious standpoint which claims superiority for itself in this respect.

7

Realism

WHAT RELIGIOUS REALISM IS NOT

Pluralism entails a realist view of religion, but what in turn that view consists in and what it implies for our understanding of religion is hard to determine. At its crudest a realist conception of religion states that there are real things corresponding to religious concepts. Michael Devitt initially defines realism about common-sense and scientific discourse in ontological terms: '*Realism* Tokens of most common sense, and scientific, physical types objectively exist independently of the mental' (1984, 22). This is to say that realism about common-sense discourse maintains the extra-mental existence of things corresponding to most common-sense concepts. Of science it maintains specifically that there are extra-mental things corresponding to most concepts of unobserved, hypothetical or theoretical entities. The non-realist in science is one who regards such concepts as having no correspondence with extra-mental reality. Do we want to define religious realism in a precisely similar fashion? Does the religious realist want to say that most religious concepts have tokens in extra-mental reality that correspond to them? Many realists in religion would balk at this, because of the difficulties in supposing that most of the entities spoken of in religious myths exist outside the human imagination, or even that there is a one-to-one correspondence between them and facets of the transcendent as it manifests itself. The lush ontologies of religious mythology are thought worth pruning by many contemporary adherents of the traditions themselves. Religious realism is more properly a minimal realism, affirming that an extra-mental entity or state corresponds to the fundamental concepts of the focus of religion, with less fundamental concepts (of angels, spirits and so forth) at best indirectly corresponding to this thing.

But this is not enough. Even the likes of Feuerbach thought there were extra-mental things corresponding to religious concepts; it was merely that these things were facets of human nature and not entities or states transcending the mundane or human world. So realism in religion looks as if it ought to be the view that some religious concepts genuinely correspond to transcendent entities and states. Put this way it is no more, and no less, than the view that there is a sacred, transcendent reality.

If this is what realism in this area essentially is, there seem to be two problems arising from it. First, it appears to be an undemonstrable doctrine in the philosophy of religion. For how could the philosophy of religion claim, in the light of its recorded history of debate, to demonstrate that there was such a sacred, transcendent reality? Second, realism, so understood, seems to have no implications for the study and description of religion in history and culture. Suppose we accept the philosophical postulate that there is an ultimate reality appropriately described as sacred and transcendent, how should this affect the way in which we understand actual religious traditions? Conceivably, there could be such an ultimate reality, yet this would have no implications for our understanding of the religions, if it merely *happened* to be the case that some of their constituent concepts corresponded to it.

The first of the problems in understanding realism can be dealt with quite easily. What is at issue in the philosophical debate about religious realism is not whether the ontological thesis apparently at the heart of the realist view can be demonstrated, but whether it is viable or plausible. Our final acceptance of the ontological thesis cannot depend on the meagre argumentative resources of philosophy but is rather a feature of our personal judgement as to the character of the world we live in. Yet it should make a difference to the character of a philosophical understanding of religion if there is something to be said for the ontological thesis behind realism. Not least, we have seen that a pluralist understanding of religion is only possible to the extent that there is some plausibility to belief in the transcendent. It is in these terms that our exploration of realism will proceed henceforth. We shall not demonstrate its truth but consider how far it is a live option in a philosophical understanding of religion.

The second initial problem in realism was: if it is merely an ontological thesis, how can it have any implications for our understanding of religion? Realism has to be more than an ontological thesis. Furthermore, the putative relation of 'correspondence' between fundamental religious concepts and an extra-mental, transcendent state has to be richer than so far suggested in order for it to affect our understanding of religion. A relationship between religious concepts and religious reality has to be something that plays some large part in the interpretation and explanation of religion. That means that in asking what religious concepts mean, in understanding why folk have come to hold them, and in explaining how they have developed, some part of our answer must make reference to the alleged correspondence between religious concepts and sacred reality.

For realism to be a justified element in a philosophical interpretation of religion, it must be at least initially plausible to suppose that correspondence between fundamental religious concepts and extra-mental, extra-mundane reality is part of the interpretation and explanation of religion. So realism has to be a semantic and epistemological thesis about religion as well as an ontological one. In other words, it has to contain an ontological claim buttressed by the thought that human beings have come into cognitive contact with the object of that claim to a degree and in a way that helps explain why they say and do what they do. The ground for the ontological, semantic and epistemological aspects of religious realism has already been laid in Chapters 5 and 2 of this study. In 'Epistemology' we tried to show how the basic ontological claim of religion is initially plausible and also how adherents might be aware of the reality which corresponds to it. In 'Reference' we tried to show how the terms of religious discourse might enable members of the traditions to latch on to that reality for all the diversity within, and inadequacy of, that discourse. In order to get clearer on the semantic and epistemological elements of realism and their relation to the ontological element certain false trails must be explored and exposed for what they are. We need to begin with the trail that starts from the notion of truth. We need to spell out why the idea of religious beliefs turning out or being true is something of a red-herring in pursuing the interrelationships between the semantic, epistemological and ontological aspects of religious realism.

On the matter of truth and realism the burden of our song is simple: emphasis on the concept of truth by itself will not link the ontological aspects to realism with the semantic and

epistemological aspects. Hick's treatment of the realist theme in
An Interpretation of Religion illustrates this point.

Hick begins his discussion of realism by giving it the ontological definition we started with. It is tantamount to the claim that
the objects of religious belief exist independently of what we
take to be our experience of them (1989, 172). He then confronts
the doubt that realism could not conceivably be true because
nothing could verify its key ontological claim. The doubt that
nothing could conceivably show the existence of extra-mental,
extra-mundane reality with any objective certainty is especially
important for Hick because of his commitment, re-affirmed in
An Interpretation of Religion, to the religious ambiguity of the
universe. This leaves the naturalist free to interpret the universe
as devoid of religious meaning. Nothing in the present life, not
even the existence and character of religious experience, puts the
truth of the religious interpretation of reality beyond reasonable
doubt. Hence Hick appeals (on 178–9) to an unambiguous post-
mortem experience as the possible means whereby the ontological claim of religion is verified. He puts the matter thus in an
earlier work: 'For if there is a further development of human
experience, beyond this present life, which is incompatible with
a naturalistic understanding of the universe but which develops
and enlarges our various religious understandings of it, this will
constitute verification of the religious side of the religious/natu-
ralist opposition' (1985b, 124–5). This 'further development of
human experience' will consist in enjoyment of 'a limitlessly good
end-state' (1989, 179), one that vindicates the 'cosmic optimism'
that is at the heart of all the post-Axial faiths according to Hick.

Now there are a number of questions one can pose about this
approach to religious realism. It may be asked, first, how far any
experience post-mortem could unambiguously vindicate belief
in the real but noumenal focus of religion Hick posits. For this
would have to be an experience which presumably vindicated
Hick's pluralist account of the ontology behind the religions and
not a confessional account of that ontology. Since it is the confessional accounts which are rich, specific and have a connection
with human concepts, room for doubt on the score of the post-
mortem verifiability of the pluralist's ontological commitment
obviously exists (as shown forcefully in Heim 1992). For our
purposes the more important worry is how far the possibility of

the religious interpretation making a difference in the light of post-mortem experience effects any alteration in how we interpret and explain the character of religion as it is manifested in the here and now. We surely want realism to alter our understanding of present religious consciousness and behaviour. Yes, Hick would say, so it does: the possibility of post-mortem verification allows us to take seriously the perspective that different traditions are the product of a genuine encounter with a non-mundane reality. But what does taking that perspective seriously mean? For it remains true that the human phenomenon of religion is ambiguous and is equally interpretable in naturalist or religious terms. Hick does of course repeatedly write of, for example, religious experience as consisting of a relationship to an extra-mental, extra-mundane reality. Yet that experience is mediated by concepts that belong to the phenomenal side of his noumenal/phenomenal divide. We must once more enter our complaint that it is human concepts which give the experience its determinate character, and that character is thus explicable in human, cultural terms. So the determinate character of the experience is a product of human construction. Each tradition provides a 'cognitive filter' (1989, 163) which determines the precise character of the experience of the Real. What then is left for the ontology demanded by religious realism to contribute to the actual character of religion?

The point against Hick's epistemology is that its great stress on cognitive freedom and on the contribution of the knowing subject to the contents of consciousness leaves links between the ontology of realism and its semantics and epistemology problematic. The ontology of realism explains nothing about the content of, or connections between, the faiths. This is a point we have already made at the end of Chapters 3 and 5. Citing Stoeber's critique (1992) of Hick's extreme constructivism concerning religious experience, we noted that it left too much (that is, all!) of the specific content of religious experience to the conceptual inheritance brought to experience by the religious subject – so much as to give the transcendent no work to do. We noted the objection that Hick's constructivism might still leave the ontological claim in realism to account for the *existence* of religious experience, rather than its character, but we also showed how this distinction (between the existence and character of experience) would not bear much weight in this context. Stoeber makes the valid point that a realist view of religious experience should leave the Real with some influence on the content of experience (1992, 110). A real influence would consist in such things as: finding overlaps between different traditions' experiences (best explicable by their contact with a common, extra-mental reality) and noting the regular occurrence of experiences which challenge pre-existing religious categories and lead to heretical ideas (Stoeber 1992, 111–12).

It must be admitted that the notion of seeing the fact of common contact with the transcendent displayed in various traditions takes us in the direction of syncretism. It brings to light once more the possibility of conjoining testimonies from various traditions to create a fuller picture.

In interpreting religion we obviously have to concentrate on pre-mortem experience and we have to ask what degree of cognitive contact between religious subjects and the transcendent Hick's constructivist epistemology allows. Brian Hebblethwaite finds three extra-mental facts in Hick's interpretation of religion which are free of being created by the knowing subject in alliance with some tradition or other (1993, 131). (1) There is an ultimate transcendent reality, to which all human religions, in their very different modes, are historically and culturally shaped responses. (2) Salvific religious experience, leading to transformation from self-centredness to Reality-centredness, is not a purely human possibility. Religion, in all its different forms, involves spiritual resources from beyond. (3) Human life will be extended, beyond death, towards some form of perfected consummation in the end. Hebblethwaite in effect judges these claims to be too exiguous to be sufficient for a religious view of religion – not enough in the way of typical religious discourses turns out to correspond to reality. Our point must be that these claims illustrate perfectly the point that ontology and epistemology are not sufficiently linked in Hick. Propositions (1) and (3) give us some minimal ontological claims which bring in realism. But they could both be true and yet have no semantic and epistemological consequences of a kind that would affect the understanding of actual religion. It could be the case that both (1) and (3) *happen* to exhibit correspondences between some religious concepts and reality without this reflecting at all on the origin or cognitive character of those concepts. All depends on (2). It could provide the missing semantic and epistemological link, but alas it does not, because Hick's constructivist, Kantian and quasi-idealist epistemology leaves the alleged salvific encounter with the transcendent interpretable in naturalistic terms and devoid of decisive religious character.

Our discussion of Hick on realism amounts to an argument for the claim that the possibility or actuality of a mode of discourse being true is not sufficient for that discourse to be interpreted realistically. In particular, the semantics of a realist outlook on a mode of discourse cannot be secured by reference to truth alone, since it may just *happen* that it is true. An argument can also be mounted for saying that truth is not a necessary condition for a realistic interpretation of a set of ideas either, at least if we mean something strict by 'truth' and 'falsity'.

It looks as if the semantic aspect of realism we are after will be found in the notion of reference, not truth. It will be the idea of reference which establishes the cognitive contact between concepts and reality which in turn grounds a realist perspective on the way of thinking that embodies those concepts. A preliminary explanation of why this is so is hinted at in Chapter 2. In discussing reference, we noted the limitations of pure descriptive theories of reference, limitations which stemmed from the fact that successful reference did not depend on speakers having true accounts of the natures of the things they were referring to. It is this fact which above all else allows us to say of proponents of quite different views about the nature of scientific, or other, reality that they nonetheless refer to the same things, offering different accounts of precisely the same things. Reference is rather a material practice in which true description plays but a small part – contexts, methods of investigation and causal links between speaker and object being primary. This all suggests that a theory can be interpreted realistically although it is to a large extent false. It can have the appropriate links – semantic and epistemological – to reality despite being riddled with falsity. This, then, is the argument for saying that strict or extensive truth in a mode of discourse is not a necessary condition for interpreting it realistically. We offer it now as food for thought. We shall see later in the discussion that its conclusion needs to be modified somewhat in the light of a fuller understanding of what realism entails. Let us for the moment sum up by saying that *strict* truth is not a necessary condition for interpretation in the realist mode.

We should perhaps welcome the outcome about truth and the necessary conditions for realism, for the internal dynamics of realism suggest difficulties in finding strict truth in many systems of ideas. Realism contains as we have seen an appropriate ontological commitment. About common-sense ways of thinking it says they correspond to extra-mental, public reality. About the theories of natural science it affirms that many of their concepts correspond to extra-mental and unobserved realities. About religion it asserts that its core concepts correspond to some extramental, extra-mundane reality. Because realism has a primary ontological aspect of this sort, an opposition to idealism seems built into it and, most importantly, it seems committed to some version of a correspondence theory of truth. This might ditch realism in many people's eyes because such theories are associated with mysterious notions concerning the ability of statements as arrays of words to mirror, picture or model facts. Few philosophers have been able to make much sense of such ideas. We ought to regard such mystery-mongering as irrelevant to the correspondence theory and look behind it for a much simpler account of what truth consists in. It is one to which the notion of reference is the key. To say that a statement is true in virtue of corresponding to reality is to affirm (after Devitt 1984, 28) something like the following. A statement is true because it has an objective structure, because the appropriate referential relations hold between its parts and reality, and because of the independent nature of that reality. This should bring home more precisely the character of the tautological truth that realism is opposed to idealism. And it naturally highlights the way in which realism is an invitation to scepticism because it creates a gap between language and thought on the one hand, and the world on the other. Accordingly, we require a substantial semantic and epistemic bridge to get across this gap.

Realism suggests that the knower does not construct or constitute the thing known (whatever that may mean) as idealism claims, so it opens the possibility that knowledge may be hard to come by and that many of our statements about the world may not possess strict truth. This problem created by a realist perspective seems particularly acute when applied to theoretical science and to religion. In the former case it is not difficult for authors to point to many past scientific theories whose precise accounts of the unobserved have been abandoned and to many present theories which cannot be known to have strict truth. In the nature of the case we may doubt how many theories pertaining to unobserved realities we could say are either strictly true or false (as Harré notes – 1986, 38). For the reasons implied in this study, and particularly in Chapter 5, matters seem to stand even worse with finding strict truth in claims about extra-mental, extra-mundane, religious reality. So, we have argued, it behoves us to use a fallibilist, gradualist epistemology to interpret claims to religious certainty and knowledge.

The sceptical difficulties created by the interaction of realism's correspondence conception of truth and the ontological commitments it suggests in relation to various systems of thought highlight once more the dangers of tying it to the notion of truth. Run through again in the light of the possibility of scepticism, the key elements of realism bring out the point about truth in a fresh way. Realism requires semantic and epistemic components to link theory to the realities posited in its ontological commitments. Because of the gap between language and reality built into realism's ontology, it provokes sceptical doubts about the judgement of strict truth and falsity in ways of speaking. Therefore strict truth cannot be at the heart of the linkage between language and reality which realism posits to accompany the appropriate ontological commitments for the sphere of language in question. Some other semantic connection with an epistemology to match is required. This is what we have begun to sketch already with our stress on reference in Chapter 2 and our mitigated scepticism in Chapter 5.

The character of the gap realism posits between knower and thing known, and hence the degree of scepticism about strict truth it entails, will depend on the nature of the ontological commitment appropriate to the subject matter in hand. It is because the appropriate ontological commitment in the case of religion is to extra-mental *and* extra-mundane reality that we endorsed a considerable degree of scepticism (and relativism) about concrete

conceptions of the transcendent found in the traditions. Therefore we can accept Hick's assertion that religious realism will
have to be of the critical variety, as opposed to the naive (Hick
1989, 175). What marks out critical realism is the recognition that
concrete conceptions in the religions do not map religious reality
in straightforward fashion but display large elements of human
interpretation of that reality, or, in other words, fall short of strict
truth. This agreement with the idea of critical realism should be
qualified by the recognition that any realist view of statements
about the extra-mental *must* be critical in the nature of the case.
A gap between the knower and thing known is an essential consequence of realism and hence the fallible character of human
perception of the object of knowledge follows axiomatically. Only
a classical foundationalist epistemology which holds that knowledge of the extra-mental can be securely grounded on self-
evident or incorrigible starting points can hold out any hope that
affirmations about the real map its character without error. But
foundationalism of this kind actually appears to be the negation
of realism proper. It seeks to close the gap between subject and
reality by finding a class of basic statements whose apparent
truth guarantees their actual truth. In this way it is akin to a form
of idealism, since it closes 'the gap between the knower and
known by bringing the world, in some sense, into the mind'
(Devitt 1984, 227).

The above points show that religious realism can escape the
charge that it constitutes a threat to human religious autonomy,
as if realism entailed that we could not but agree on the character of religious reality and its demands on us. The question mark
about the utility of strict truth as a mode of judging religious
conceptions shows that such fears are largely misguided. If realism is true, knowledge of the real is set as a task and the task is
not going to be an easy one to fulfil. However, realism does have
an argument with some defenders of human autonomy in religion
about the extent to which the human religious quest is subject to
appraisal by objective norms and criteria, as the next section will
indicate. All-in-all, our realism allows for a middle path between,
on the one hand, those who opt for rampant subjectivism in
religion as the only means to save ourselves from intolerant,
authoritarian dogmatism and, on the other hand, those who think
that strict truth must attach to the dogmas of some confession or

other if we are not to fall into the pit of out and out relativism and non-cognitivism (as claimed in Kellenberger 1985 and Trigg 1983). The displacement of strict truth for the most part from the characterisation of realism shows that these are not exhaustive alternatives.

If strict truth becomes a goal which religious conceptions seek but rarely if ever obtain, then it follows that religion must make do with the other, looser semantic and epistemological links with religious reality suggested in this chapter. In particular, referential success and all that attends it will have to be seen as an acceptable substitute for strict truth. Thus, in relation to salvation, the realism we say attends pluralism entails that being in cognitive contact with the sacred will be sufficient for success in the absence of assurance that the beliefs which frame religious practices are strictly true of religious reality. In this respect our realism captures some of the spirit of claims made by Hick and Cantwell Smith. For both these authors have maintained that personal, authentic existence in relation to the ultimate is primary in salvation whereas truth of doctrine is secondary. Interpreted via our account of the notion of reference, this turns out to have something to be said for it.

One thing the abandonment of strict truth as a concomitant part of realism should enable us to avoid is the Kantian apparatus of phenomenal versus noumenal reality with its attendant tales of the knower constituting and creating reality. Idealism of this kind is at the heart of Hick's religious epistemology. At a very general level it can be seen as a response to the huge gap between knower and known that realism throws up if we view it in the light of the demands of the concept of truth. That gap can be closed if we make the *immediate* object of knowledge something mind-dependent, which is what the language of constructing and constituting reality has to imply (Devitt 1984, 140 and 192), while leaving the *mediate* object of knowledge mind-independent. We endeavour to avoid the complications and mysteries of Kantian idealism by coping with the gap in another way: abandoning, for the most part, strict truth as a feature of ordinary, workaday discourse about religious reality yet maintaining looser epistemological and semantic links between language and reality in this area. Thus we do not need to say that what we are in cognitive contact with is phenomenal religious reality, while noumenal reality is beyond our reach. We change our notion of cognitive contact rather than erect mysterious-sounding distinctions between levels of reality.

WHAT RELIGIOUS REALISM IS

Our aim in this section will be to bring out in detail the positive implications for a picture of religion entailed by adopting the referential realism we have borrowed from the philosophy of science. First let us set out more of what that realism entails in the scientific context.

Referential realism as characterised by Harré (1972, 1986 and 1987) is built around the thought that there is a permanent achievement in science, namely the establishment of the existence of an ever-increasing range of things and stuffs. In other words, reliable existential beliefs about the constitution of the physical world are gradually built up during the course of scientific history. Science has established that there are electrons, acids, genes, super-conductors and so on. So of course there are matters of truth and falsity on which it pronounces. Strict truth has still been displaced to a considerable extent, however. For we hold on to the notion that knowledge of the stuff of the world is possible and survives though theories about the detailed character, behaviour and cause of the things that make up the stuff of the world change as one theory gives way to another. What survives radical changes in the precise definition and explanation of the entities which make up the stuff of the world as described by science are a set of existential generalisations ('There are electrons', 'There are genes') plus some reliable beliefs about the make up of the things referred to in these generalisations. As we noted in Chapter 2, reference once made can survive massive deletions from, and additions to, descriptions of the object of reference.

We suggest that this accumulation of existential knowledge is to be seen as the aspect of science best explained by realism and, therefore, as the fact which provides realism with its greatest support. Some authors want to characterise the 'success' which realism in science latches on to differently, as if it were the convergence of scientific theorising on some unified, overall true theory of the world which was in question. This kind of alleged success is open to the well-known objections that the past and present of science shows no such convergence, while the numerous occasions on which past theories are rejected as blind alleys tells positively against it. (Putnam 1990, 163–78 marshals arguments against this convergence view of scientific advance.) Our view can accept advances in theorising while rejecting belief in the steady convergence of theories upon an overall account of material reality.

The essential claim of a realist view of science is that the referential success of science, shown in its accumulated existential knowledge of the stuff of the world, is sufficient reason for saying that scientific discourse has strong semantic and epistemological links with observable and unobservable reality. Positing such links is the best way of accounting for accumulated existential knowledge. Opposed to this interpretation of scientific discourse will be that of the so-called strong programme in the sociology of knowledge, which claims that personal and social factors of a non-rational kind are a sufficient explanation for the emergence and development of scientific theories. A chief target of these latter explanations of scientific discourse will be the perception that there is accumulated referential success, and thus reliable belief within the scientific past and present. Strongly descriptive theories of reference are often at the heart of this kind of scepticism. Since there is frequent and radical change in theoretical notions within science, and thus in the descriptions of the stuff of the world they inspire, one can conclude that there is no referential continuity across theory change and that the 'world changes' as theories change. The heavy dilution of description in a proper account of reference which was argued for in Chapter 2 is the appropriate response to these doubts. Realism of the kind we are defending seems a distinct possibility once we abandon the notion that the reference and meaning of terms must alter as the theoretical contexts in which they are embedded alter. We have implicitly set ourselves against this notion on a number of occasions in this study.

If the positive conception of scientific realism implicit in Chapter 2 and briefly sketched above is useful, it should apply *mutatis mutandis* to the religious case. Religious realism should be based on a recognition of existential and referential success similar to that which is the basis of its scientific counterpart. We should be able to point to a continuity of referential and existential knowledge. This would have to be characterised by the accumulation of some reliable beliefs about the stuff ('transcendent stuff' we might say) referred to across a number of traditions, hence truth enters in in a weaker fashion and by the back door. Religious realism would have to face off a parallel challenge to that pressed against its scientific cousin. It would have to provide arguments for saying that non-rational social and personal factors were not a sufficient explanation of whatever apparent referential and existential success was to be found. It would need to suggest that such success was best accounted for by saying that there were semantic and epistemological links between religious discourse and religious reality. These parallels with scientific realism would have to be pressed while noting the significant difference between the two realisms documented in the first section of this chapter. In the religious case, but not in the scientific, no direct links are posited between religious concepts in all their variety and a corresponding variety of religious 'stuffs'. For the reasons advanced above a cruder link between religious discourse and a single, though perhaps multi-faceted, transcendent stuff is all that is in question. So from the beginning religious realism is only able to apply the scientific parallel with qualification. A more modest, qualified realism is then all that is in question.

Should realism in religion look for a convergence of religious doctrines and thus for a possible future synthesis of religions? This point will be taken up below, but we can say now that we certainly should expect to find convergence at the level of basic characterisations of the sacred, and thus some possibility of synthesising those characterisations. But if the agnosticism behind pluralism is valid, we should not expect to find convergence at the level of detailed doctrines. The reply offered highlights once more the need for pluralist realism to show the coherence of uniting a measure of realism and scepticism toward the religions.

The positive case for scientific realism has a number of aspects. First one must establish that there is an apparent accumulation of referential success and existential knowledge which realism might be the best explanation for. We have already seen how this might be done. Then one must argue that realism gives the best explanation of this. The argument for realism has the basic form of an abductive case from fact to an hypothesis which is the best explanation of that fact. Some preliminary points will set up the appeal to this abductive inference.

One of the facets of scientific cognition which directly supports the realist explanation of its character is the fact that scientific history appears to exhibit a clear pattern of success in using referential concepts denoting the unobserved to anticipate reality. In the manner indicated in Chapter 2, a concept like virus will be introduced to denote whatever thing of a certain sort is the cause of various effects. Science is then set a task of discovering whether there are viruses. Theoretical and technical advance eventually leads to fashioning the means of detecting viruses – through the development of the electron microscope. Here we seem to have an instance of a repeated achievement in the history of science: referential terms are introduced to refer hypothetically to new facets of reality and later ostensive knowledge of that reality is obtained through technical and theoretical advance.

Science also uses concepts which refer to unobservables which can never become observables because, for example, their character and the physics of processes of observation so dictate. Deep physics contains many such concepts. An anti-realist interpretation of these parts of science can be avoided if they can be seen to be continuous in modes of thinking and argument to other parts of science which appear to have their referential pretensions vindicated (as explained by Harré 1986, 314–16).

The appeal to realism as the best explanation of apparent accumulation of referential success and of reliable beliefs about the stuff of the world is further strengthened by pointing to what Harré styles the moral achievement of the scientific community (1986, 1). Those who want to explain away scientific 'progress' as a non-rational process may point to the personal and institutional factors that seem to determine which scientific enterprises are taken up and which are set aside. Harré does not in general deny the fact that the study of the scientific community and its systems of authority leads to an understanding of how scientific success and failure is determined. Yet he insists that this study throws up the community's continued commitment to honesty, publicity and trustworthiness in the testing and communication of ideas. In other words, the community is run by reference to standards that are in the broadest sense rational, for all that they are embodied in tradition and in systems of authority. The community and its standards exhibit a drive to identify cheats, charlatans and eschew merely private intuitions and guesses.

Seen in the light of the above points, the ground is prepared for the fundamental abductive inference behind realism. There is an apparent cognitive success in science consisting in the steady accumulation of reliable beliefs principally about matters referential and existential. The best explanation for this success is that there are extra-mental, unobserved realities to which scientific concepts in large measure correspond. The inference here can be seen as partaking of the causal. The apparent success documented is best seen as caused by the fact that scientific cognition is in contact with extra-mental and unobserved realities. Forms of anti-realism are by contrast left with the implausible task of saying such success is unreal, or of relying on the sociology of knowledge to provide a sufficient explanation of it, or of leaving it an unexplained anomaly.

Anti-realists, and surprisingly some realists (see Harré 1986, 35), deny the cogency of this best-explanation argument for realism. They can argue that the fact that the realist hypothesis would explain apparent accumulation of reliable beliefs about the stuff of the world does not entail its truth. For any true proposition there is an infinite number of other propositions that imply it, and hence an infinite number of false ones. But the realist case is not of course that realism's truth is *entailed* by the fact that it would explain this apparent success. It is rather that it is made plausible by it (Banner 1990, 62). We rely, necessarily, on an inference to the best explanation throughout our reasoning. What defeats general scepticism about it is that it is employed in context and in context we do not have an infinite number of live hypotheses to choose from to explain the facts. Contextual factors give meaning to notions of plausibility, economy, fruitfulness and the like in determining which hypotheses are the best in explaining admitted phenomena.

The upshot of the realist case with respect to science is a perspective on science's history. It is contended that it is best viewed as the history of an attempt to engage with reality. It is the history of an enterprise where the character of the real has influenced the flux of human thought. We have seen how the case for realism might go in general in the scientific case. How then might it look in the religious?

If religious thought showed a like engagement with reality, we should expect to see a similar structure of apparent cognitive success and to point to realism as the best explanation of that success. The apparent cognitive success would have to be the accumulation of existential and referential knowledge about transcendent reality. Here is the point to remind ourselves of the argument of Chapter 5. Such an accumulation could be seen in the ubiquity of religious experience, provided that ways are on hand to find convergences and overlaps in it. The force of religious experience can be supported by the experience of transcendence in the moral life and by the experience of sanctification across many traditions made so much of by Hick. The religious realist's case must be that these phenomena amount to the basis for reliable beliefs about the existence and general character of sacred reality. Religion is best seen as an age-old attempt to refer to and engage with an extra-mental and extra-mundane reality. That is the best explanation of the character of at least significant parts of evolving religious thought. I think this view entails that the realist must see some *direction* in the history of religion and its spirituality, such as is indicated in Hick's account of the move from pre-Axial to post-Axial faith. Without that, the talk of 'accumulation' and 'convergence' within religious experience can be accused of lacking a clear grounding.

Behind the above sketch lurk major problems. First some of the supports of a best explanation argument to realism in science are apparently lacking in the religious case. The fact of referential guesses being rewarded with later ostensive demonstration of the existence of stuffs which correspond to those guesses does not appear to obtain. Nothing neatly matches the schema whereby viruses are introduced as the cause of bodily symptoms and later that reference is borne out by development of the relevant sense-extending instrument. It will be alleged against the realist that there is no proven record of referential anticipations being rewarded in this way. The religious realist may concede this point, thus making the background case for realism weaker, or endeavour to argue that the phenomena of mystical and religious experience provide at least analogues to referential vindication. It may be argued that paths of mystical exploration or paths of sanctification provide parallel evidence of anticipations of reality 'paying off' with direct encounter with realities sought. It could be maintained that spiritual disciplines of this kind exhibit a broadly similar pattern of experiential encounters rewarding, or disappointing as the case may be, expectations and thus providing a control over the formation of belief. The resolution of this argument is difficult because the extent of the analogies between religious and other forms of experience are indeterminate and disputable (see Franks Davis 1989 for a fuller discussion).

The anti-realist will also maintain that religious thought exhibits nothing like the moral structure displayed in science. It is controlled not by norms favouring criticism, publicity and accountability. Systems of authority control it that are morally unchecked, depending instead on the influence of power, emotion and the like. We are familiar with classic exposés of the amoral character of the forces that determine religious change and assent such as Hume's *The Natural History of Religion*. The realist will have to concede much to this picture of the prevalence of broadly superstitious motives in the formation of religious opinion. Yet there is of course another side to the coin, shown in the morality of genuine intellectual and spiritual disciplines within the religions. It could be conceded, however, that religious thinking is much less clearly a moral order in its character than science.

The key to the realist case must be the finding of a body of accumulating reliable belief about extra-mental, extra-mundane reality. Only this would provide clear-cut evidence (via a best explanation abduction) for the conclusion that religion was the outcome of cognitive contact with the real. Where could such reliable belief be found? From the terms of the argument offered so far it will not be found in *positive, detailed* claims about the character of the level of reality postulated. In regard to this area of belief we find no accumulation. At a more general level of claim, we can note the arguments of authors like Ward (1987) as an attempt to show an accumulation and convergence of basic characterisations of the transcendent across traditions. Moreover, the realist will point to what he or she must see as accumulation of reliable beliefs of a negative or relational kind about the transcendent. These will include beliefs about the moral and spiritual demands alleged contact with the transcendent invokes.

In this context the debates about salvific convergence between the faiths and about pragmatic confirmation of salvific expectations in the lives of believers become crucial. The realist must see, in the manner of Hick and Cantwell Smith, an accumulation of what we can call 'personalistic/pragmatic truth' as the justification for saying that religions both contain key concepts that correspond to the appropriate reality and are in part to be explained as outcomes of cognitive contact with that reality (compare Twiss 1990, 565–6).

This talk of personalistic and pragmatic truth entails the religious realist taking a considerable hostage to fortune. To vindicate this talk something must be made of the idea that the religions yield moral insight. That idea in turn has to face the rigours of the Humean critique and its portrayal of religion as more likely to lead to intolerant and vicious behaviour than to good. The realist must somehow show that religion has been a significant agent in the moral development of humanity – and, indeed, that there has been such a moral development.

The above points reinforce earlier discussions in this study highlighting the need for pluralism to show overlaps and convergences between the faiths. Two aims depend on the extent to which this can be done. On it hangs, first, the endeavour to show that there is a body of reliable belief (theoretical and pragmatic in character) which can serve as the basis for an argument to a realist interpretation of religion. On it hangs also the matter of *which* traditions can be encompassed by the realist and thus the pluralist hypothesis. To the degree that some traditions (such as the pre-Axial ones, or perhaps the absolute-rejecting strands of Buddhism) do not partake in this alleged accumulation of belief, then to that degree we shall have to say that they only partly refer to transcendent reality, if at all, and can only be partly explained through cognitive contact with the real. It is vital to note that pluralism cannot avoid being judgmental in this matter. Judgement and discrimination of alleged cognitive achievements in religion and the religions are required to establish the basic datum of the realist hypothesis, namely that there is some cognitive success to be explained. Judgement and discrimination are also required to determine which traditions fall under the scope of the hypothesis. This is the occasion to underscore a point already made more than once in this study: pluralism, being judgemental, cannot remain absolutely neutral with regard to the key notions of all traditions and it moves closer to inclusivism as a result.

As we have said, it is down to a review of the ubiquity and reliability of certain forms of human experience (perhaps aided by some general reflections of a natural theological kind) to establish whether there is a datum on which the realist hypothesis might rest. The further intellectual challenge facing pluralism is to show this datum to be best explained through the hypothesis of cognitive contact with the transcendent real. The complete vindication of this explanatory conclusion, as opposed to the establishment of some plausibility for it, would be a mammoth task. It would involve the refutation of all plausible versions of naturalistic explanations of religion and, amongst other things, the establishment of an account of the human subject such that cognitive contact between it and the transcendent was thinkable. One can indeed indicate in a preliminary fashion why alternative explanations of the alleged datum of cognitive success are questionable. It is relatively easy to point to two related failings of radical explanations of religion of the kind familiar from the writings of the likes of Feuerbach, Marx and Freud. The first is their dependence on an atheism (usually in the guise of materialism) which holds a priori that there can be no sacred reality for human beings to be in contact with via religion. The arguments, if any there be, for this methodological atheism usually exhibit the kind of dogmatism its proponents stigmatise in religion. The second weakness in such standard naturalistic explanations is the sketchiness and tendentiousness of the explanatory mechanisms held to account for religion. None of these explanations has anything like a well-developed and proven theory of human nature and society that would enable it to account for religion in a cogent fashion. (Both these weaknesses are fully explored in relation to a variety of theories of religion in Clarke and Byrne 1993.)

Anti-realist explanations of religion would appear to be on firmer ground in targeting the datum held to provoke the need for a realist interpretation of religion, namely an alleged record of cognitive success across the faiths. For if there is nothing to provoke a realist interpretation, there is no need to put up a fully-fledged rival.

So far we have treated the issues as if there were but two explanatory choices on offer: realist-pluralism and anti-realist naturalism. This is not so and the exploration of further rivals will enable the issues to become clearer.

Confessional explanations of religion that are inclusivist share the realist interpretation of religion held by pluralism and they extend that interpretation to a range of traditions in a parallel fashion. Yet confessional inclusivism must interpret the cognitive success which is the datum for realism differently. It must see that success as paradigmatically displayed in one confession and must see other confessions as converging in their reliable cognitive achievements upon the successes of the favoured tradition. If there is no such convergence, then there is no reason to bring other faiths under the umbrella of a realist hypothesis. The justice of this way of viewing the matter depends on the ins and outs of the epistemology of experience, revelation and apologetics discussed in Chapter 5. The crucial point to be reminded of is that inclusivist realism which is confessional requires cognitive success as to the *details* of the character of the sacred to be established in order for that success then to be interpreted primarily by the concepts of one, favoured confession. This in turn entails that the character of inclusivism's realism is different, since it can expect that one tradition more or less achieves *detailed*, authoritative beliefs about extra-mental, extra-mundane reality.

Confessional exclusivism must exhibit a similar discriminatory realism, but implies an even stronger contrast between the cognitive state of two parts of humanity. Those in the favoured confession are in cognitive contact with the appropriate level of reality. Those outside just are not. Presumably something like the strong programme for the sociology of knowledge works for the non-favoured traditions. The exclusivist thus has a stake in the success of naturalistic explanations of religion, in so far as he or she must maintain that something like them is appropriate for those outside the fold. Those inside are a different kind of cognitive animal altogether.

Confessionalism shows room for the interpretation of the *scope* of realism in religion, but there is also room for manoeuvre on the *character* of realism. Between realism and anti-realism there lies revisionary realism in regard to religion. Relativistic responses to religious plurality exhibit revisionary realism. They assert that religions are about something real, but deny that that something is extra-mental and extra-mundane. Since the basic standpoint of relativistic responses is that each religion focuses on a different real, because it is, or is part of, a conceptual schema that constitutes its own world, they maintain that the world of religious knowledge is not separate from the human subject. Relativism partakes of idealism in making the character of reality dependent on human subjects and their cognitive activity (as explained and espoused in Runzo 1993). This at least allows relativism to produce a realist-sounding conclusion. We have argued, however, that the substance of the relativistic response takes us back to anti-realism, in that it denies human beings are in contact with properly extra-human reality. We might be revisionary in more subtle ways, by reinterpreting, in the fashion of many a modern Western philosopher of religion, the character of the transcendent reality religions are allegedly about. We may interpret religions as being primarily in contact with *moral* reality, allowing this to transcend the human subject in ways which give us some scope for a realist interpretation of religious concepts (as does Sutherland 1984).

The plausibility or otherwise of revisionary religious realism is beyond the scope of the present discussion. It fits into the characterisation of the issues offered here when it is seen as one means of securing a cognitive success which might then become a datum for realist interpretation. The revisionist's point will be that, without drastic reinterpretation, we shall not be able to see religion as producing an accumulating cognitive success. Taken at face value, religion is a relative cognitive failure. The reinterpretation required to see it as a cognitive success may easily lead to forms of pluralism. We can however justly set them aside as departing from the spirit of religious pluralism defined in this study.

The motives behind philosophical revisionary realism point to the disputable and disputed character of the cumulative cognitive success pluralism purports to find in religion. From this chapter and from Chapter 5, we can see why thinkers might not wish to commit themselves to a realist interpretation of religion. There is yet one further option open to such thinkers, this being a methodologically neutral interpretation of religion. Realist pluralism and confessionalism in its various forms are built on what may be styled, for want of a better phrase, methodological theism. They are interpretations of religion dependent on showing at least some aspects of religious life and thought to be the outcome of cognitive contact with a transcendent reality. Naturalist interpretations of religion are built on a corresponding methodological scepticism. They depend on showing how religion in all its aspects arises out of forms of illusion, human projection, and superstition. For realist pluralism and confessionalism, the logic of religion is at least in part the logic of discovery, anticipation and encounter with reality. For naturalism the logic of religion is the logic of illusion. Those who are committed on methodological or general philosophical grounds to a thoroughgoing agnosticism about transcendent reality can still interpret religion. They can indeed rely on the beliefs of the religious to interpret religion. They can take seriously the content of the experiences and faith commitments of religion's adherents. That content gives religious experience and belief a variety of intentional objects: they appear to be of Christ, Krishna, sunyata and so on.

The neutral interpretation of religion simply refuses to adjudicate on whether there is anything real corresponding to these intentional objects and *ipso facto* on whether there is a single transcendent reality to which they all correspond. This is the stance of methodological agnosticism. It allows interpreters to take seriously the operation of reason in the religious traditions, in some weak sense of reason whereby it explains but does not justify. Religious beliefs and actions are intelligible in a minimally rational manner, because they connect with other religious beliefs and actions. Religion has, in other words and for the most part, an internal logic the bringing out of which makes religion intelligible. Contrary to typical naturalism, the neutral, agnostic view allows there to be a minimal rationality to religion. Contrary to pluralism, a more thoroughgoing agnosticism in the interpretation of religion refuses to be drawn on whether this rational structure justifies the various elements and commitments of realism.

Such neutralism (set out at length in Clarke and Byrne 1993) represents a clear alternative to realism and pluralism, and perhaps the best alternative to these if confessionalism is discounted. What would defeat it would be the demonstration of the spread and accumulation of apparent reliable insight into transcendent reality across one or more traditions. Neutralism evinces the consistent application of the cultural-linguistic approach to religious discourse described at the beginning of Chapter 6. Religions are examples of rule-governed forms of social life, the languages of which make possible certain forms of believing, acting and experiencing. It is not important for understanding such forms of social life to decide whether they are really about the objects allegedly encountered in them. All the referential expressions they contain can thus be 'bracketed' (Clarke and Byrne 1993, 51). In this respect these forms of social life can be treated in the manner of games: we understand them just in understanding their internal logic and what participants *think* the point of them is. But their relation to reality is not vital in explaining them.

It is important to get clear about the connection between this perspective on religion and that of pluralism. Pluralism depends on seeing religion as in some large measure explicable in cultural-linguistic terms (Twiss 1990, 534–5). For the pluralist, we know, remains agnostic as to many of the detailed claims of the religions and so he or she brackets out the truth of those claims and sees their point rather in the forms of life and experience they make possible and contribute to. Yet the pluralist sees a redeeming logic of discovery, anticipation and encounter behind some aspects of the religions. As well as being cultural-linguistic systems making forms of life and experience possible, religions also exhibit the human ability over many centuries and in many parts of the world to reach out to, and achieve cognitive contact with, extra-linguistic, extra-social, extra-mundane reality. So key aspects of the experiential, conceptual and doxastic array of human religion across many traditions can be best explained as arising out of that outreach and contact. This is, if you like, the redeeming trans-human, trans-cultural sense that pluralism sees in the religious life of humankind. And all depends on the plausible diagnosis of cognitive success across the traditions, as I have shown.

8
Conclusion

REVIEWING THE ARGUMENT

The aim of this book has been to show that pluralism is a viable and plausible philosophical interpretation of religion. In this section we review the strength of the case offered for these conclusions. Pluralism's viability and plausibility depend in part on two matters so far not discussed at length in these pages: the overall interpretation of religious life offered by pluralism and the impact of pluralism on first-order engagement with the faiths. The second section of this chapter takes up these two remaining issues.

The three defining theses of our version of pluralism are as follows. (1) All major religious traditions are equal in respect of making common reference to a single, transcendent reality. (2) All major traditions are likewise equal in respect of offering some means or other to human salvation. (3) All major traditions are to be seen as containing revisable, limited accounts of the nature of this reality: none is certain enough in its dogmatic formulations to provide the norm for interpreting the others.

The viability of thesis (1) rests squarely on the non-descriptivist account of reference offered in Chapter 2. If that is plausible, then it enables us to detach reference to the transcendent in the traditions from the detailed accounts they give of the transcendent. We saw that reference is not purely an extensional notion and that some crude identificatory knowledge underlies successful reference. But if we can use the philosophical notion of the ultimate both to provide the essence of the identificatory knowledge we need and to define the basic ontological category to which the transcendent might belong, then there is ground for saying that all major traditions designate one and the same sacred. A caveat to this claim must be entered in the case of certain strands of Buddhism which appear to deny that there is a positive reality denoted by words for the sacred.

191

The viability of the single reference thesis becomes plausibility if we can move from a conditional reference thesis ('If anyone refers, then it is likely that most refer') to an unconditional one. This move depends on showing grounds in the cognitive success of the religions for saying that they latch on to extra-mental, extra-mundane reality. The case for this conclusion was outlined in Chapters 5 and 7, and rested on forms of religious experience, broadly conceived. It also depended on rebutting naturalistic explanations of religious experience and life, and upon the fruitfulness or otherwise of taking a reference claim on behalf of the religions seriously in the actual study of religious change and development.

The case for the viability and plausibility of pluralism so far summarised argues for either the truth of pluralism or the truth of some confessional inclusivist interpretation of religion. Points made in favour of thesis (1) tell against naturalism, relativism and neutralism. Arguments in favour of thesis (2) begin to distinguish pluralism from confessionalism. Thesis (2) points to a very minimal view of salvific success indeed. It has to be minimal for a variety of reasons. In the working out of the thesis in Chapter 4, and elsewhere in this study, a cultural-linguistic account of religious language is accepted in large measure. This emphasises the extent to which religious discourses create unique forms of practice and experience through their containing doctrinal sentences which function as sets of rules. Hence there is no single, detailed and concrete way of life that they all preach. The anti-descriptivism implicit in thesis (1) and the agnosticism in thesis (3) add to the salvific minimalism entailed by pluralism. The contention that the detailed descriptions offered by the traditions of the transcendent cannot be known to be true, entails that the pictures of salvific paths within them cannot be known to be appropriate in detail. Hence, thesis (2) makes salvific success to be both something that consists in a second-order property, supervenient on the detailed pictures of modes of living in the traditions, and something minimal. It is minimal in consisting in a basic orientation toward the eternal that might be present in all faiths and in being something that might flow from simply making contact with the sacred, rather than in arriving at a true, detailed portrait of its nature and requirements. Such an interpretation of salvific success immediately runs counter to the claims of confessional exclusivism. It also tells against inclusivism of a non-prospective kind, for that type of inclusivism sees 'the other religions' as preparing their adherents for a saved life whose character is defined by the favoured confession.

Pluralism's third thesis reaffirms its realism, while containing the vital assertions that are its main rebuttal of confessionalism. The agnosticism preached in (3) is compatible with the referential realism implicit in (1) and (2) to the extent that one can allow reference to proceed under conditions of great ignorance as to the precise nature of the referent. The arguments of Chapters 2, 6 and 7 all try to support this position. It is those arguments which should offer some plausible ground for not getting a neutralist or relativist reading out of the case made in this book. The arguments in these chapters tell equally against the certainties of confessionalism. It is characteristic of the case offered here, as it must be of any version of pluralism, that it uses the very fact of religious diversity in respect of cognitive claims to tell against confessionalism. Disagreement entails doubt to the extent that there is no publicly available means of resolving disagreement. So, of course, the agnostic dismissal of confessionalism in the interpretation of religion can be rebutted by the offer of successful apologetic arguments in favour of the claims of one confession or another. And this study has by no means shown that such arguments cannot be offered. We noted in Chapter 5 that behind the epistemology relied on here is one thing inherited from the Enlightenment – the dislike of claims to epistemic privilege. There is a corresponding drive in philosophical pluralism toward universalist and egalitarian ideas about cognition (compare McLeod 1993, 127–9). That is to say, pluralism's tendency is to say that, since we all live in the same world, the experience of all of us should count in determining its character. We should be suspicious of anyone or any group who claims to have access to certainty about this common world which others cannot have. It is this universalism and egalitarianism which leads to the conclusion that cognitive conflicts which cannot be resolved by publicly assessable arguments are good indicators of the need to be agnostic about the subject matter in question. Readers must judge whether this is a fair way of dealing with the claims of individual confessions to have the detailed truth about the transcendent on the basis of some unique revelation or founding experience.

We have already indicated that there are points at which pluralism is vulnerable to refutation. It could be defeated by appropriate proof of naturalism or of the revealed status of some kind of confessionalism. Moreover it us under some internal strain, for its heavy agnosticism is combined with a form of realism and an acceptance of salvific success in the religions. No interpretation of religion is without such weaknesses and strains. In thinking about the difficulties and strengths in a pluralist interpretation, we should above all recall the fundamental picture it has of the relation between human discourse and the world. Pluralism, as outlined here, combines both a severe correspondence idea of truth and a strong realist commitment. The former opens up a large gap between religious discourse and the world, the latter asserts that the gap can be and is bridged. The notion of truth it has feeds the agnosticism it uses against confessionalism. So it must employ something other than the notion of truth to bridge the gap thus opened up and used against other positions, hence the role of referential realism vital to this study. If that notion fails, then relativism or neutralism might be correct. It might be better either to seek another way of closing the gap between religious discourse and the world (relativism), or to set aside the relation between discourse and reality in interpreting religion (neutralism).

So referential realism is the distinctive underpinning of this version of pluralism. It is what makes it possible and what sets it apart from the pluralisms of Hick, Cantwell Smith and others. They can, however, be seen to be working on the same very general lines. They too open up a gap between religious reality and confessional, doctrinal accounts of it and then seek to create a new bridge from religion to reality without giving unequivocal truth back to confession-based doctrines. Hick's Kantian phenomenal/noumenal distinction and Smith's faith/belief distinction can be seen as devices to this end. Our implicit argument has been that they do not do the job as well as referential realism, in particular because they cannot sufficiently close the gap between language and reality they have opened up. They are not realist enough.

THE BIG PICTURE

The title of this section is definitely euphemistic, since our discussion leaves open to considerable question how far a defensible pluralism does have a large-scale portrait of religious life or a philosophy of history into which religion fits.

We have associated a few general remarks about the character of religion in history with the three main theses of pluralism. So we have said that we should see the religions as connected, overlapping attempts on the part of human beings to understand, and orient themselves toward, the sacred. They are limited to some degree by the historical and cultural basis of human understanding, but they are stepping stones toward right relation to the transcendent. Pluralism accepts that religions are in large measure socio-cultural systems which are the product of history and circumstance, yet it also sees a redeeming logic of discovery, anticipation and encounter behind some of their aspects. As well as being cultural-linguistic systems making forms of life and experience possible, religions also exhibit the human ability over many centuries and cultures to reach out and achieve cognitive contact with transcendent reality.

In filling out this picture, we can say that it is broadly evolutionary. It posits a human tendency to cognitive and moral self-transcendence which is exhibited in and through the development of life in culture. The picture is broadly evolutionary, because it can take into account the accumulation of experience and insight and the widening of human contacts which is a feature of human history. The passage from pre-Axial to post-Axial faiths can be seen as an instance of this evolution, marking a key stage in cognitive and moral self-transcendence as folk sought more in their religious life than mere confirmation of societal goals and aims. General movements in religious history away from crudely anthropomorphic conceptions of the sacred can also be seen as facets of a cognitive evolution in religion. In particular, pluralism sees religion, despite its all too manifest failings, as something which completes a movement toward self-transcendence implicit in human nature, human epistemic activities and, particularly, morality. In morality it sees the movement toward pursuit and acknowledgement of the good in itself. So in sum, the pluralist will want to combine the basics of an anthropological approach to religions as cultural systems (see Chapter 3) with the cognitive viewpoint of philosophy toward religion and mix both these viewpoints with some thoughts about limited progress in human history. As noted in the previous chapter, it is another matter whether the perception of progress in religious history is at all justified.

These modest thoughts about self-transcendence and accumulation of insight and experience across human history show why pluralism is distinct from relativism, for I take it that relativism would have difficulty in saying, for example, that twentieth-century English citizens know more about the world than their counterparts in ancient Britain, or that their religious life had advanced beyond that of Druidic worshippers. Nonetheless there are good reasons why pluralism should go little further than this in the way of providing a philosophy of history or an overall meaning to history.

We can see why this is so by contrasting our pluralism with that of more confident followers of the Enlightenment paradigm. Kant in *Religion within the Limits of Reason Alone* offers a kind of pluralism based on essentialism. There is an essence to all genuine religion consisting in pure moral faith. Many major religions possess pure moral faith as the kernel which redeems their ecclesiastical and merely historical trappings. There is a slow progress in history which begins with humans enjoying a purely instinctual being and which works toward the completion of rational and moral life. In parallel, religion develops from slavish worship of gods and spirits toward its true nature as a vehicle of pure moral faith and the creation of an ethical commonwealth. It is characteristic of this kind of vision of religion that it redeems and unites religions only at the cost of making them the contingent, ultimately dispensable, means of expressing something which the philosopher, the author of the pluralist hypothesis, finally states. Kant is at one with a number of modern thinkers (one could also cite Hegel) who absolutise their own teaching by making history, including religious history, lead up to it. The hubris involved in this is not merely funny. What it fails to do is be consistent with its own acknowledgement of the principles of historical and cultural criticism. It uses those principles in offering a critique which sets aside the absolute claims of the religions of history, while supposing that the philosopher who offers the critique can then produce a fully worked-out philosophy of history that is absolutely true.

Our pluralism must be true to its own agnosticism. As well as recognising itself as a view which is highly defeasible by argument, it can offer no grand, detailed philosophy of history or of the absolute. So it has no basis for seeing the religions as leading up to it. It uncovers no essential truth which they could not recognise in themselves and which once brought into the open makes them redundant.

The Enlightenment project represented by Kant came under fierce attack, even before Kant's death, from the likes of Herder and Schleiermacher. One of the key features of that attack consisted in pressing the claims of religious experience against those of reason narrowly conceived. Pluralism as advanced here is in part the heir to that attack. The stress on religious experience provides another reason why pluralism cannot see itself as a rival to historical faiths which preaches their dispensability. This study has joined in the emphasis on modes of experience as the characteristic evidence of the human claim to have contact with the transcendent, the modes of experience running from certain moral ones not confined to religion to forms of felt liberation or sanctification. This fits in with reference to the sacred being grounded in practices not descriptions, these practices getting their vindication in felt encounters with transcendence. No one has a true, detailed doctrine of the divine according to our pluralism, so we see cognitive success in this area lying in practice appropriately vindicated. This of course implies that only within forms of practice that constitute living in harmony with ultimate reality – that is, in religions – can any worthwhile relationship with the sacred be achieved. So there can be no preaching that the messy, historically and culturally conditioned faiths should give way to the truths of philosophy.

So far the general philosophy of religion implied by pluralism seems to contain elements of the Enlightenment but only as these are softened and transmuted by the Romantics. In particular, the stress upon practice and experience calls to mind some of Schleiermacher's key ideas in the fifth of *The Speeches on Religion*: that cognitive success in religion consists in relation to the infinite vouched by experience; that each religion is a form of relationship to the infinite; and that each is in consequence one of the modes of relationship humankind had to accept at some time and some place. The philosophy of history implied by pluralism is similar to some of the message of Herder's *Yet Another Philosophy of History*. This affirms that there must be some relationship to the divine exhibited in human history (1891, 559) and decries those who think they know the plan of history, and particularly those philosophers who see a uniform progress in human history from superstitious past to a liberated present identified as such by their own achievements (1891, 527). Pointing to such parallels does not at all amount to saying that our pluralism is just a reworking of Herder's and Schleiermacher's. There is much in these thinkers that goes way beyond the ideas offered in this study.

One item in the Romantic inheritance which this study does not reaffirm is the doctrine of progressive and general revelation that dominated so much philosophy and theology of world religions in the nineteenth century (see Byrne 1989, 181–3). Descending from Herder and Schleiermacher via Hegel, this gave pioneer historians of religion like Max Müller the following general picture. The history of religions was the story of the unfolding of religion's essence, of the religion behind the religions. Religion's essence consisted in a primal and core experience or form of spirituality which underlies all religions worthy of the name. It evolves and perfects itself through religious history, for example, by becoming slowly more integrated with moral notions. This primal experience is at once human and divine in origin. It is a form of human experience which can be documented by the science of religion. The unfolding meaning to human religious history also has its divine aspect, since it is also the history of the working out of general revelation. The historian of religion studies not only the evolving human story of religion, but also the evolving divine revelation, which is hidden, like an implicit message, in the history of human religions.

What prevents our pluralism from following this ambitious path is its agnosticism toward the sacred and its general cultural-linguistic approach to religious discourse. The agnosticism pluralism preaches is severe. It suggests that, though contact with the transcendent is present in the practices and experiences of the faiths, the detailed character of the transcendent (if such detail is available at all) cannot be read off from those contacts. The formal doctrine of the transcendent implied in this study places its true nature at the outer limits of human thought. When this is allied with our stress on the socio-cultural basis of religious thought, then there is no reason to suppose that pluralism ushers in the successful search for a general revelation vindicated by the whole of human history. The socio-cultural basis of thought ties in with the cultural-linguistic view of religious discourse. This entails a modest constructivism in the interpretation of religious experience. While this does not prevent our seeing some general overlaps in religious experience, it should preclude postulating a core religious experience as the basis for an essence to all religions, whose unfolding we can then see at work in religious history.

So far, then, pluralism does not seem to have much of a big picture which will enable it to provide a philosophy of religious history. Its ambitions in this area are seen to be becomingly modest. There is nothing wrong in this if pluralism arises out of the analytical philosophy of religion. It remains a doctrine combining an assertion of minimal referential and salvific success in the religions with agnosticism about more detailed dogmatic accounts of these. Its very agnosticism entails its minimalism.

We must now turn to the question of what implications our pluralism might have for the first-order practice of religion. It should be evident that our pluralism is modest enough not to offer itself as a philosophical replacement for religion. It holds out absolutely no promise that philosophical reflection is an alternative or better route to cognitive and salvific contact with sacred reality. Rather, as we have seen, it points to modes of practice vindicated by experience as the appropriate source of access to the sacred. So far pluralism's 'big picture' has consequences which leave the distinction between first-order religious life and second-order reflection on it intact. Moreover, it looks as though our pluralism does not have the consequence of privatising religions or of turning them into commodities between which one can choose, as is claimed by post-modernist critics of pluralism (see the end of Chapter 1). The alliance our pluralism forges with Schleiermacher's thoughts about the centrality and inescapability of living modes of experience in gaining relationship with the transcendent means that this criticism is out of place. Reference to the sacred is based in forms of experience and practice which are traditionally and communally grounded. The project of putting together an ideal religion for oneself by taking bits and pieces from the global religious supermarket is completely at odds with these thoughts about practice and experience. The pluralist could make a similar point about moral insight. He or she might justly embrace a moral epistemology which grounds moral insight in communally anchored modes of perception and habits of choice. Moral knowledge becomes a tradition-based activity too, which is not to say that different traditions cannot have the same or similar insights. To get an implication of 'consumerism' from pluralism, pluralism has to be allied to an individualism about the grounds of experience, insight and reference. But there is no reason why pluralists have to be individualists of this kind.

Pluralism's reflections on the relativity of the doctrinal claims of traditions is not then a plea to escape such relativity by selecting the 'good' bits and pieces of extant traditions in order to construct a superior version of religious faith free of the limitations of those currently on the market. Pluralism alleges that the culturally conditioned and limited character of human religious thought is evidence against taking the confessions' accounts of their own status, with their portraits of their role in human religious history, to be true. Pluralism's own account of the meaning of religion is a better response to the fact of relativity, it claims. But these are all arguments about the adequacy of second-order interpretations of religion. They do not, in isolation, have any clear implications for the construction of a form of faith that somehow escapes this relativity. To be sure, the fact that pluralism sees individual traditions as aspects of an overlapping encounter with the one reality does indeed imply that as traditions they may well profit from sharing insights, spiritualities and the like. (We have also noted that at a very general level one should be able to put together different views about the fundamental character of the sacred.) But, with its Romantic inheritance, the test for pluralism of whether engagements between the faiths of this kind yield insight of a religiously useful and valid kind would lie in the enrichment, or otherwise, of communally bound forms of religious life.

There is a paradox here that needs exploring further. If pluralism is true, then rich, living, doctrinally loaded accounts of the

nature of transcendent reality and of salvation are both necessary and inevitably flawed. They are necessary for the moulding
of the practical and experiential complexes by means of which
humankind can genuinely relate to the sacred. They are inevitably flawed, for from the nature of the case they cannot claim
strict truth with any certainty. That is to say, taken literally and
positively they cannot claim with certainty to correspond in detail
with the reality they refer to. The pluralist does not know which
of these detailed, first-order beliefs is false. Some may be true.
He or she considers that they are all radically uncertain. Therefore, they are no basis for any interpretation of religion we can
now offer. In particular, they are no basis for absolutist claims
about salvation, revelation and the like.

This paradox does generate some first-order problems from
pluralism's second-order reflections, but we have to be absolutely clear what these problems are. The problems lie in this
general area: does not pluralism imply that doctrinal utterances
in the traditions affirm nothing worthy of belief? Is it not, then,
a recipe for the abandonment of belief in these utterances or at
least for the drastic modification of how they are affirmed? The
doctrinal utterances in question will include all those from within
the traditions which imply absoluteness and uniqueness for their
messages. So, in Christianity for example, it will include that
class of doctrinal statements which claim unique status, authority and the like for Christ and his redemption. If affirmation of
statements of this type is ruled out or drastically modified by
pluralism, then is it not finally destructive of the very traditions
it is supposed to interpret? Two points may be offered in support of this last claim. On the one hand the very identity of
traditions seems to be bound up with their claims to absoluteness and uniqueness, so that nothing could count as a Christian
view of life that was not bound by commitment to the uniqueness and absoluteness of God's revelation in Christ (Hastings
1990, 235). On the other hand one can offer the general thought
that it is deeply characteristic of religious traditions that they
offer absolute visions of the world and humanity from a local-
ised, historically particular perspective. If you object to this mixture, you object to them. The upshot of this case against pluralism
is that it is, when all is said and done, a form of scepticism and
like all scepticism destructive.

These criticisms of pluralism's destructive first-order implications can be deflected, but only partly. First we must begin by noting that pluralists are mitigated sceptics. They do declare religious reality to be unknowable in large measure. They do not declare that they have a disproof of the absolutist claims of any religion. They can accept that it is logically possible for religious reality to be just as one of the traditions claims it to be. What pluralism preaches is an agnosticism which makes the possibility of absolute truth in one of the confessions too unlikely to serve as the basis for interpreting religion as a whole. Agnosticism has to be the basis for any reasonable interpretation of the religions we can now offer. So pluralism does not affirm that an affirmation such as 'Jesus is *the* Son of God' is proved false. And it can and does affirm that such an affirmation belongs to a set of doctrinal statements which have cognitive point. The point is two-fold. The set will help constitute, in rule-like fashion, modes of practice and experience from which access to the sacred is enabled. Further, and in consequence, the set of doctrinal statements that define a particular faith may have referential success, metaphorical truth and thereby a referential intent which is vindicated.

The critic will not be content with this. It will be said in reply that pluralism affirms that one cannot say 'Jesus is the Son of God' and reasonably believe it to be true, in the sense of corresponding to reality. Doctrinal statements may refer to religious reality, but they are presumed by pluralism not to describe that reality truly, in detail and with any certainty, since no one can do that. So someone who affirms doctrinal statements after going through the reflective process which leads to embracing pluralism as a philosophical thesis cannot affirm doctrinal statements to be unequivocally, categorically true. 'I believe' cannot mean the same for such a person in 'I believe Jesus is Son of God' as it means in 'I believe that grass is green'.

This much must be conceded by the pluralist. It must be granted that, despite all the cognitive point pluralism gives to doctrinal affirmations, it does not leave everything as it is. The doctrinal stance is altered by pluralism. Here, if nowhere else, the second-order leaks into the first-order.

What if the faithful take their stand and insist that without assured, detailed, literal and positive truth to doctrine, traditions cannot maintain their identity and authenticity? Well, then pluralism really does have to swallow its paradoxical consequence: on its view the traditions are indispensable but also cognitively flawed.

Works Cited

Abe, M. 1993 '"Dazzling Darkness": the Understanding of "Ultimate Reality" in Buddhism' in Huschel, K.-J. and Häring, H. eds *Hans Küng: New Horizons for Faith and Thought*. London: S.C.M. Press. 306–25.

Abraham, W.J. 1982 *Divine Revelation and the Limits of Historical Criticism*. Oxford: Clarendon Press.

Alston, W.P. 1989a 'Functionalism and Theological Language' in Alston, W.P. *Divine Nature and Human Language*. Ithaca: Cornell University Press. 64–80.

—— 1989b 'Irreducible Metaphors in Theology' in Alston, W.P. *Divine Nature and Human Language*. Ithaca: Cornell University Press. 17–37.

—— 1989c 'Referring to God' in Alston, W.P. *Divine Nature and Human Language*. Ithaca: Cornell University Press. 103–17.

—— 1991 *Perceiving God*. Ithaca: Cornell University Press.

Apczynski, J.V. 1992 'John Hick's Theocentrism: Revolutionary or Implicitly Exclusivist?' *Modern Theology*. 8, 40–52.

Aquinas, St Thomas 1964a *Summa Theologiae* vol 2. McDermott, T. tr. London: Blackfriars/Eyre and Spottiswoode.

—— 1964b *Summa Theologiae* vol 3. McCabe, H. tr. London: Blackfriars/Eyre and Spottiswoode.

Banner, M.C. 1990 *The Justification of Science and the Rationality of Religious Belief*. Oxford: Clarendon Press.

Boyd, R. 1979 'Metaphor and Theory Change: What is "Metaphor" a Metaphor for?' in Ortony, A. ed. *Metaphor and Thought*. Cambridge: Cambridge University Press. 356–408.

Burrell, D. 1973 *Analogy and Philosophical Language*. New Haven: Yale University Press.

—— 1986 *Knowing the Unknowable God: Ibn-Sina, Maimonides, Aquinas*. Notre Dame: University of Notre Dame Press.

Byrne, P. 1982 'John Hick's Philosophy of World Religions' *Scottish Journal of Theology*. 35, 289–301.

—— 1984 'Mysticism, Identity and Realism: a Debate Reviewed' *International Journal for the Philosophy of Religion*. 16, 237–43.

—— 1985 'F.R. Leavis and the Religious Dimension in Literature' *Modern Theology*. 2, 119–30.

—— 1989 *Natural Religion and the Nature of Religion: the Legacy of Deism*. London: Routledge.

—— 1992 *The Philosophical and Theological Foundations of Ethics*. London and Basingstoke: Macmillan.

—— 1993 'A Defence of Christian Revelation' *Religious Studies*. 29, 381–94.

Christian, W.A. 1964 *Meaning and Truth in Religion*. Princeton: Princeton University Press.

Clarke, B. 1992 'Identity and the Divinities' *International Journal for the Philosophy of Religion*. 31, 133–48.

Clarke, P.B. and Byrne, P. 1993 *Religion Defined and Explained*. London and Basingstoke: Macmillan.

Cobb, J. 1990 'Beyond Pluralism' in D'Costa, G. ed. *Christian Uniqueness Reconsidered: the Myth of a Pluralist Theology of Religions*. Maryknoll: Orbis. 81–95.

D'Costa, G. 1986 *Theology and Religious Pluralism: the Challenge of Other Religions*. Oxford: Blackwell.

—— 1990 'Christ, the Trinity and Religious Plurality' in D'Costa, G. ed. *Christian Uniqueness Reconsidered: the Myth of a Pluralist Theology of Religions*. Maryknoll: Orbis. 16–29.

—— 1993 'Whose Objectivity? Which Neutrality?: the Doomed Quest for a Neutral Vantage Point from which to Judge Religions' *Religious Studies*. 29, 1. 79–95.

Devitt, M. 1981 *Designation*. New York: Columbia University Press.

—— 1984 *Realism and Truth*. Oxford: Blackwell.

DiNoia, J.A. 1990a 'Pluralist Theology of Religions: Pluralistic or Non-Pluralistic?' in D'Costa, G. ed. *Christian Uniqueness Reconsidered: the Myth of a Pluralist Theology of Religions*. Maryknoll: Orbis. 119–34.

—— 1990b 'Varieties of Religious Aims: Beyond Exclusivism, Inclusivism and Pluralism' in Marshall, B.D. ed. *Theology and Dialogue*. Notre Dame: University of Notre Dame. 249–74.

—— 1992 *The Diversity of Religions*. Washington D.C.: the Catholic University Press of America.

Donnellan, K.S. 1977 'Reference and Definite Descriptions' in Schwartz, S.P. ed. *Naming, Necessity and Natural Kinds*. Ithaca: Cornell University Press. 42–65.

Donovan, P. 1993 'The Intolerance of Religious Pluralism' *Religious Studies*. 29, 217–29.

Evans, G. 1977 'The Causal Theory of Names' in Schwartz, S.P. ed. *Naming, Necessity and Natural Kinds*. Ithaca: Cornell University Press. 192–215.

Ferré, N. 1967 *Basic Modern Philosophy of Religion*. New York: Scribners.

Foreman, R.K.C. ed. 1990 *The Problem of Pure Consciousness*. New York: Oxford University Press.

—— 1991 'Reply to Bagger' *Religious Studies*. 27, 413–20.

Forgie, J.W. 1994 'Pike's *Mystic Union* and the Possibility of Theistic Experience' *Religious Studies*. 30, 231–42.

Franks Davis, C. 1989 *The Evidential Force of Religious Experience*. Oxford: Clarendon Press.

Gale, R.M. 1991 *On the Nature and Existence of God*. Cambridge: Cambridge University Press.

Geertz, C. 1975 *The Interpretation of Culture*. London: Hutchinson.

Gellman, J.I. 1993 'Naming and Naming God' *Religious Studies*. 29, 193–216.

Gellner, E. 1992 *Postmodernism, Reason and Religion*. London: Routledge.

Gilkey, L. 1988 'Plurality and its Theological Implications' in Hick, J.

and Knitter, P.F. eds *The Myth of Christian Uniqueness*. London: S.C.M. Press. 37–50.

Gillis, C. 1989 *A Question of Final Belief*. London and Basingstoke: Macmillan.

Goodman, N. 1976 *The Languages of Art*. Indianapolis: Hackett.

Griffiths, P. 1990 'The Uniqueness of Christian Doctrine Defended' in D'Costa, G. ed. *Christian Uniqueness Reconsidered: the Myth of a Pluralist Theology of Religions*. Maryknoll: Orbis. 157–73.

—— 1991 *An Apology for Apolgetics: a Study in the Logic of Interreligious Dialogue*. Maryknoll: Orbis.

Hardy, F. 1994 *The Religious Culture of India: Power, Love and Wisdom*. Cambridge: Cambridge University Press.

Harré, R. 1972 *The Philosophies of Science*. Oxford: Oxford University Press.

—— 1986 *The Varieties of Realism*. Oxford: Blackwell.

—— 1987 'The Displacement of Truth' in Abraham, W.J. and Holtzer, S.W. eds *The Rationality of Religious Belief*. Oxford: Clarendon Press. 85–104.

Harvey, P. 1990 *An Introduction to Buddhism*. Cambridge: Cambridge University Press.

Hastings, A. 1990 'Pluralism: the Relationship of Theology to Religious Studies' in Hamnet, I. ed. *Religious Pluralism and Unbelief*. London: Routledge. 226–40.

Hebblethwaite, B. 1993 'John Hick and the Question of Truth in Religion' in Sharma, A. ed. *God, Truth and Reality: Essays in Honour of John Hick*. London and Basingstoke: Macmillan. 124–34.

Heim, S.M. 1992 'The Pluralistic Hypothesis, Realism and Post-Eschatology' *Religious Studies*. 28, 207–22.

Herder, J.G. 1891 *Auch eine Philosophie der Geschichte zur Bildung der Menscheit. Sämmtliche Werke* vol 5. Suphan, B. ed. Berlin: Weidmansche.

Hick, J. 1981 'On Grading Religions' *Religious Studies*. 17, 451–67.

—— 1983 'On Conflicting Religious Truth-Claims' *Religious Studies*. 19, 485–91.

—— 1985a *Death and Eternal Life*. London and Basingstoke: Macmillan.

—— 1985b *Problems of Religious Pluralism*. London and Basingstoke: Macmillan.

—— 1989 *An Interpretation of Religion*. London and Basingstoke: Macmillan.

—— 1990 'Straightening the Record: Some Responses to Critics' *Modern Theology*. 6, 187–95.

—— 1991 'Reply [to Gavin D'Costa]' in Hewitt, H. ed. *Problems in the Philosophy of Religion*. London and Basingstoke: Macmillan. 24–7.

—— 1993a *Disputed Questions in Theology and Philosophy of Religion*. London and Basingstoke: Macmillan.

—— 1993b *The Metaphor of God Incarnate*. London: S.C.M. Press.

Hughes, G.J. 1987 'Aquinas and the Limits of Agnosticism' in Hughes, G.J. ed. *The Philosophical Assessment of Theology*. Tunbridge Wells: Search Press. 35–64.

Hume, D. 1976 *The Natural History of Religion* and *Dialogues Concerning*

Natural Religion. Colver, A.W. and Price, J.V. eds. Oxford: Clarendon Press.

Jantzen, G.M. 1984 'Human Diversity and Salvation in Christ' *Religious Studies.* 20, 579–92.

—— 1987 'Conspicuous Sanctity and Religious Belief' in Abraham, W.J. and Holtzer, S.W. eds *The Rationality of Religious Belief.* Oxford: Clarendon Press. 121–40.

Jennings, T.W. 1985 *Beyond Theism.* New York: Oxford University Press.

Kant, I. 1960 *Religion within the Limits of Reason Alone.* Greene, T.M. and Hudson, H.H. trs. New York: Harper and Row.

Katz, S. 1978 'Language, Epistemology and Mysticism' in Katz, S. ed. *Mysticism and Philosophical Analysis.* London: Sheldon Press. 22–74.

Keelenberger, J. 1985 'The Slippery Slope of Religious Relativism' *Religious Studies.* 21, 39–52.

Kenny, A. 1992 *What is Faith?* Oxford: Oxford University Press.

Kent, B. 1994 'Moral Provincialism' *Religious Studies.* 30, 269–85.

Keown, D. 1992 *The Nature of Buddhist Ethics.* London and Basingstoke: Macmillan.

Knitter, P.F. 1985 *No Other Name: a Critical Survey of Christian Attitudes toward the World Religions.* London: S.C.M. Press.

—— 1988 'Toward a Liberation Theology of Religions' in Hick, J. and Knitter, P.F. eds *The Myth of Christian Uniqueness.* London: S.C.M. Press. 178–200.

Lindbeck, G. 1984 *The Nature of Doctrine: Religion and Theology in a Post-Liberal Age.* London: S.P.C.K.

McFague, S. 1983 *Metaphorical Theology.* London: S.C.M. Press.

—— 1987 *Models of God: Theology for an Ecological, Nuclear Age.* London: S.C.M. Press.

McKim, R. 1988 'Could God Have More than One Nature?' *Faith and Philosophy.* 5, 378–98.

MacIntyre, A. 1988 *Whose Justice? Which Rationality?* Notre Dame: University of Notre Dame Press.

—— 1990 *Three Rival Versions of Moral Enquiry: Encyclopedia, Genealogy and Tradition.* Notre Dame: University of Notre Dame Press.

McLeod, M. 1993 *Rationality and Theistic Belief: an Essay on Reformed Epistemology.* Ithaca: Cornell University Press.

Markham, I. 1991 'Faith and Reason: Reflections on MacIntyre's "Tradition-Constituted Enquiry"' *Religious Studies.* 27, 259–67.

Martin Soskice, J. 1981 'Metaphor amongst Tropes' *Religious Studies.* 17, 55–66.

—— 1985 *Metaphor and Religious Language.* Oxford: Clarendon Press.

—— 1987 'Theological Realism' in Abraham, W.J. and Holtzer, S.W. eds *The Rationality of Religious Belief.* Oxford: Clarendon Press. 105–19.

Meynell, H. 1981 *Freud, Marx and Morals.* London and Basingstoke: Macmillan.

Milbank, J. 1990 'The End of Dialogue' in D'Costa, G. ed. *Christian Uniqueness Reconsidered: the Myth of a Pluralist Theology of Religions.* Maryknoll: Orbis. 174–91.

Miller, R.B. 1986 'The Reference of "God"' *Faith and Philosophy.* 3, 3–15.

Morris, P. 1990 'Judaism and Pluralism: the Price of "Religious Freedom"' in Hamnet, I. ed. *Religious Pluralism and Unbelief*. London: Routledge. 179–201.

Müller, F.M. 1893 *Introduction to the Science of Religion*. London: Longmans.

Netland, H.A. 1986 'Professor Hick and Religious Pluralism' *Religious Studies*. 22, 249–62.

—— 1991 *Dissonant Voices: Religious Pluralism and the Question of Truth*. Grand Rapids: Eerdmans.

Newbiggen, L. 1990 'Religion for the Market Place' in D'Costa, G. ed. *Christian Uniqueness Reconsidered: the Myth of a Pluralist Theology of Religions*. Maryknoll: Orbis. 135–48.

Otto, R. 1958 *The Idea of the Holy*. Harvey, J.W. tr. New York: Oxford University Press.

Outka, G. and Reeder, J.P. 1992 *Prospects for a Common Morality*. Princeton: Princeton University Press.

Pailin, D. 1990 *The Anthropological Character of Theology*. Cambridge: Cambridge University Press.

Pannikkar, R. 1988 'The Jordan, the Tiber and the Ganges: Three Kairological Moments of Christian Self-Consciousness' in Hick, J. and Knitter, P.F. eds *The Myth of Christian Uniqueness*. London: S.C.M. Press. 89–116.

Penelhum, T. 1971 *Problems of Religious Knowledge*. London and Basingstoke: Macmillan.

Pentz, R. 1991 'Hick and Saints: Is Saint-Production a valid Test?' *Faith and Philosophy*. 8, 96–103.

Proudfoot, W. 1985 *Religious Experience*. Berkeley and Los Angeles: University of California Press.

Prozesky, M. 1984 *Religion and Ultimate Well-Being*. London and Basingstoke: Macmillan.

Putnam, H. 1990 *Realism with a Human Face*. Cambridge, Mass.: Harvard University Press.

Richards, G. 1989 *Towards a Theology of Religions*. London: Routledge.

Runzo, J. 1986 *Reason, Relativism and God*. London and Basingstoke: Macmillan.

—— 1993 *World Views and Perceiving God*. London and Basingstoke: Macmillan.

Schellenberg, J.L. 1993 *Divine Hiddenness and Human Reason*. Ithaca: Cornell University Press.

Schleiermacher, F.D.E. 1958 *On Religion: Speeches to its Cultured Despisers*. Oman, J. tr. New York: Harper and Row.

Schwöbel, C. 1990 'Particularity, Universality and the Religions' in D'Costa, G. ed. *ChristianUniqueness Reconsidered: the Myth of a Pluralist Theology of Religions*. Maryknoll: Orbis. 30–46.

Searle, J.R. 1979 'Metaphor' in Ortony, A. ed. *Metaphor and Thought*. Cambridge: Cambridge University Press. 92–123.

Senor, T.D. 1991 'God, Supernatual Kinds and the Incarnation' *Religious Studies*. 27, 353–70.

Shaw, P. 1992 'On Worshipping the Same God' *Religious Studies*. 28, 511–32.

Sherman, N. 1989 *The Fabric of Character*. Oxford: Clarendon Press.
Smart, N. 1993 'A Contemplation of Absolutes' in Sharma, A. ed. *God, Truth and Reality: Essays in Honour of John Hick*. London and Basingstoke: Macmillan. 176–88.
Smith, P. 1981 *Realism and the Progress of Science*. Cambridge: Cambridge University Press.
Smith, W.C. 1978 *The Meaning and End of Religion*. London: S.P.C.K.
—— 1979 *Faith and Belief*. Princeton: Princeton University Press.
—— 1981 *Towards a World Theology: Faith and the Comparative History of Religion*. London and Basingstoke: Macmillan.
Stoeber, M. 1992 'Constructivist Epistemologies of Mysticism: a Critique and a Revision' *Religious Studies*. 28, 107–16.
Stone, J. 1991 'A Theory of Religion' *Religious Studies*. 27, 337–51.
Surin, K. 1983 'Revelation, Salvation and the Uniqueness of Christ and other Religions' *Religious Studies*. 19, 323–43.
—— 1990a 'A Politics of Speech: Religious Pluralism in the Age of the McDonald's Hamburger' in D'Costa, G. ed. *Christian Uniqueness Reconsidered: the Myth of a Pluralist Theology of Religions*. Maryknoll: Orbis. 192–212.
1990b 'Toward a "Materialist" Critique of Religious Pluralism: an Examination of the Discourse of John Hick and Wilfred Cantwell Smith' in Hamnet, I. ed. *Religious Pluralism and Unbelief*. London: Routledge. 114–29.
Sutherland, S.R. 1979 'God, Time and Eternity' *Proceedings of the Aristotelian Society*. 79, 103–21.
—— 1984 *God, Jesus and Belief*. Oxford: Blackwell.
Swinburne, R. 1977 *The Coherence of Theism*. Oxford: Clarendon Press.
—— 1989 *Responsibility and Atonement*. Oxford: Clarendon Press.
Taylor, C. 1989 *Sources of the Self*. Cambridge: Cambridge University Press.
Trigg, R. 1983 'Religion and the Threat of Relativism' *Religious Studies*. 19, 297–310.
Twiss, S.B. 1990 'The Philosophy of Religious Pluralism: a Critical Appraisal of John Hick and his Critics' *Journal of Religion*. 70, 533–68.
von Glasenapp, H. 1970 *Buddhism: a Non-Theistic Religion*. Schlögel, I. tr. London: Allen and Unwin.
Vroom, H. 1990 'Do all Religions Worship the Same God?' *Religious Studies*. 26, 73–90.
Wainwright, W.J. 1984 'Wilfred Cantwell Smith on Faith and Belief' *Religious Studies*. 20, 353–66.
Ward, K. 1987 *Images of Eternity*. London: Darton, Longman and Todd.
—— 1990 'Truth and the Diversity of Religions' *Religious Studies*. 26, 1–18.
Williams, P. 1991 'Some Dimensions of the Recent Work of Raimundo Panikkar: a Buddhist Perspective' *Religious Studies*. 27, 511–21.
Yinger, J.M. 1970 *The Scientific Study of Religion*. New York: Macmillan.
Yob, I.M. 1992 'Religious Metaphor and Scientific Model: Grounds for Comparison' *Religious Studies*. 28, 475–85.

Index

211